50
FAMOUS
RAILWAYMEN

50
FAMOUS
RAILWAYMEN

The engineers and
entrepreneurs who
shaped Britain's
railways

Chris de Winter Hebron

Silver Link Publishing Ltd

First published in 2005

British Library Cataloguing in Publication Data

A catalogue record for this book is available from the British Library.

ISBN 1 85794 248 5

Silver Link Publishing Ltd
The Trundle
Ringstead Road
Great Addington
Kettering
Northants NN14 4BW

Tel/Fax: 01536 330588
email: sales@nostalgiacollection.com
Website: www.nostalgiacollection.com

Printed and bound in Great Britain

Contents

Introduction

When the subject of this book was first proposed to me, it was suggested it be called *50 Famous Railway Engineers*, and I was left to pick the list for inclusion – there are of course many more than 50 who deserve the title! – myself. However, as I began to ponder who should be included and who left out, several things became clear, which have influenced me in what was inevitably always going to be a personal and idiosyncratic choice from so large a field.

First, I rapidly began to realise that the greatest men in our railway history were not all simply locomotive engineers – though many, of course, were, and in this book they do by and large predominate. Railways need many other kinds of great men to make their trains run, as well as great locomotive builders – they need civil engineers to survey and lay out the track, carriage designers to further passenger comfort, and managers and entrepreneurs to conceive and control services and operations. Especially in the early days, many of these tasks were performed by the same people – Brunel, for instance, was actually a much better civil engineer than he was a locomotive man, and much, much later both Gresley and Stanier designed excellent carriages as well as locomotives (and Gresley also had a distinct 'feel' for entrepreneurial operations). On other occasions, they were most definitely split – on the Midland, Johnson built some of the world's most elegant single-driving-wheel locos, but it was Thomas Clayton who produced the prize-winning carriages they hauled; while Georges Nagelmackers never designed a locomotive in his life (and only sketched out his carriages), but nonetheless gave birth to the most famous train of all time, the 'Orient Express'.

Our 'famous railwaymen' therefore did not have to be restricted to just famous engineers; indeed, there positively had to be a sprinkling among them of the other sorts of fame I've just listed. Nor did they necessarily have to be ultimately successful – George Hudson ended his days in scandal and disgrace, but without him there might well never have been a Midland Railway at all.

A further question concerned what nationalities should be represented on the list. The book is aimed primarily at British readers, so Britons would obviously be in the majority, but at least some other railwaymen, especially entrepreneurs like Pullman from the USA and Nagelmackers from Belgium, were so influential on British practice that they clearly had to be included. But in that case, where would one stop? In the matter of compounding, for example, did it make sense to include (as I have done) Francis Webb and R. M. Deeley, but to exclude (as I also have done) Samuel Vauclain of the USA or (especially!) André Chapelon of France?

The truth, though, is that in Britain we followed a particular engineering tradition, which was different from both that of the USA and that of continental Europe, and it is this that my selection is attempting to represent. In Britain, for the most part, railway companies designed and built their own locomotives, so the Chief Mechanical Engineer was a truly crucial appointment. In Britain, too, railway engineering was through most of the railway age a 'hands-on' profession, learned through premium apprenticeship rather than academic study. In the USA this was often true also, but most railways ordered locomotives designed and built by one of the great locomotive-building firms, such as Alco or Baldwin, rather than building their own (though on the exceptions, such as the Pennsylvania, the line's Master Mechanic was every bit as powerful as the British CME). And in mainland Europe, with its radically different higher education system, though railways often built their own locomotives (as in Britain), locomotive design was a much more academic profession, taught from a very early period in technical universities – Austria's Karl Gölsdorf, for example, was Herr Doktor Ingenieur.

Thus – with the very few exceptions I have noted above – this book celebrates the first of those traditions, the premium apprentice made good, building locos or carriages for his own railway, and its equivalent in the fields of management and finance. Ross Winans, Samuel Vauclain, Karl Gölsdorf or André Chapelon are omitted, not because they are any less important, but because they belong to the other two traditions. It would, of course, be an easy matter – archival research aside! – to create a book about 50 famous railwaymen from each of the other traditions too.

One final point needs also to be made about these vignettes. The biographical summary with which each one opens varies in completeness, not because of my especial indolence, but because although all 50 of my subjects are famous as 'railwaymen', the amount that is on record about them as people varies tremendously. On the one hand you have, say, George Stephenson, about whom everything knowable seems to be already recorded (sometimes in several versions), while at the other extreme you have someone like Thomas Clayton, about whom so little seems to be recorded outside his inimitable carriage drawings that we even have some difficulty in establishing whether his first name was indeed Thomas, or whether it was James (I myself called him 'James' in *Dining at Speed*, following a reference in Roy Williams's history of the Midland Railway, which now turns out to use both forenames at different points for the same man!). Understandably, the biographical summaries tend to reflect this variability, and thus contain some gaps here and there. If any reader happens to have information that would fill one of those gaps, I'd be delighted if they could write to me about it, care of the publishers.

Acknowledgements

Once again, this is a work that could not have been accomplished without the help of many other people. First and foremost, I would like to acknowledge the diligence of the many authors whose books I have consulted in preparing these accounts: their titles are to be found in the Bibliography. I would also like to thank the staff of Cambridge University Library reference and periodicals reading rooms, for guiding me through the sometimes complex process of tracking down particular journal entries (and especially the somewhat fugitive family history material by Deeley), Liz Butler of QFHS and the staff of Friends House Library for help with Digest records for John Ellis, and most especially the staff of Norfolk County Library, Holt, who dealt assiduously with almost weekly demands both for inter-library loans and for books from the most inaccessible parts of the Central Store stacks in the Millennium Library at Norwich. I would also like to pay tribute to the assiduity of the compilers of www.steamindex.com, whose entries have been of great use in filling in the gaps in other accounts of many of my 'famous railwaymen'.

I am also particularly grateful to Brian Radford and A. E. Overton for supplying information on both Deeley and the enigmatic Tom Clayton, to Michael Farr for performing a similar service for Thomas Edmondson, to the archive staff of the Festiniog Railway for help with information on Robert Fairlie, to Elaine Stanier of the Mitchell Library Glasgow for finding portraits of Dugald Drummond and J. F. McIntosh, to Edward Beach of St Vincent Philatelic Services Ltd and Aviva Susman of the Inter-Governmental Philatelic Corporation New York, for kind permission to use the portraits of famous railwaymen on stamps, and to Hamp Smith of the Minnesota Historical Society and Kathryn Santos and Ellen Halteman of the California State Railroad Museum Library for assisting me in searching for photos and primary source material on Henry Villard and George Pullman (the photo of Villard in particular is courtesy of CSRM Archives). I would also like to take this opportunity to thank Andrew Bullen of the ELI Illinois digitisation project and the Pullman Preservation Alliance for permission to reproduce the photograph of George Pullman.

Abbreviations

CIWL	Compagnie Internationale des Wagons-Lits
CME	Chief Mechanical Engineer
CR	Caledonian Railway
DNB	*Dictionary of National Biography*
ECJS	East Coast Joint Stock
GNR	Great Northern Railway
LBSCR	London, Brighton & South Coast Railway
LMS	London, Midland & Scottish Railway
LNWR	London & North Western Railway
LSWR	London & South Western Railway
LYR	Lancashire & Yorkshire Railway
M&GNR	Midland & Great Northern Joint Railway
MSLR	Manchester, Sheffield & Lincolnshire Railway
MSWJR	Midland & South Western Junction Railway
NBR	North British Railway
NER	North Eastern Railway
psi	Pounds per square inch (pressure)
ROD	Railway Operating Division (British Army Royal Engineers)
SDJR	Somerset & Dorset Joint Railway
SECR	South Eastern & Chatham Railway
TE	Tractive effort

James Allport
1811-92

Railway Manager

Born	Birmingham, 27 February 1811
Education	Belgium
Married	Ann Gold, Birmingham, 1832
Best-known works	Midland Railway's 'London Extension', St Pancras Station, Settle & Carlisle line, introduction of 3rd Class on all trains, abolition of 2nd Class and upgrading of 3rd to 2nd standard, introduction of Pullman cars to UK
Honours	Knighthood, April 1884 (the first railway manager to receive this honour); JP for Derby (borough and county)
Died	Midland Grand Hotel, St Pancras, 25 April 1892
Buried	Belper Cemetery, Derby

The son of a Birmingham small-arms manufacturer, James Joseph Allport first entered the railway world at the age of 28, when in 1839 he joined the small and somewhat impecunious Birmingham & Derby Junction Railway as a junior, rising, however, to be manager of the line in 1843. When the line was amalgamated under Hudson's chairmanship the following year to form the nucleus of the Midland Railway, Allport moved to the Newcastle & Darlington Junction Railway (an early constituent of the NER), where he held the same position until 1850. He was then appointed manager of the Manchester Sheffield & Lincolnshire Railway (later the Great Central), whence John Ellis, who had become Chairman of the Midland Railway following Hudson's fall in 1849, head-hunted him to become that company's first General Manager.

When Ellis appointed Allport, the Midland faced a series of problems. Although one of the largest provincial companies, equalled only by the LYR and the MSLR, it was 'landlocked' on all sides by competitors. It lacked any direct access to London – the natural destination for its coal and iron products, and for its business travellers – or to Scotland, the natural destination for its wealthier potential tourists now Queen Victoria had begun the fashion for Scottish holidays. Partly because of this, and partly because of the Hudson scandal, its finances were also in a poor way, and it lacked business confidence. The reputation of Ellis (and his immediate successors) was able to repair the problem of confidence, but his brief to Allport was to undertake the strategic management tasks necessary to counter the practical problems of 'landlocking' and access to remunerative markets.

Allport proved to be something of a commercial genius. Although concentrating initially on the direct London extension – a job that one way or another was to take him ten years, and would culminate in the building of the famous St Pancras station – he never lost sight of a strategic vision for the line that would make it one of the premier railway lines in Britain, rivalling the LNWR and the East Coast cartel. This strategy, which he successfully brought to fruition, had several overlapping phases.

The first phase, centred on the key London traffic, was to complete the direct London extension, with adequate spare capacity for both fast passenger and heavy goods movements, and the Midland's own terminus at St Pancras. This involved laying quadruple track on most of the line from north of Kettering to London, with the up slow lines used by a near unending succession of coal trains, while expresses cavorted merrily along on the fast lines. The original southwards extension of 1858 had run from Leicester via Bedford to Hitchin on the Great Northern Railway, reaching London via the GNR thanks to running powers negotiated by Allport against some resistance from that company, and the Midland's own line was finally completed throughout to St Pancras by 1867. This included the new terminus at St Pancras, under a roof of iron spans manufactured by the Butterley Company and transported direct via the Midland's own lines, and fronted by what was at that point London's premier hotel, elevated above Euston Road with cellars housing Burton beer (one of the Midland's main goods).

The second phase was to negotiate a joint agreement with the Glasgow & South Western Railway (currently not linked to any major English company) for Anglo-Scottish expresses via Carlisle. Allport initially used existing running powers over the 'little North Western' (Clapham (Yorks)/Ingleton/Sedbergh/Low Gill) to get there, but as soon as possible, because of frustrations and delays caused by LNWR ownership of certain key sections of this route, he needed to create an independent Midland line to Carlisle to avoid depending on running powers. Financial limitations meant that work on this and the London extension could not be carried on simultaneously, but in 1866 an Act was obtained for the construction of the Settle & Carlisle route – the highest main line in England, running through spectacular scenery – and this was finally opened for through Anglo-Scottish services ten years later, in 1876.

Together with his negotiation of running powers over the MSLR into Manchester, this successfully solved the 'landlocking' problem, but Allport still needed to upgrade the Midland's Manchester, Sheffield and other Northern business services to compete directly with those of the LNWR and GNR, and to create a quality through Anglo-Scottish passenger service using the new line to compete with, and preferably surpass, those of the existing West Coast and East Coast joint routes. Because of route lengths and gradients, the possibility for competition by cutting journey times was very limited (Allport did a little, but his rivals matched it); he therefore, in the 1870s, took a deliberate decision to compete instead on journey quality.

In this area, Allport realised two things just fractionally ahead of his competitors. The first was that, as the LNWR's Sir Frank Ree put it a little later,

'It requires but a trifling inducement to influence the travelling public in the choice of route'

and the second was that there was by now for the first time a substantial long-haul market in 3rd Class travel. Most other companies at this period attempted, without too much success, to divert this demand towards the purchase of more expensive 2nd or 1st Class tickets, by severely limiting the availability of 3rd Class on long-distance trains; Allport, by contrast, realised that there was substantial money to be made from long-haul 3rd Class *per se*, provided the facilities were good enough to induce the new travellers to use it in sufficient numbers. These two concepts together formed the core of Allport's 'comfort revolution', which again had several phases.

Allport began by persuading the Midland Board, in April 1872, to admit 3rd Class passengers to all trains, partly on social reformist and humanitarian grounds (a common element in his reforming arguments, as with other reformers of the period), but also with a very clear eye to the possibility of obtaining increased revenue from fewer trains, if 3rd Class trains no longer had to run separately. Next, in 1873, Allport created a new post of Carriage & Wagon Superintendent to which he appointed Thomas Clayton, specially head-hunted from the GWR at Swindon. Interior upgrades were started immediately, upholstering seats in the 3rd Class carriages to 2nd Class standard for the new all-class fast trains. Then, in 1875, he persuaded the Board to simultaneously abolish 2nd Class, upgrade existing 2nd Class stock to 1st Class standards and reclassify it, and drop 1st Class fare levels to those of the former 2nd Class. Now 3rd Class on the Midland was the equivalent in comfort of 2nd Class anywhere else, and 1st Class was available at 2nd Class prices.

The only market that these reforms between them did not capture was thus what today would be called 'premium first', and Allport's final reform, in parallel with those above, was to address this market by means of introducing Pullman carriages (at that time ultra-luxurious sleepers and day cars rather than diners). In the autumn of 1872 he obtained permission from the Board to carry out a fact-finding visit to America to examine that country's carriage practice, and in particular that of George Pullman, whom he persuaded the Midland Board to invite to address the regular half-yearly shareholders' meeting for February 1873. This resulted in an agreement with the Pullman Company to provide Pullman day and sleeper coaches 'as demand warranted' for a period of 15 years, and allowed Pullman the use of two erecting sheds at Derby Works to erect cars both for the Midland and for any other railway. Thus Allport was responsible for initiating not only Pullmans on the Midland, but also the entire Pullman tradition in England, though diners, which we now most associate with Pullman, had to wait – on the Midland anyway – until after his retirement as General Manager in 1880 to become a member of the Midland Board.

John Aspinall
1851-1937

Locomotive Engineer and Manager

Born	Liverpool, 25 August 1851
Education	Beaumont College, Old Windsor, followed by pupillage at Crewe under Ramsbottom and subsequently F. W. Webb, who sent him on a tour of the USA
Married	Gertrude Schrader, Edge Hill, 2 September 1874 (d 13 March 1920)
Best-known works	Development of automatic vacuum brake, completion of Horwich Works (LYR), development of standardisation and 'large engine' policies, Liverpool-Southport and Manchester-Bury electrification
Honours	President, Inst of Civil Engineers of Ireland 1885; Telford Premium of Inst of Civil Engineers 1888 and James Watt Gold Medal 1901-02; Associate Professor of Railway Engineering, Liverpool University, 1902, and Chairman of Engineering Faculty 1908-15; President, Inst of Mechanical Engineers, 1909 and 1910; knighthood 1917; Hon DEng, Liverpool University, 1922; President, Inst of Civil Engineers, 1918; President, Smeatonian Society, 1931; James Watt International Medal of Inst of Mechanical Engineers, 1936; Knight of Grace of the Order of St John of Jerusalem; Knight of the Order of Leopold

Died	Deerstead House, Woking, 19 January 1937
Buried	St Edward's Cemetery, Sutton Park

Although John Audley Frederick Aspinall's immediate ancestry was one of lawyers and churchmen, his family background included an engineering tradition: his great-great-grandfather was James Wyatt, inventor of the spinning machine. After training at Crewe under two of the seminal locomotive engineers of the 19th century (Ramsbottom and Webb), in a group of pupils that also included H. A. Ivatt, he became first Works Manager then Locomotive Superintendent of the Great Southern & Western Railway of Ireland (on the second move appointing Ivatt to be his deputy as Works Manager). Here he began a policy of locomotive standardisation and 'large engine' development (the latter especially noticeable in his 4-4-0s of Class 60), which he later continued back on the mainland during his time as CME of the LYR. One of the first duties of the new 4-4-0 class was to haul the Irish Royal Train of 1885, the construction of which Aspinall also oversaw. During this period he also designed and patented his continuous vacuum brake.

In 1886 Aspinall was appointed Chief Mechanical Engineer of the Lancashire & Yorkshire Railway, a position he held till 1899, when he was appointed General Manager of the same company – the first locomotive engineer ever to attain a General Manager's post. During his time as CME, he oversaw the development and completion of Horwich Works (the central replacement for the older small works at Bury and Miles Platting begun by his predecessor Barton Wright with Ramsbottom as Consulting Engineer), with a logical and efficient layout and facilities for mechanical handling and hydraulic riveting. He also designed improved coal-handling and watering facilities at Oldham and Southport. On the locomotive front, he continued Barton Wright's policy of standardisation (which fitted well with his own ideas worked out while in Ireland) and continued his 'large engine' development, standardising on 0-6-0s and 0-8-0s for freight, 4-4-0s and 'Highflier' 4-4-2s for passenger work, and the famous 'Lanky' 2-4-2Ts for local services (all further developed by his successors after 1900).

Aspinall's term as General Manager combined diplomatic persuasiveness with careful logical analysis of strategic issues. He was the first railway manager to fit communication cords to all carriages, and also one of the very few to appreciate the exact distinction between the concepts of 'economy' and 'advantage' in strategic decision-making – a distinction that informed his pioneering decision to electrify the Liverpool-Southport line, experiments for which began as early as 1901. He also carried out experiments on wind resistance and locomotive 'front-end shaping' (a precursor of streamlining), which demonstrated that, for the speeds then obtaining, savings would be negligible compared with side-resistance effects. On the operational side, he initiated one of the earliest 'fixed-interval' passenger services – the hourly 40-minute Manchester-Liverpool expresses – promoted the Hull-Zeebrugge ferry service with mainland Europe, and oversaw the completion of the Dearne Valley railway, serving 11 collieries, to secure freight traffic from the new South Yorkshire coalfield. He also saw through a no-competition and revenue-sharing 'tripartite agreement' with the Midland and the LNWR, which eventually became the basis for the formation of the LMS at the 1923 Grouping.

The latter part of Aspinall's term of office was overshadowed by the First World War, which led to Horwich Works being diverted from locomotive building to war construction (and also, briefly, to his own internment as a prisoner of war at Munsterlager – he had been on holiday in Bad Homburg when war broke out). Nevertheless he was able to complete a second electrification scheme, Manchester-Bury, which featured all-metal stock with electric lighting, running on a 10-minute fixed-interval headway, and to institute central train control for the whole LYR system from the Manchester control room. He resigned in 1919, however, on being appointed Consulting Mechanical Engineer to the newly formed Ministry of Transport.

During this final phase of his career Aspinall was a prime mover in several major advances in railway engineering and management. He played a major part in shaping the 1923 'Big Four' grouping of companies, and was a major advocate of the 1920s West Coast main line electrification scheme (killed off, alas, by the Depression). Between 1924 and 1928 he returned to the LMS as an engineering consultant, where he championed the 'big engine' policy that led to the building of the 'Royal Scot' 4-6-0s.

Aspinall also had throughout his life a major interest in engineering education, insisting that Horwich Works from the outset had dedicated space for a Mechanics' Institute, fund-raising for Liverpool University's Engineering Faculty (where he was appointed Associate Professor in Railway Engineering in 1903), and advising on the structure of sandwich courses to provide a balance of practical and theoretical training.

Isambard Kingdom Brunel
1806-59

Civil Engineer

Born	Portsea, Portsmouth, 9 April 1806
Education	Dr Morell's School, Hove; Caen College, Lycée Henri IV, Paris; failed entrance exam to Grand École Polytechnique but was apprenticed to Louis Breguet, Paris
Married	Mary Horsley, Kensington, 5 July 1836
Best-known works	London & Bristol Railway (later Great Western), especially use of broad (7ft 0¼in) gauge, Maidenhead Bridge, Box Tunnel, Swindon Works, Royal Albert Bridge, Saltash; also Thames Tunnel (with father Marc), Clifton Suspension Bridge (completed after his death), and steamships *Great Western*, *Great Britain* and *Great Eastern*
Honours	Elected FRS 1830 for work on Thames Tunnel and Clifton Suspension Bridge
Died	18 Duke St, London, 15 September 1859
Buried	Kensal Green Cemetery, London

Isambard Kingdom Brunel was one of the three or four greatest (some would say, the greatest) engineering geniuses of the early 19th century – he himself recognised only Robert Stephenson as his equal. Born into an engineering family – his father Marc, a French émigré inventor and entrepreneur, had taken out 17 patents by 1825 – Brunel received what was probably the best formal engineering education of any of his British contemporaries, in France, alongside the apprenticeship more usual at the period, first under Louis Breguet, the Paris manufacturer of chronometers, and subsequently under his father, working on the Thames Tunnel. At this time civil, marine and mechanical engineering had not yet separated into distinct professions, and Brunel's energy and inventiveness – and his drive to 'be somebody', as he himself put it – were such that he was constantly embarking on new schemes and adding new projects to his portfolio (of which he periodically took explicit stock), be they tunnels, docks and harbours, railway works, bridges, or steamships. A list of his most famous works is given above: this summary will concentrate on those directly relevant to his status as a railway engineer.

Brunel's first – unsuccessful – application for a railway engineer's post was to the Newcastle & Carlisle Railway, in 1829 (the actual appointee was Francis Giles, an old rival of his on the Thames Tunnel project). Two years later, in December 1831, he obtained his first personal experience of an existing railway: en route home from an interview for the post of engineer (successful this time) to Monkwearmouth Docks, he called on his then girlfriend, Ellen Hulme, in Manchester and travelled on the Liverpool & Manchester Railway. His response to the shaky and bumpy motion of early carriages on the 'Stephenson gauge' was to try drawing freehand circles and lines in his notebook, with the note

'I record this specimen of the shaking on the Manchester Railway. The time is not far off when we shall be able to take our coffee and write whilst going noiselessly and smoothly at 45mph. Let me try…'

Although Brunel himself never indicated any one clear moment when the idea of the 'broad gauge' was fully formed in his mind, it seems likely that this desire for greater stability, quiet and speed was the beginning of that process (it is also one of the first British suggestions for on-train refreshment, though Brunel never developed this side of the proposal).

Brunel's selection of the broad gauge for the London & Bristol – later the Great Western – Railway, to which he was appointed Engineer in March 1833, was only part of his proposal to create the 'finest line of railway' in Britain – 'not the cheapest, but the best', as he put it himself. The line, which he conceived as a strategic trunk link between London and what was then England's largest commercial port, was to be as straight and level as possible; the permanent way, constructed to dimensions sufficient to take his 7-foot gauge, was specially engineered to maintain a smooth and level surface both lengthwise and crosswise; Maidenhead Bridge and Box Tunnel, the two major works on the original line, were similarly designed to combine elegance with working efficiency (the flat arches of Maidenhead Bridge in particular led to contemporary fears about its ability to stand up – it is, of course, still standing and HST 125s run over it regularly!). The combination of these factors led to a railway line that, during the 1840s and 1850s, gave the smoothest ride and returned the highest average express speeds of any English railway, and has in the ensuing 150 years required remarkably little structural upgrading for modern traffic.

What it did not do, though, was keep to budget. Brunel's original estimate for constructing the line was £2.5 million; the final cost was nearly three times as much. This led to considerable friction between him and the Board, which was in turn responsible for one of his greatest strategic mistakes. By the time Swindon station and works, with its associated workmen's housing, was under construction, Brunel was under very considerable pressure to save money on the project; he therefore agreed when the Rigby brothers, his contractors for this part of the project, undertook to build the station and the housing at their own expense, in return for rents from the housing and a 99-year lease on the station refreshment rooms, and the GWR contracted to stop all trains except those sent 'express for special purposes' at Swindon station for 10 minutes during that period, and not to offer any competitive catering facilities elsewhere on the line. The Great Western was thus saddled with a high-speed line on which every train had to stop at Swindon, much too close to London to be convenient as the only refreshment stop on longer journeys. It took till 1895 before the company could buy out the monopoly contract.

Brunel's other major strategic mistake was, as it turned out, the broad gauge itself, which had so contributed to the line's speed and comfort. Most railways in Britain (and indeed elsewhere in Europe and America) opted to use Stephenson's gauge of 4ft 8½in, and as the UK railway map steadily filled up, problems of 'break of gauge', with its resultant need to tranship both goods and passengers – at times even including Queen Victoria – became more frequent. Gloucester was a particular case in point, the transhipment chaos there becoming so scandalous that it engendered a famous cartoon in *Punch*. In 1845 a Royal Commission on Gauges was set up, which recommended that the Stephenson gauge become standard, and the Gauge Act of 1846 gave this the force of law. Railways whose Parliamentary Acts contained 'special enactment defining the gauge' otherwise – which included the Great Western and its Brunel-designed subsidiaries – were exempt, but eventually (after Brunel's death) the costs and inconvenience of transhipment meant that conversion to standard gauge became inevitable, with all its attendant expense and knock-on effects on carriage and locomotive design.

Despite this, though, Brunel in his work for the Great Western and its subsidiaries such as the Bristol & Exeter remained at the forefront of early Victorian railway civil engineering. He built a series of impressive timber viaducts on the South Devon and South Wales Railways, and for the Cornwall Railway created probably his bridge masterpiece, the Royal Albert Bridge at Saltash with its sharply curving approaches, using wrought iron spans – again still in use today. He experimented with atmospheric traction on the South Devon Railway (not a success— rats ate the greased flaps that were supposed to retain the piston vacuum below the power cars), and at Swindon created in 1842 one of the first integrated carriage and wagon works on any railway in Britain. Even his first steamship project, the *Great Western* of 1837, was designed to extend the railway's influence by a linking liner service from Bristol to New York.

Brunel's only major railway engineering weakness lay in locomotive design – at that time often built by external contractors to railway engineers' specifications. Brunel's specifications resulted in underpowered locomotives that did not steam well, but luckily he had appointed a brilliant mechanical engineer in Daniel Gooch, his Locomotive Superintendent (though because of his competitive nature and need to be seen to be in control, he disliked Gooch's increasing independence in that post).

Oliver Bulleid
1882-1970
Locomotive and Carriage Engineer

Born   Invercargill, New Zealand,
                  19 September 1882; family returned
                  to UK 1889-91 after father's death

Education   Middle School, Jed Street,
                  Invercargill, 1888-89; Llanfyllin
                  Church School, 1891-92; Spa College,
                  Bridge of Allan, 1892-94; Accrington
                  Technical School 1894-99; Premium
                  Apprentice under H. A. Ivatt (qv),
                  Doncaster, 1901-06; also attended
                  Doncaster Technical School and
                  lectures at Sheffield and Leeds
                  Universities. Introduced to US
                  locomotive practice while at
                  Doncaster Machine Shop

Married   Marjorie Ivatt, Christ Church,
                  Doncaster, 19 November 1908

Best-known works 'Bognor Buffet Cars', 1938;
                  'Merchant Navy' and 'West Country'
                  'Pacifics', 1941/1945; Co-Co electric
                  locomotive, 1941; 'Q1' 0-6-0s, 1942;
                  'Leader' Class 0-6-6-0s, double-
                  decker suburban stock and 'Tavern
                  Cars', all 1949; 1-Co-Co-1 diesel-
                  electric loco, 1951; 'Turf burner'
                  0-6-6-0 for CIE, 1957

Honours   President, Inst of Locomotive
                  Engineers, 1939-44; Member,
                  Permanent Commission of
                  International Railway Congress,
                  1939; President, Inst of Mechanical
                  Engineers, 1946-47; CBE, 1949;

27

	Hon Member, American Society of Mechanical Engineers, 1949; President, Inst of Welding, 1949-50; Hon DSc, University of Bath, May 1967; Drivers' Testimonial, Exeter, August 1967
Died	Malta, 25 April 1970
Buried	Balzan, Malta

O. V. S. (Oliver Vaughan Snell) Bulleid has been described as 'the last giant of steam', although his engineering record is in fact much wider, also taking in innovations in carriage and wagon design, electric locomotive and multiple-unit building, and the mechanical side of early UK diesel-electric practice. Curiously, unlike many of the 'famous railwaymen' recorded in these pages, he does not seem to have been overwhelmingly attracted to locomotive engineering from an early age: his childhood was marked by a brilliant, inquisitive mind about most things, a somewhat unruly nature (which he retained all his life!) and no particularly clear idea about what he wanted to become. Indeed, he became apprenticed under Ivatt almost by accident, on the urging of a clerical relative with a living at Doncaster who wanted to keep him firmly in the High Anglican faith, which he feared would be lost by a proposed legal apprenticeship back in New Zealand. (The move was if anything too successful – Bulleid eventually converted to Roman Catholicism.) Thus throughout his career his primary engineering commitment was perhaps to scientific and technological enquiry and experiment (both successful and not-so-successful) rather than to locomotive engineering as such.

Although the work for which Bulleid is best remembered in the UK (see list above) was all done after he became CME of the Southern Railway in 1937, it followed a long period of equally important development work. From 1907 to 1937, with the exceptions of four years spent abroad with Westinghouse (1908-12) – where he first encountered French chain drive – and the British Exhibitions division of the Board of Trade, and wartime service with the Division of Railway Transport (1915-19), Bulleid served as a personal assistant at Doncaster, first to the Locomotive Running Superintendent, then to the Works Manager, under whom he introduced a machine forging and drop stamping plant, and finally to Nigel (later Sir Nigel) Gresley (qv).

Bulleid's initial contributions as personal assistant to Gresley were in carriage design – an aspect of the CME's remit that was to continue to interest him when he joined the Southern. In 1921 he pioneered the 'quint-art' dining set for the London-Leeds service (five coaches – Brake Composite, 1st Diner, Kitchen, 3rd Diner, Brake Composite – on six bogies, the first set to cook entirely by electricity), and in 1922 a pair of twin-articulated ECJS sleeping-cars that set the standard for inter-war sleepers on all three Scottish routes (and incidentally the first railway vehicle to use the 'crank to close the window if you sneeze' made famous in the railway episode of T. S. Eliot's 'Practical Cats'). He also initiated welded carriage underframes. On the locomotive side, it was Bulleid who was responsible for the balancing design for Gresley's three-cylinder locomotives; he was also closely associated with the 'P2' design – especially the prototype *Cock o' the North*, the testing of which he oversaw at the French national testing plant at Vitry-sur-Seine. He accompanied Gresley on various Continental visits in connection with his high-speed streamlined designs, and was personally responsible for the aerofoil design of the wheel valances of the 'A4' 'Pacifics'.

In 1937 Bulleid was appointed CME of the Southern Railway, to succeed R. E. L. Maunsell. His initial inspections uncovered a line on which steam-haulage improvements and updating had been systematically sacrificed by top management to push forward electrification, a stance highly appropriate to both London suburban traffic and the Central and Eastern Divisions generally, but which had left the old LSWR main line, the heavy Dover and Southampton boat trains, and goods traffic all seriously underpowered. The line's flagship express engines – the 'Lord Nelsons' – were consistent under-performers as built; the 'Schools' 4-4-0s were excellent but too small for projected West Country traffic levels (though they did perform magnificently on tests on the 'Atlantic Coast Express' in 1939); and Maunsell's last freight design, the 'Q' Class 0-6-0s, had parts to designs dating back to Wainwright's day and were again underpowered for future demand.

Bulleid began by rebuilding the 'Nelsons' with Lemaître exhausts and Chapelon-style cylinder internal streamlining, in which condition they gave yeoman service, but they were still more than ten years old and wearing fast, even at the outbreak of war. He also experimented briefly in 1939 with a streamlined casing for the 'Schools' Class, for use on fast lightweight limited expresses, but appears to have thought better of it, and returned the test loco (No 935 *Sevenoaks*) to its original state. Of the 'Qs', he simply remarked that 'they arrived too late to stop being built'. It was clear that, apart from additional electrification designs (which duly arrived in the form first of the 'Bognor buffet' sets and later – in 1941 – of the Co-Co electric locomotives designed jointly with Raworth), the Southern's most pressing needs were for a really modern and powerful express locomotive, capable of hauling 500-600-ton trains at a 70mph average, and a widely available heavy-duty freight workhorse. It was these that Bulleid provided in his most important designs – the 'Merchant Navy' and 'West Country' 'Pacifics', and the 'Q1' Austerity 0-6-0s – even though the 'Merchant Navy' Class had to be slipped in under the wartime net as mixed traffic.

An analysis of Bulleid's original designs, both for these locomotives and for his carriages (and even for the 0-6-6-0T 'Leaders', his last design for mainland Britain, which proved to be such a disaster), demonstrates that they were based on three guiding influences – French practice, particularly over such matters as internal streamlining, large blast-pipes, thermic siphons and welded construction, and even chain-driven gearing; his experience under Gresley, evident for example in the scalloped table edges of the 'Bognor buffets', reminiscent of the LNER 'Coronation' coaching stock; and American practice, gleaned from his work with the International Railway Congress and avid reading of American technical journals since youth. (Perhaps the best example of this last is found in the 'Tavern Cars' and inward-facing restaurant seating for the post-war 'Atlantic Coast Express', both of which are clearly highly influenced, both in concept and in layout, by the 'Moderne' design produced by Pullman-Standard for a range of US railways from 1937.)

Bulleid's main designs, from the 'air-smoothed' 'Merchant Navy' 4-6-2s to the 'Tavern Cars', characteristically engendered controversy by their very radical nature when viewed from a traditional 'Stephenson' UK standpoint. You either loved them or you hated them – there was almost no middle way. This makes objective assessment of his work singularly difficult (a characteristic he shares with Francis Webb).

As with those of Webb (qv), his designs have certain well-noticed drawbacks. The 'Pacifics' were horribly prone to wheel-slip and burned a lot of coal, and the oil-bath-enclosed chain-driven valve-gear was much too complicated for post-war British conditions (it might have done better in France); the inward-facing restaurant car seats were cramped by having to fit within the UK loading gauge (they'd worked fine on the New Haven Railroad, but that was to the much larger American gauge), and diners disliked sitting with their backs to the view; and the Methodist Union and Temperance League were horrified by actually having a pub on a train – though that was their prejudice rather than a fault of Bulleid's design. On the other hand, the 'Pacifics' were certainly speedy (in my youth, I used regularly to record speeds over 90mph behind them in 1947-49), steady runners when they weren't slipping, and magnificent at hill climbing with heavy trains. The 'Q1s' looked like something out of a nightmare, but reliably hauled heavy goods loads throughout and after the war, and were able to run at speeds up to 75mph despite having only 5ft 1in wheels. And the 'Tavern Cars', despite the furore they caused, returned the best financial profits of any Southern catering vehicle.

Bulleid's last three designs, however, were a different matter. The 0-6-6-0T 'Leader' was intended to be a general-purpose steam locomotive with the overall availability of a diesel, able to be simply lifted off its bogies and on to new ones in a matter of minutes and, if (as Bulleid assumed) eventually oil-fired, to be operated from a single forward-facing cab – one at each end, so no need for turntables – if necessary in remote tandem. The concept was certainly intriguing and innovative. However, the detail design was even 'fussier' than the 'Pacifics', though various experiments had been carried out previously on some of its elements, eg sleeve valves, and since the UK government countermanded the oil-firing proposal for exchange rate reasons, the centrally positioned fireman's cubby-hole would have been unbearably hot in regular operation. Had Bulleid remained in full charge after nationalisation, he might (just possibly!) have overcome the major problems with the class, but he was now subject to central overruling from British Railways, and in 1949 resigned from BR in favour of a post with CIE in Dublin, first as Consulting Engineer, then in 1951 as CME – the same year that the first really successful readily available diesel-electric 1-Co-Co-1 locomotive (for which he had designed the mechanical parts) was delivered to the Southern Region of BR.

The second of his last three designs, the double-decker electric suburban train, again suffered from the restricted British loading gauge. Intended as a response to overcrowding on the Charing Cross-Dartford line, where sets could not be lengthened because of platform restrictions, it made use of an ingenious 'up and down' design with staggered upper and lower compartments, to increase capacity by roughly 50%. Double-decker trains, as we have since seen, operate well to larger loading gauges, for example in America and France, but here, as in the 'Tavern' diners, the restrictions of the British loading gauge seem to have finally defeated the designers. The problem was not capacity, but that the upper and lower compartments were so 'squashed up' by loading gauge constrictions that boarding and alighting took almost as long again as with normal stock, effectively cancelling out any savings from increased capacity.

Bulleid's final design, a sort of lightweight and modified 'Leader', designed to burn turf, emerged from CIE in 1957. Like the 'Leaders' proper, it seems to have been envisaged ultimately to burn oil, but even in its turf-burning mode it appears to have steamed well, and been a fast and reasonably powerful locomotive, with few of the problems that dogged the original 'Leader' Class back in Britain. However, both Bulleid and steam traction were now reaching retirement age; Bulleid retired from CIE in 1958 (aged 76!), and Ireland committed completely to dieselisation.

George Churchward
1857-1933

Locomotive Engineer

Born	Rowes Farm, Stoke Gabriel, Devon, 31 January 1857, son of the younger brother of a Devon squire
Education	Totnes Grammar School, and private tutor at home; apprenticed to John Wright, Newton Abbot Works (South Devon Railway), 1873, then transferred to Swindon, under Joseph Armstrong, in 1876 when GWR absorbed SDR
Married	Remained single
Best-known works	CME of GWR following William Dean (qv); introduced standard designs, boiler and part interchangeability, superheating, taper boilers and long lap valve travel; designed '2800' and '4700' Class 2-8-0s, '4300' Class 2-6-0s, '4500' Class 2-6-2Ts, '2900' ('Saint') and '4000' ('Star', four-cylinder) 4-6-0s, *The Great Bear* (first British 4-6-2); oversaw building of first successful European locomotive testing plant
Honours	Mayor of Swindon, 1900, and Hon Freeman, 1920; President, Assoc of Railway Locomotive Engineers, 1917; CBE 1918
Died	Swindon, 19 December 1933 – run down by GWR express outside his house while inspecting track
Buried	Swindon parish churchyard

George Jackson Churchward was a Great Western man through and through. Born in Devon, the son of a country squire's younger brother, he trained first with the South Devon Railway – to all intents and purposes the GWR – then, when that line was fully absorbed by the GWR, transferred to Swindon, where he completed his apprenticeship under first Armstrong, then Dean. In 1885 he became Carriage Works Manager, then Works Manager 11 years later (he re-equipped Swindon Works with modern machine tools and 30hp electric motors), and Dean's Chief Assistant in 1898. Dean retired in June 1902, and Churchward succeeded him.

Churchward's locomotives were marked by a radical shift in both design and appearance from those of his predecessor's major design period, incorporating many features closer to American than current British practice, especially in cylinder arrangement, front-end framing and boiler design, probably due to his long-standing friendship with A. W. Gibbs of the Pennsylvania Railroad. His first few years as CME at Swindon, 1902-07, were spent in extensive design trials and prototype experiments, with a view to establishing design criteria for the standard locomotive designs with interchangeable parts that he had in mind. Prototype locomotives built during this period included the 4-6-0s Nos 100 (built during the handover period between Dean and Churchward), 98 (the first to have the full taper boiler) and 171 *Albion*, with 225psi pressure (later briefly converted to a 4-4-2 for more direct comparison with three French de Glehn compounds bought in experimentally for testing and trial purposes), together with the four-cylinder simple 4-4-2 No 40 *North Star*, produced in 1907, also to form part of the extended express locomotive tests.

However, the compounds did not show sufficient superiority over the simple machines to warrant the adoption of compound expansion, and the running departments preferred the greater adhesion of the 4-6-0s to the 4-4-2 types. Consequently the Great Western express engine under Churchward was standardised on two simple-expansion designs – a two-cylinder 4-6-0 descended from *Albion* (the 'Saint' class) and a four-cylinder 4-6-0 version of *North Star*. Other prototypes produced during this period included No 97, the first freight 2-8-0, and No 99, the first 2-6-2T.

The upshot of all this experimental design was the standardisation of Swindon design on taper boilers to improve water flow, long travel and long lap valves to ensure good exhaust, short straight steam passages for the same purpose, fireboxes with curved side plates and crown (for good circulation) and a backward-sloping top to guard against loss of water cover in sudden braking, and low-temperature superheating to ensure dry steam and avoid cylinder condensation (the famous 'Ramsbottom Effect' [qv]). Four standard boilers proved sufficient to fit all the classes envisaged (though a fifth, the 'No 7', was added in 1921, the year of his retirement), at just two pressures – 225psi for the 'No 1' fitted to all express 4-6-0s and the 2800 Class of 2-8-0s descended from No 97 (and later the 'No 7'), and 200psi for the other three, among other designs fitted on the three different sizes of standard 2-6-2T descended from No 99.

Subsequent design work by Churchward followed the same pattern of a search for standardisation, with one exception. In 1908 he obtained permission to build one experimental large engine, a 4-6-2, at an estimated cost of £4,400. The locomotive that emerged, *The Great Bear*, used a 'Star' Class front end (though with larger cylinders), but both the boiler – a comparatively poor steamer when handled by GWR firemen used to the narrow grates, but excellent when handled properly – and the firebox were specially designed non-standard items. It seems probable that Churchward never intended his 4-6-2 to be a genuine prototype (or he would have incorporated more standard components), and there remains some doubt as to just why he did build it, though he does seem to have envisaged a lengthy and strenuous experimental testing of the design, which still remained incomplete when the First World War brought it to a halt.

The Great Bear's axle weights restricted it to the London-Bristol route, where it performed regularly on daytime down expresses, returning overnight on up fast fitted freights. It is possible that Churchward may have intended the locomotive as a practical challenge to Civil Engineering weight restrictions, by showing what could be done with heavier weights; at that time he was still on excellent terms with James Inglis, the Chief Engineer, though they became estranged later when Inglis became General Manager. Alternatively, A. W. Gibbs's influence might possibly have been behind the choice of wheelbase – the Pennsylvania RR brought out its prototype 4-6-2 (Class 'K28', the ancestor of the famous 'K4s') in 1907. A further alternative is that the wide firebox – an American design feature that, as Churchward commented, 'English locomotive engineers are within measurable distance of adopting' as early as 1903 – looked forward to the days when the GWR would need to burn inferior coal.

Experience with *The Great Bear* did, however, produce one important insight: the increasing need for locomotives that could handle passenger and fast freight traffic equally well – 'mixed traffic' locomotives, in fact. The result was two further prototypes, both with the 5ft 8in wheels of the larger 2-6-2T – the '4300' Class, Britain's first mixed traffic 2-6-0 and one of the Great Western's most ubiquitous and numerous classes, in 1911, and the '4700' Class large-wheeled 2-8-0s, even more directly inspired by the schedules and activities of the 'Pacific', following the First World War hiatus in 1919. The '4700s', a comparatively small class, eventually used a special new (and specially large) boiler, the 'No 7' referred to above, though the prototype had the express 4-6-0 'No 1'. However, the '4300' 'Moguls' had both their boiler and many other parts interchangeable with the large 2-6-2Ts, making them in effect tank and tender versions of the same design.

Churchward retired in 1921, taking C. B. Collett (qv), his Principal Assistant, into virtual partnership during 1920 to ease the transition, just as Dean had done with him. Always a keen fly fisherman, he asked for a fishing rod as a retirement present (and of course got it). In retirement he continued to live in the official GWR CME's residence, 'Newburn', opposite Swindon Works. In 1933, with failing eyesight and hearing, he was knocked down by one of his own locomotives while inspecting the track one foggy December morning. He left behind him an unrivalled fleet of standardised locomotives, arguably of the most advanced design in Britain.

Thomas Clayton
1831-1916

Carriage Designer

Born	Madeley, Shropshire, early 1831, son of a blacksmith who later became an engineer and boilermaker/ foundrymaster; exact date of birth not recorded, but baptised on 12 June 1831.
Education	Initial engineering education as patternmaker in father's shops, followed in 1850 or 1851 by apprenticeship in locomotive department of Shrewsbury & Birmingham Railway (absorbed by GWR 1854). (He seems also to have gained experience working for several other lines at this time, including the LBSCR.)
Married	(1) Emily Baker, Bridgnorth, 5 June 1854 (d Swindon, 18 August 1871); (2) Mary Elizabeth Gough (widow), Bethnal Green, 16 October 1873
Best-known works	Building of Derby Carriage & Wagon Works, 1873-77; redesign and refurbishment of 3rd Class to 2nd Class standard, 1875; bogie 12-wheel composites and eight-wheel 3rds for Scottish expresses, 1876; universal brake hose coupling between carriages, 1878; Travelling Post Office, 1879; 12-wheel bogie diners, 1892-93; 'clerestory-balloon' coaches from 1897 for Manchester services

Honours	Bogie Composite No 916 awarded
	Grand Prix at Paris Exhibition 1889
Died	Bournemouth, 12 April 1916 (of
	heart disease)
Buried	Wimborne Road Cemetery,
	Bournemouth

Of all the 50 men featured in this book, Thomas Clayton is perhaps the most elusive. Apart from the somewhat sparse marital and educational details listed above, his life outside of his work at Derby seems almost impossible to track down – though a photograph of circa 1899 currently in the National Railway Museum collection shows him and S. W. Johnson (qv) posed in a 'family group' setting with what appear to be the mothers, wives and daughters of their two families. Even his first name is not given as the same in all sources: both Hamilton Ellis and David Jenkinson call him Thomas throughout, as does J. B. Radford, but Roy Williams, in *The Midland Railway: A New History*, refers to him sometimes as Thomas and sometimes as James Clayton. It is certain from MR Locomotive Committee minutes of his appointment that Thomas is the correct forename, but just to complicate matters there was indeed another, slightly later, Clayton called James, working for the Midland under Deeley and Paget. However, he was a locomotive draughtsman rather than a specialist carriage designer; in 1913 he moved to the SECR to form part of Maunsell's team, and as late as 1937-38, 20 years after the death of 'our' Clayton, was still working (though in ill health) for the Southern under Bulleid. It is not clear whether or not the two Claytons were related, though A. E. Overton records that Tom Clayton did have four sons by his second wife.

However, notwithstanding his personal elusiveness, Clayton is one of the most important figures in British railway carriage design. In 1873 he was head-hunted by Allport (qv) of the Midland as part of the latter's drive to upgrade the railway, and its passenger-carrying ability, to national status. At Swindon Clayton had already come to prominence first by overseeing construction of the Swindon Carriage Works from 1863 onwards, then by designing and building the Great Western's second (bogie) Royal Saloon, much to Queen Victoria's approval. Under Kirtley (qv) the posts of Locomotive Superintendent and Carriage Superintendent had been combined, but following Kirtley's death in harness in 1873 Allport determined to split the two posts, appointing a leading specialist for each, the Locomotive Superintendent being S. W. Johnson (qv). Clayton was appointed specifically to execute Allport's planned reform of passenger comfort; as the summary at the head of the entry shows, he did so to the highest standards, as a result of which the Midland led all other railways for passenger comfort for many years.

Clayton began, in 1873, virtually as soon as he was appointed, by overseeing the creation of a new and (for the period) massive Carriage & Wagon Works at Derby, involving substantial technological advance in the use of both steam and hydraulic power. This process took in all some four years, till 1877, but at the same time he was also redesigning and refurbishing 3rd Class stock to 2nd Class standard (Allport was about to phase out 2nd Class altogether). From 1875 this involved providing upholstered seats for 3rd Class passengers – something hitherto unheard-of – causing something of a furore in the railway world.

Still more luxury was to come. In 1876 there followed a series of bogie 12-wheel Composites and eight-wheel 3rds for the new London-Scotland expresses, to the unprecedented height of 8ft 4½in. The 3rd class seats were of repp stuffed with horsehair, while 1st Class were of sprung and overstuffed broadcloth. All the door bottoms had draught excluders. Initially the Composites offered four 3rd Class compartments, three 1st Class, and a luggage compartment; in later years the design was modified to include toilet facilities (at the cost of one 3rd Class compartment), and steam heating and oil-gas lighting were added. It was in this form that one of the composites, No 916, won the Grand Prix at the 1889 Paris Exhibition.

Clayton's later coaches continued to set the standard not only for the Midland but for other UK railways, both in comfort and in safety. In 1878 he was responsible for introducing the universal brake hose coupling (adopted by most major lines at a conference called by F. W. Webb (qv) in 1881 and still in use to the very end of steam in the UK), allowing a single pipe to replace the complex dual-pipe arrangement with separate male and female hose connectors that had been in use up to that point. In the following year he introduced a 30-foot Travelling Post Office vehicle complete with mailbag exchange apparatus. Among his finest late coaches were his 12-wheel bogie diners of 1892-96 (one of which was fitted out by Gillow's of Lancaster as a showpiece 'regardless of cost'); these were 1st and 3rd Kitchen-Diners in pairs, gangwayed together at the kitchen ends but not through-connected to the rest of the train, with full-width kitchens with Fletcher-Russell oil-gas cookers. His best late non-dining stock was the 1897 'clerestory balloon' series for the Manchester business services, with internal corridors but not through-gangwayed; they featured toilets (though not on every coach!), steam heating with extra radiators below the door-space, and electric bell communication between passengers and train staff.

The one area where Clayton was behind his rivals in design was the introduction of through-gangwayed corridor trains; these did not appear on the Midland until the very end of the 19th century, only a few years before his retirement in 1902. The reason may well have been a desire to save train weight, especially on dining-car services, where non-corridor diners meant that the vehicle also carried revenue-earning seats –

both factors especially important on a heavily graded line with a small-engine policy.

Like a number of other Victorian engineer-managers we shall meet in this book, Clayton appears to have been something of an autocrat, despite the fact that he never entirely lost traces of his bluff working-class origins in the Wolverhampton GWR patternmakers' shop. In *Midland Railway Memories* (1924), George Pratt comments of him that 'the carpenter's cap and apron seemed to cling to him to the end of his life' (quoting his somewhat awkward epistolary style as evidence), but also remarks of him that '"his" men were always treated as mice'.

To some extent, however, this autocratic stance may well have been a matter of meeting the needs of the situation. At least up until 1878 he had to carry through a revolution in working practices and standards, getting rid of the older and more hidebound workers, recruiting new ones to meet exacting quality standards, and moving an entire labour force on to piecework (apparently Allport's idea rather than his), and at the same time defending 'his' carriage rebuilds from staff on the running side who constantly sought to borrow them from the shops before they were completely ready to help out in traffic emergencies. Perhaps the one real management oddity of his régime was his persistent refusal to allow his staff to join the Midland's superannuation scheme, for which there seems little rational explanation – especially when at the same time he made it a point of honour to give staff widows preferential employment in the upholstery shops, despite some union objections.

As remarked above, Clayton retired in 1902 (succeeded by Thomas Bain), and he and his second wife Mary Elizabeth went at some point after that to live in Bournemouth, where he died of heart problems in 1910. Mary, who is buried with him, survived him by a further 18 years.

Charles Collett
1871-1952

Locomotive Engineer

Born	Grafton Manor, Worcs, 10 September 1871
Education	Merchant Taylors' School, then pupillage with Maudslay Son & Field (marine engineers) and studies at City & Guilds Engineering College, South Kensington (now Imperial College). Joined Swindon Works as draughtsman, 1893
Married	Ethelwyn Mary Simon, St George's, Bloomsbury, 4 November 1896
Best-known works	Designed 'Castle' and 'King' Class 4-6-0s (enlarged from Churchward 'Star' design) and 'Hall', 'Grange' and 'Manor' mixed traffic 4-6-0s (derived from Churchward 'Saint' design); re-equipped Swindon Works (especially erecting shop) and modernised testing plant; extended automatic train control to all important GWR routes
Honours	OBE 1918; JP 1921; Collett Avenue, Swindon, named after him in 1938
Died	Melrose, Wimbledon, 23 August 1952
Buried	Not known

Like his predecessor Churchward (qv), Charles Benjamin Collett was a product completely of the Great Western as far as locomotive engineering went; following his pupillage in marine engineering, he joined Swindon drawing office in 1893, as a young man of 22, and rose successively to be Assistant Works Manager in 1900, Works Manager in 1902, and Churchward's deputy in 1920, the year before the latter's retirement. He took over from Churchward as CME at the turn of the year 1921/22; because of the usual transitional arrangements falling across the turn of year period, different authorities have quoted his taking office as either of these years. His first two or three years in office were occupied by two completely different problems – the absorption by the new post-Grouping GWR of a large number of smaller railways, mainly in South Wales, of extremely varied sizes and locomotive fleets, and the simultaneous need in the GWR's original heartland for a new and more powerful express engine for the reviving post-First World War traffic.

The first problem, indeed, became for a while something a preoccupation with Collett (though it never prevented him from addressing the second one also). It is sometimes assumed that, because the Great Western was never merged with other companies of similar size, it therefore in some ways 'had it easy' compared with the other 'Big Four'. This, however, is not really true: while it was saved from the 'amalgamation infighting' that bedevilled the pre-Stanier LMS, and possibly also the first couple of years of the Southern (till Walker took it firmly in hand), it did face an almost equally daunting administrative and engineering task. On the 'old' GWR, locomotive and part standardisation had under Churchward proceeded further than on any other British railway, and most if not all of its repair and running practices were governed by this fact, but suddenly here were entire series of new locomotives and lines to be incorporated into this system, the locos totally non-standard in design and the lines in many cases fiercely independent in nature. How on earth were they to be fitted into the Swindon way of doing things?

Collett's initial response was to conduct an audit of

all the multifarious locomotives taken over, to see how many could be rebuilt, as need arose, to incorporate standard Swindon parts (particularly boilers). Those that could be so rebuilt, would be – the rest would be scrapped and replaced by GWR standard types. At this point, however, a problem arose: in the South Wales Valleys in particular, track and traffic conditions had given rise to a characteristic locomotive type of which there was no direct Great Western equivalent – the large but compact 0-6-2T. Standard GWR 'pannier' 0-6-0Ts were too light (and didn't have the fuel and water capacity for the runs involved), though panniers could be fitted on existing Welsh 0-6-0Ts readily enough; and standard GWR outside-cylinder 2-6-2Ts, though in some cases large enough, found it difficult to handle the clearances and track curvature. Collett's response, partly it would appear at the suggestion of the Great Western's new General Manager, Felix Pole, was a classic managerial and engineering compromise – the Great Western's very own brand new 0-6-2T design, the '5600' Class of 1924, with standard GWR pistons and valves, and the Swindon No 2 boiler. Two hundred were eventually built, replacing the older Welsh 0-6-2Ts as they became due for withdrawal.

Collett's response to his other initial problem – the need for a more powerful express engine – was also a compromise, though a highly triumphant one. His initial design, building on Churchward's 'Star' Class four-cylinder 4-6-0s, was to generate additional power from the Swindon No 7 boiler, as fitted to the '4700' mixed traffic 2-8-0s. However, the Civil Engineer wouldn't have it – that would have made the locos too heavy for all but the 'full-strength' sections of the line (a feature that likewise restricted the route availability of the later 'Kings'). Collett compromised again, designing a new, lighter standard boiler (the Swindon No 8). The result was the 'Castle' Class, a triumphant success from the word go, and frequently regarded as the best Great Western express engines ever, even including the more powerful (and heavier) 'Kings' that appeared three years later and did have a (lengthened) version of that troublesome No 7 boiler. A 'Castle' was shown at the Wembley Exhibition, while *King George V* appeared – yet again thanks to Pole – at the B&O Centenary celebrations in the USA. Collett's name and fame were assured. There were only ever 30 'Kings', but the total build of 'Castles' eventually reached 171.

Collett's other main claim to fame as a locomotive designer rests on his two-cylinder mixed traffic 4-6-0s, the 'Halls', 'Granges' and 'Manors'. The first of these three designs was pure Churchward, constructed by simply replacing the 6ft 8½in wheels of *Saint Martin* with 6ft 0in drivers, though further modifications to cabs and centring arrangements were made in the later locos of the series. The 1936 'Granges' had smaller wheels still (5ft 8in) and thus a somewhat higher tractive effort; they were particularly intended to supplement Churchward's '4300' Class 2-6-0s (which Collett had continued to build until 1932!) and were specially useful on fast perishable traffic, such as fruit and veg. The 'Manors' of 1938 were a lighter version of the 'Granges', with a 17-ton axle-loading offering very wide route availability. All three types were successful in traffic.

Similarly successful, though less obviously spectacular, were the '2251' Class taper-boilered 0-6-0s of 1930 for lighter duties, and the many and various new and Churchward 0-6-0PTs and 2-6-2Ts produced throughout Collett's reign. There was also, however, one very curious departure from Collett's standard 'post-Churchward' locomotive practice during the 1930s: a revival of several modernised Dean designs – notably 0-6-0PTs and 0-4-2Ts, primarily for auto-train working, and a group of refurbished 4-4-0s (the so-called 'Dukedogs') for the former Cambrian Railways holiday traffic. Possibly, like the GWR's diesel railcars, also constructed under Collett, these resurrections and renewals were a response to the pressures of the Depression years: they were certainly cheaper to produce than an entirely new branch-line design would have been.

At the other end of the scale, Collett also schemed out in 1937 a proposal for a massive 2-10-2T, using the '4700' Class No 7 standard boiler, for Ebbw Vale iron ore traffic, which often needed double-heading plus a banker. The projected 2-10-2T would certainly have been powerful enough to handle the trains on its own – but how it might have dealt with Ebbw Vale curves one hates to think! In the event, the Locomotive Committee didn't approve it, and the onset of war just two years later put an end to any design revisions that might have been in Collett's mind.

Outside of locomotive design pure and simple, Collett played two other important roles in the Great Western's inter-war development. He substantially modernised both Swindon Works (especially the erecting shop and, in 1936, the testing plant) with new equipment, making possible considerably greater mileages between major overhauls, and similarly modernised Wolverhampton and Caerphilly Works to make repairs of heavy engines possible there, avoiding the need to send locos to Swindon. He also widely extended the use of the Automatic Train Control safety system across the Great Western's routes (and recommended its extension to the other 'Big Four', though this never happened). His last two years in office were preoccupied by the onset of the Second World War; he attempted to minimise the extent to which Swindon Works was called upon for non-railway war work (such as munitions manufacture), and resisted the employment of women in railway trades. Less than wholly successful on both these wartime fronts, Collett retired as CME in 1941, and died in 1952.

Davison Dalziel
1854-1928

Financier and Travel Entrepreneur

Born	London, 17 October 1854, nephew of George Dalziel and his brothers, the London wood-engravers
Education	London and USA
Married	Harriet Danning, Edinburgh, 1876
Best-known works	Chairman of Pullman Company Ltd, London, 1907-28 (and sole owner 1907-15); refashioned Pullman in UK as primarily a luxury at-seat dining service; introduced 3rd Class Pullman cars; joined CIWL Board in 1903, becoming Chief Executive, 1919, and Chairman, 1924; co-ordinated activities of CIWL, Pullman and Thomas Cook between wars
Honours	Elected MP for Brixton, 1910; baronetcy, 1919, and ennobled in 1927 as Lord Dalziel of Wooler, for services during First World War
Died	London, 18 April 1928
Buried	Highgate Cemetery (East), London, opposite cemetery entrance

Like Villard (qv) in USA, Davison Dalziel came to railways via journalism and high finance, though his association with them lasted much longer and was substantially more financially successful, while being equally influential on travel comfort and style. He made his initial fortune in journalism in San Francisco and Chicago in 1878/9 onwards, then moved to London and set up a news agency (1893) and also London's first motor taxi service (1908). In 1907 he bought out the Pullman Company (UK), of which he was sole owner until he floated it as a public company in 1915, and of which he remained Chairman until his death in 1928. In the early 1920s he was also briefly owner of the *Evening Standard* and the *Pall Mall Gazette*, but resold them within the newspaper world to concentrate on his railway interests.

Dalziel was also active in mainland Europe. He joined the Board of Wagons-Lits in 1903, with a remit to overhaul the company's then ailing finances (they had taken a considerable loss on the 1900 Paris Exhibition); this he did successfully, also masterminding the purchase by Wagons-Lits of Thomas Cook. While already involved with Pullman (but before his 1907 takeover), he married his daughter to Nagelmackers's son René, thus ensuring a dynastic as well as financial link between what were in effect to become 'his' two major companies (although his daughter, alas, died young in 1910). In 1919 he became Chief Executive of Wagons-Lits, and in 1924 Chairman, again remaining so until his death.

Dalziel's influence on luxury train travel in Britain and Europe, especially after the First World War, was profound. When he bought out the Pullman Company, and took over the financial control of Wagons-Lits, both concerns were struggling, Pullman because it had few economically viable contracts and Wagons-Lits because of the losses sustained on the 1900 Paris Exhibition. Dalziel turned both companies round financially, but, more importantly, in so doing he changed significantly the nature of their product and image in each case, effectively creating the company images that became standard from then till the end of luxury rail travel.

In Britain he modified the Pullman offer in several important ways. Initially in the USA, the essence of Pullman travel had been luxurious day and night accommodation, especially overnight, purchased by paying a premium. However, in Britain there was little call for luxury sleepers (and what demand there was, was satisfied mainly by the railway companies themselves), so it was unclear just what prospective passengers were being asked to pay their premium supplements for. As part of his drive to regain viable markets, Dalziel conceived of the key Pullman 'marque' as being luxury daytime travel with an at-seat catering service at every seat. His test-bed for this concept was the 'Southern Belle', which ran between London and Brighton twice daily (except during the war years) from November 1908. In 1915, initially to offset the wartime decline in 1st Class traffic, he added 3rd Class Pullmans to the service, with slightly denser seating (2+1 replacing 1+1) and a few other simplifications, including carriage numbers instead of names. Both experiments were resounding successes, and set the standard format for Pullman trains in Britain from then on. He also ordered new carriage designs, from British rather than US builders.

His other main changes were to rationalise the existing Pullman contracts, seeking to focus on and add to profitable routes and 'drop' unprofitable ones – a policy continued by his successors and one that was assisted by Sir Ralph Wedgwood of the LNER and Sir Herbert Walker of the Southern (qqv) – and to integrate his British and continental ventures to provide through London-Paris services. In particular he created in 1924 the 'Golden Arrow' (Pullman)/ 'Flèche D'Or' (Wagons-Lits) cross-Channel service, complete with its own steamer (the *Canterbury*), though the onset of the 1929 Depression meant, alas, that for much of its life this political flagship international rail service was not a financial success.

In his dealings with Wagons-Lits, Dalziel's innovations were similar. Co-operation between CIWL and Pullman replaced the competition verging on enmity that had existed in George Pullman's and Georges Nagelmackers's days. International Pullman services, such as the Londres-Vichy Pullman, were introduced, making use of Wagons-Lits contracts, and again British and mainland European firms were induced to co-operate over the design and furnishing of Wagons-Lits dining-cars. 2nd Class (which still existed in mainland Europe, fulfilling the upper part of the role of 3rd Class in the UK) was introduced to most Wagons-Lits expresses, though not at this point to the 'Orient Express'. The latter was itself expanded following 1919 into an entire 'suite' of trains – 'Direct Orient', 'Simplon Orient', 'Arlberg Orient', 'Tauern Orient' and a range of feeder trains both in Europe and in the Middle East. And by integrating the workings of Pullman, CIWL and Thomas Cook, Dalziel made it very much easier to make international bookings right across Britain and mainland Europe.

Although he married and had a family, Dalziel never retired. He was still at work overseeing his companies virtually to the day of his death in April 1928, in his 75th year.

William Dean
1840-1905

Locomotive, Carriage and Wagon Engineer

Born	London, 9 January 1840, son of Henry Dean, manager of Hawes's soap factory
Education	Haberdasher's Company's School, apprenticed from October 1855 under Joseph Armstrong at the GWR's Northern Division Wolverhampton Works
Married	Twice: his first wife died after the birth of their third child, his second (1878) died 1889
Best-known works	Under Gooch's chairmanship, presided over final stages of conversion from broad to standard gauge; introduced first transverse-compartment sleepers (1881) and first all-corridor through-gangwayed carriage set (1891); improved vacuum brake and established Swindon technical and materials laboratory; designed 0-6-0 'Dean Goods', 'Aberdare' 2-6-0s, 'Duke' and 'Bulldog' 4-4-0s, 4-2-2 express 'singles'; also built several experimental early 4-6-0s, for both freight and passenger service (the latter at the very end of his term, jointly with Churchward – qv)
Honours	Major, Swindon Volunteers; JP for Wiltshire; MIME 1868; MICE 1878; Dean Street, Swindon, named after him in 1890

| *Died* | Folkestone, 24 September 1905 |
| *Buried* | Folkestone Cemetery |

Like his predecessor, Armstrong, and his successors, Churchward and Collett, William Dean was essentially a Great Western man in both training and earlier career. Indeed, the GWR was one of the few pre-Grouping railways of sufficiently large size to be able to fill all its senior posts by internal appointment (there was a carefully controlled series of criteria for entry to the various career steps within the company). There were, however, two separate 'Great Western traditions' in locomotive practice, resulting from the line's initial mixture of broad and standard gauge: the original Gooch tradition was located at broad gauge Swindon, while the 'Wolverhampton' tradition was located in the virtually autonomous standard gauge works at Stafford Road in that city. Dean essentially belonged to the second of those traditions.

Dean served his initial apprenticeship under Joseph Armstrong, at Stafford Road Works, where he then remained. When Armstrong moved to Swindon to succeed Gooch in 1864, his brother George took over as Wolverhampton Locomotive Superintendent, with Dean as Works Manager. However, following the decision in 1866 to phase out the broad gauge in stages, a number of leading 'Wolverhampton' men were transferred to Swindon to assist Joseph Armstrong, including Dean as his Principal Assistant and W. H. Stanier (Sir William Stanier's father) as Dean's confidential clerk. Joseph Armstrong's tenure at Swindon was, however, much shorter than anyone might have expected; worn out by pressure of work, he died in harness in 1877, and William Dean succeeded him as Locomotive Superintendent with some 15 years of the broad gauge liquidation process still to run.

Dean's career as Locomotive Superintendent thus fell into two distinct but unequal halves – a 15-year period presiding over the death of the 'old' (broad gauge) GWR, and a further ten years (1892-1902) concerned with re-stocking what was in effect a new, all-standard-gauge, railway. In the first period most of the broad gauge locomotive needs were met by continuing earlier Armstrong and Gooch designs, but increasingly through this period Dean began to produced 'convertible' locomotives, with cylinders, wheels, boiler and firebox fitted to broad gauge chassis in such a way that a simple alteration to the frames could make them standard-gauge-compatible. The process could also work in the opposite direction if extra broad gauge locomotive power was temporarily needed. A number of classic standard gauge designs were also produced in this period, the most famous and long-lasting being the '2301' Class 0-6-0 freight engines (some produced as convertibles, though none actually ran on the broad gauge), which ultimately numbered 280 and, after Dean's death, were adopted as an ROD standard design during the First World War.

This period also saw a number of important non-locomotive developments. Principal among these was the introduction of the first modern-style 'transverse' sleepers (with corridor) in 1881, to a convertible design and initially on broad gauge bogies, since they were to run through to Penzance. Also introduced were a chemicals and testing laboratory in 1882, under the aegis of W. H. Stanier (who also began the technical classes as the Swindon Mechanics Institute that formed the basis of the Swindon & North Wilts Technical Institute), and a design of improved vacuum brake. This last, which gave excellent service for the next 70 years, was designed for Dean by Joseph Armstrong junior – his former chief's talented son.

The second part of Dean's career as Locomotive Superintendent was dominated by the need to provide adequate and reasonably standardised rolling-stock for the now all-standard-gauge Great Western. To this period belong his best-known locomotive classes – the '3001' and '3031' Classes of 4-2-2, the 'Armstrong' and 'Badminton' 4-4-0s (the latter being the first GWR engines to sport a Belpaire firebox), and the smaller-wheeled 'Duke' and 'Bulldog' Class 4-4-0s, the former especially for service west of Exeter. (These two classes were so successful that more than 30 years later Collett (qv) married the frames and boilers of the remaining examples to form the '3250' Class 'Dukedog' light 4-4-0s for use in West Wales.) The sturdy '2301' 0-6-0s continued to handle most freight traffic, but Dean also experimented with 4-6-0s and 2-6-0s for heavy freight, the latter eventually becoming standard as the 'Aberdare' ('2500') Class, 31 of which were still at work in 1944. On the carriage side, 1891 saw the first through-gangwayed all-corridor train in Britain running on the GWR (though it had no dining-car – the Swindon refreshment room contract had not yet been bought out).

From about 1896 Dean's health began to fail, and he increasingly took his Principal Assistant and nominated successor, G. J. Churchward (qv), into partnership. During this period much of the updating and reboilering of the classes described above took place, often replacing Dean's lovely copper-domed parallel boiler with Churchward's domeless trademark design (in both parallel and taper version), as well as a series of highly original 'transitional' experimental designs, including the GWR's first express 4-6-0s and 4-4-2s, which are described more fully in the entry under Churchward. Dean finally relinquished office in 1902, and died in 1905.

Richard Deeley
1855-1944

Locomotive Engineer and Scientist

Born	Chester, 24 October 1855, son of a Midland Railway accounts office employee also called Richard Mountford Deeley
Education	Chester Cathedral Grammar School, followed by pupillage under E. B. Ellington, MD of Hydraulic Engineering Co, 1873-75, and S. W. Johnson (qv) at Derby, 6 December 1875-April 1879
Married	Deeley remained single
Best-known works	Modification and rebuilding of Johnson 4-4-0s and 0-6-0s; development of the Smith-Johnson three-cylinder compounds, and design of a simple counterpart ('999' Class); introduction of power classification and class numbering systems; Morecambe electrification; studies of lubricants and of meteorology, following his resignation from MR
Honours	MIME 1890; MICE 1906; Fellow, Geological Society, 1885, Member of Council, 1914-19, Vice-President 1917-19; Fellow, Royal Meteorological Society
Died	41 The Grove, Isleworth, 19 June 1944
Buried	Derby Cemetery

Richard Mountford Deeley is just about the only locomotive engineer not accorded any entry in the *Oxford Companion to British Railway History*, and his time 'at the top' on the Midland Railway was only five years, though he had for a number of years previously been first Chief of Testing (including important work on piston valves), then Works Manager and finally Assistant Locomotive Superintendent to S. W. Johnson (qv), under whom he had been initially apprenticed. During his short time in charge, however, he made several key contributions to Midland locomotive practice, which were continued under his successor Sir Henry Fowler (qv) into LMS and even eventually into BR practice; indeed, it can be argued that he created the conditions whereby Midland supremacy in locomotive matters was later assured.

Deeley's first major contribution to the Midland locomotive fleet consisted of rebuilding (or in some cases redesigning and building new) his predecessor's 4-4-0 and 0-6-0 designs; these were worthy (and sometimes beautiful) engines, but in most cases were under-boilered. Though he did not superheat them – Fowler was to do that – Deeley fitted them with larger boilers (boiler design had been one of his fortes since 1893), operating at increased pressure (200psi for the '700' Class, for example), thus substantially increasing their power – essential for the heavier corridor trains that were then coming into use, and also for the increased weights of the Midland coal traffic. Even more importantly, however, Deeley's rebuilding programme resulted in the creation of much more standard forms of motive power – neither the 4-4-0s nor the 0-6-0s were all identical, but many parts were standard among them.

His major personal success in locomotive design formed part of this improving and standardising process. This was of course the famous Midland compound 4-4-0s – the Midland's most powerful passenger locomotive, and one of the most successful compound designs to run anywhere in the world outside France. The initial five engines had once again been built by Johnson to a patent by W. M. Smith. They were a good design in any case, but Deeley's redesign made them quite outstanding. He made two important changes to them – a new and higher-pressed boiler, and, his master-stroke, a complete redesign of the regulator system.

One of the problems with compound locomotives is the need for simple or semi-compound working on starting. The Smith-Johnson compound design achieved this via a spring-loaded regulator valve controlled by the driver from the cab – a good but rather 'fiddly' design (and thus able to be mis-set rather more easily than one might perhaps have wished). Deeley's improvement was to do away with the 'fiddle', and introduce instead a single lever that moved the machine from simple to compound by stages automatically, according to the level of cut-off. Once again, the importance of this development lay not simply in the converting of a good locomotive into an outstanding one, but in forming the basis for a standard class eventually totalling 240 and used right across the LMS system. Ten large simple 4-4-0s (the '999' Class) were also built for comparison.

Deeley's other major contributions also had to do with standardisation — this time, of classification and numbering. It was Deeley who devised the Midland power classification system (3F, 4P, etc) defining exactly the type of work a locomotive was sufficient to do. It was he also who re-organised the locomotive fleet numbering system, so that locomotives of the same general type (express passenger, freight, passenger tank, shunting tank) were numbered together, with the numbers painted large on the tank or tender sides, visible at a glance. This may sound like organisational obsessiveness, but its importance was crucial; it played a major role in the introduction of centralised train control, in which the Midland led the field, pioneered – though not without some opposition – by Deeley's contemporary, General Traffic Superintendent Cecil Paget, during 1907-09.

This brings us to the vexed matter of Deeley's resignation – why should a notable engineer, at the height of his powers, suddenly leave office after only five years as CME, and never have anything to do with railways or locomotives again (for that apparently is the case)? The problem appears to have been one of personalities, stemming back to Johnson's day. Under Johnson Deeley was Works Manager, and Cecil Paget his assistant. When Deeley became Assistant Locomotive Superintendent, Paget became Works Manager. The two men were both brilliant engineers, but of very different temperaments, even though they had slightly earlier carried out a successful joint fact-finding tour of the USA and Johnson himself seems on at least one occasion to have publicly 'havered' over which one he was going to recommend to succeed him.

To add to the problem, Paget, though technically reporting to Deeley, was the son of the Midland Chairman, Sir Ernest Paget – and he had himself designed a pioneering locomotive, a multi-cylindered 2-6-2 something like an early 'Leader' (but with a more conventional appearance), which was being built and tested at Derby, under Deeley's nose. Meanwhile Deeley's own 'large engine' proposals for a compound 4-6-0 and a freight 0-8-0 were substantially ignored, and his Morecambe-Heysham electrification scheme of 1908, which he had intended as a field trial for main-line electrification between Derby and Manchester, was taken no further. The younger Paget even became General Superintendent, and thus Deeley's superior, in 1907, as noted above. Further, though an excellent locomotive engineer, Deeley seems not to have been as single-mindedly dedicated to railways and railway engineering as most of his locomotive superintendent contemporaries (including Paget!), having a wide range of other scientific and technical interests ranging from glaciation to metallurgy, even during his time at Derby.

In 1909 these tensions all boiled over with the proposal to 'split' the post of Locomotive Superintendent into CME and Chief Motive Power Superintendent, and Deeley resigned – though the Hamilton Ellis story of him stalking into Derby Works with a workman, removing his nameplate from the door, and vanishing never to be seen again, turns out in fact to be apocryphal, and he seems to have maintained a personal friendship with several of his old Midland colleague – including, surprisingly, Paget! On his resignation, the Directors awarded him a substantial retirement pension for life, and he used this 'window of opportunity' to return to more general scientific fields, including his first love, geology, on which he had already published while still with the Midland; he published first on lubricants, jointly with his former Midland colleague Archbutt, and then, in 1935, aged 80, on meteorology. He died in 1944, a reserved, private man to the last – even his own 1941 genealogical history of his family omitted any mention of his own immediate circumstances apart from his position with the Midland Railway.

Deeley hardly ever designed a poor locomotive – though on the one occasion when he did, the 'hole-in-the-wall' or 'flatiron' 0-6-4Ts, the design was so bad that nobody could find any real use for them, even after Fowler rebuilt them. Since his proposed 4-6-0 was never built, the compound 4-4-0s must remain his lasting masterpiece, but there is also one curious 'ghost engine' – a might-have-been that never got beyond the drawing-board that is more than a little intriguing. This was a design, dated 1906, for a four-cylinder 2-4-4-2 compound tank engine, with wheels divided but not articulated, an un-superheated boiler carrying 220psi pressure, and 5-foot coupled wheels. The high-pressure cylinders (13in by 26in) were at the rear, and the low-pressure (20in by 26in) at the front. It is not clear just what duties this large and apparently quite handsome locomotive was intended for. More power for the Toton coal trains, as an alternative to the proposed 0-8-0s? A counterblast to the Paget 2-6-2? Who knows?

Dugald Drummond
1840-1912

Locomotive Engineer

Born	Ardrossan, Ayrshire, 1 January 1840, son of a locomotive inspector
Education	Engineering apprenticeship with Forrest & Barr, Glasgow (including both marine and locomotive engineering)
Married	Recorded as being married in the Census of 1881, in which year the NBR Board refused his request for a shopping pass for his wife; the on-line Oxford *Dictionary of National Biography* states that he had one son and four daughters, but does not give his wife's name
Best-known works	Father of the 'Scottish' 4-4-0, beginning with the 'Abbotsford' Class of 1876 on NBR and continuing on CR with '66' Class and 'Gourock Bogies', and (south of the border) with 'C8', 'T9' and 'D15' Classes on LSWR; popularised 0-4-4T type on all three railways concerned, and produced four-cylinder 4-6-0s for the LSWR, notably the 'Paddlebox' 'T14' Class; modernised works on all three railways (Cowlairs, St Rollox and Eastleigh as a replacement for Nine Elms); design improvements including firebox water-tubes, smokebox steam-driers and feedwater heating
Honours	Two gold medals at Edinburgh

	International Exhibition 1886; Telford Medal, Inst of Civil Engineering, 1897
Died	Surbiton, 8 November 1912, following leg amputation after accident at Eastleigh
Buried	Brookwood Cemetery, Plot 38 (grave restored and re-dedicated April 1995)

Most of the '50 famous railwaymen' recorded in this book either worked entirely for or made their name on a specific company. Dugald Drummond's fame, however, depends not on the work he did for a specific company so much as the way he initiated and popularised specific types of locomotive, notably the 'Scottish' 4-4-0, the passenger 0-4-4T and a sturdy version of the goods 0-6-0, across a wide range of companies – three for which he worked, the North British, Caledonian and LSWR, and in Scotland particularly on a wide range of other companies.

Following his apprenticeship, Drummond became Assistant Works Manager at Cowlairs under Stroudley (qv). In 1865 he followed Stroudley to the Highland Railway, serving as his Works Manager, then followed him again in the same capacity to the LBSCR at Brighton. In 1875, however, Drummond struck out on his own, becoming Locomotive Superintendent of the North British Railway, where he introduced a number of Stroudley features, such as 'improved engine green' livery and local names for the locomotives, and also modernised Cowlairs Works. He left the NBR in 1882, apparently under something of a cloud despite his fine technical record (there appear to have been financial problems at Cowlairs), to join the Caledonian, where he remained until 1890, again modernising its works (St Rollox this time). After a brief spell running his own railway engineering firm, he moved south in 1895 to the CME's post on the LSWR, which he held till his death in 1912.

This list of appointments, however, tells little about what made Dugald Drummond great. His long association with Stroudley meant that he developed a strong aesthetic sense (it is said that he never designed a bad-looking locomotive), but it also enabled him to see two areas in which Stroudley's designs had decided weaknesses, certainly as far as work in his native Scotland was concerned, with its harsh climate, sharp curves and steep gradients – Stroudley's aversion to leading bogies on express engines and his generally light and low-powered designs. He applied these insights to the machines he found when he returned home, to develop a characteristically sturdy and versatile Scottish locomotive design practice, which influenced his successors and which he re-exported to England during his period as CME of the London & South Western.

Perhaps the most important of these designs were those developing the 4-4-0 type. Although author Tom Middlemass describes him as 'the real patriarch of the Scottish 4-4-0', Drummond was not the originator of the 4-4-0 type in Scotland – that was William Cowan on the Great North of Scotland Railway – and on the North British Wheatley had already designed 4-4-0s with the characteristic 'Scottish' combination of inside cylinders (unlike the GNSR) and inside frames by the time Drummond arrived. But Drummond added one crucial feature – power. In 1876 the Midland-NBR 'Waverley Route' to Edinburgh was at long last open throughout, and it rapidly became apparent that Wheatley's engines, though sturdy, simply could not keep time with main-line trains on the fearsome Border Counties gradients unassisted. Drummond provided a design, the 'Abbotsford' Class, with larger cylinders (18in by 26in against 17in by 24in), a larger boiler, and a fifth more starting tractive effort. In both appearance and overall design it was the clear ancestor of both Drummond's later designs for the Caledonian, the racing Class '66s' and the smaller-wheeled but equally nippy 'Gourock bogies' for the Clyde excursion traffic, the famous 'Dunalastairs' by McIntosh (qv) that followed them, and their progenitor's own later successively larger designs for the LSWR.

Drummond thus both initiated and personally developed, across some 35 years, the 'Scottish' (and South Western!) passenger 4-4-0 with designs of ever-increasing power and speed, adding as he went such refinements as firebox water-tubes, smokebox steam-driers and feedwater heating (though providing superheaters was left to his successors). He even attempted four-cylinder propulsion in the LSWR 'T7' and 'E10' Classes, though by making them uncoupled 'double singles' (ie 4-2-2-0s) in the classic Webb manner, he undid most of the benefits of the added cylinder power – they were persistently short of steam, and slipped badly. Almost all of his 4-4-0 locomotives proper, however, survived the 1923 Grouping, and his last four classes – 'L11', 'S11', 'L12' and 'D15', all for the LSWR – not only entered the Southern's stock intact, but also (almost entirely) that of British Railways. His last and most powerful 4-4-0 design, the 'D15s', were truly magnificent machines, particularly as superheated by Maunsell (qv); however, his attempts at four-cylinder 4-6-0s were less successful.

Drummond was also responsible for initiating and developing a series of increasingly powerful 0-4-4T designs, again culminating in a design for the LSWR – the well-known 'M7' – 100 of which survived to enter British Railways stock, and again on his earlier railways systematically further developed and enlarged by his successors, particularly McIntosh. He also developed characteristically sturdy 0-6-0 freight designs, the two most famous being the Caledonian 'Jumbos' (again perpetuated by his successors and again all but six taken over by BR) and the '700s' on the LSWR.

In personality, for all his engineering brilliance, Drummond was as dour and rough as his mentor Stroudley was suave and gentlemanly, with an unmodified Scottish Calvinist insistence on telling the truth as he saw it. It is possible in this respect that his unequivocal evidence to the Tay Bridge enquiry (which offended several NBR Directors) may have been a contributory factor to his departure to the Caledonian. Likewise, his short-lived foray into the world of private engineering manufacture may have suffered from this constitutional inability to 'make friends and influence people', and his appointment to Nine Elms was similarly followed by a spate of resignations (his response was to import a quantity of Scottish replacement personnel, including his successor D. C. Urie as Works Manager, and to replace Nine Elms altogether with the new Eastleigh Works). Even the steam scalding at Eastleigh that resulted in his death seems partly to have been the result of his own pig-headedness. But there is no doubt at all that he was a great and very influential locomotive designer.

Thomas Edmondson
1792-1851
Inventor

Born	Moor Lane, Stonewell, Lancaster, 30 June 1792, of a Quaker family
Education	At home, then apprenticed to Gillows & Co, the Lancaster cabinet-making firm (later Waring & Gillow)
Married	(1) Hannah Satterthwaite, Colthouse, Lancs, 11 November 1822; (2) Rachel Hodgson (née Beeby), Maryport, 26 August 1829
Best-known works	Inventor of the card-based printed railway ticket system
Honours	Specimen press exhibited at British Association meeting, Newcastle, September 1838
Died	Meltonville, Crumpsall, Manchester, 22 June 1851
Buried	Friends' Burial Ground, Mount Street, Manchester

If it had not been for his company failing, Thomas Edmondson might never have taken an interest in railway matters at all (though as we shall see the stamped ticket would probably still have come into existence in one or other of two different forms). Born into a Lancaster Quaker family in 1792, Edmondson was by training a cabinet-maker (like Pullman), though he seems from an early age to have had a mechanical bent – his mother reportedly taught him knitting at home 'to keep him out of mischief', and one of his earlier inventions, while still an apprentice, was a device whereby a housewife could churn butter and rock a cradle simultaneously (one wonders just how many of these Gillows of Lancaster actually sold!). More to the point perhaps, during the journeyman phase of his apprenticeship he also made several improvements to the cabinet-making implements of the day.

On the completion of his apprenticeship, Edmondson moved to Carlisle, where he started up a furniture business in partnership with a colleague. However, the venture was not successful, and its consequent bankruptcy forced Edmondson in 1836 to seek employment with the newly formed and still uncompleted Newcastle & Carlisle Railway, which had begun running trains over its western section in the previous year. He was appointed 'railway clerk' (ie station master) at the Cumbrian station of Milton (now Brampton), some 14 miles from Carlisle, and among his various duties in this capacity were issuing tickets and accounting for monies received.

The form of ticketing that Edmondson found in place at Brampton was the old coaching-style paper ticket, laboriously written out by hand for each customer, which he found irksome to write out, slow to deliver to the customer, and insecure in accounting terms – once again, as with refreshment room stops, a technology that had been perfectly adequate in coaching days was foundering under the pressure of the larger numbers conveyed even by the earliest of trains. By 1837 Edmondson had had enough, and was casting his mind around for an alternative that would be both faster and more secure. He found it in the shape of the pre-printed ticket, individually numbered in sequence and valid only when date-stamped on issue, that bears his name.

Edmondson was not the only person or concern to find the old coaching-style ticket and waybill system ineffective for the new means of transport. The Leicester & Swannington had begun using stamped metal tickets (a little like the discs or strips one used to make on those station platform printing machines) in 1832. However, they could only record the issuing station name and the passenger number, and were handed in at the other end for potential reuse – and thus potential fraud. Cardboard tickets had also begun to appear, in Germany, around 1835, but although with true German thoroughness they even recorded the train departure time and the coach number in which the traveller was entitled to a seat, they too lacked any unique ticket number and so were open to potential illegal reuse on the same train on another day.

It is not clear whether Edmondson knew of these developments or not; but in any case his own idea, which he claimed occurred to him whole and entire while walking in a Northumbrian field (he even took his family to show them the exact spot!), had a number of characteristic features that set it apart from any of the others. In the first place, all tickets were sequentially numbered and issued in numerical order; in the second place, each ticket was validated by being date-stamped upon issue. Thus every ticket was uniquely traceable, rendering the entire revenue operation very much more secure.

Initially, all the destinations were handwritten on the tickets, but by the time Edmondson moved in 1839 from the Newcastle & Carlisle, which had been slow in taking up the device on the rest of its system, to the much larger Manchester & Leeds, which had asked him to take charge of its revenue operation at twice the N&C's salary, separate numerical series starting with '0' had been established for each of the most commonly requested journeys, enabling the entire ticket to be pre-printed, and issued simply by taking it from the storage rack for that series and running it through the dating press. Because each series began with 0 rather than 1, a 'checking machine' carrying the highest number left in each rack enabled the number of tickets issued to be counted automatically at the end of each day.

It was in fact this series of mechanical racks, presses and checking machines that formed the mechanical heart of Edmondson's system, and it was for these that we have to thank his inventive skill and initial cabinet-making training in equal measure. In designing the fine mechanical detail of his devices he was helped by Ralph Cairns, a Brampton watchmaker, and John Blaylock, a Carlisle clockmaker and iron-founder of Irish extraction. (The 1892 *DNB* entry on Edmondson seems to conflate the two men, quoting only Blaylock and calling him a 'Dublin watchmaker'; certainly one of the earliest uses of the Edmondson system outside Manchester was in Dublin.) Subsequent refinements to the system were made by James Carson, but the basic 'Edmondson system' remained standard on railways around the world as late as the 1990s, despite competition from technological advances such as mechanised 'blank ticket' production (GWR 1911 onwards) and paper-roll printing (London Underground and BR, 1950s onwards). Indeed, Edmondson's system was only fully superseded when computerised ticket issue systems became generally available. (Most 'heritage' lines still use Edmondson tickets, though that may partly be for reasons of nostalgia.)

Edmondson patented his system, and left the Manchester & Leeds, in 1841 according to the *Oxford Companion*, but his son John's 1878 note suggests a possible date of anything up to ten years later (although the full ten years would put his move very close to his actual death date!). He set up the firm of John Edmondson to produce and sell tickets (from card stocks manufactured by De La Rue of playing-card fame!) and ticket machines; the firm was registered in the name of his eldest son because, as a former bankrupt, Thomas could not own a business, even after he had discharged his debts. His patent royalties, though individually modest (a mere 10 shillings a mile

71

per annum), in keeping with good Quaker practice eventually left him a considerably wealthy man. He died in 1851, and it is perhaps significant of what people thought of him at the time that within a year of his death a special article about him called 'Our Railway Ticket System' was being published in Dickens's famous magazine *Household Words*.

John Ellis
1789-1862

Railway Manager

Born	Sharman's Lodge, Leicester, 3 August 1789, son of Quaker farmer Joseph Ellis
Education	Nothing recorded (though his descendants by his second marriage attended Ackworth and Bootham schools)
Married	(1) Martha (no further details given), probably 1816; their son E. S. Ellis was born 7 January 1817 and Martha died 2 February that year; (2) Priscilla Evans, Warwick, 18 October 1820
Best-known works	Joint backer (with William Stenton) of Leicester & Swannington Railway; succeeded George Hudson (qv) as Chairman of Midland Railway; overcame Midland's post-Hudson financial crisis by concentrating on building up coal and mineral traffic; oversaw acquisition of Bristol & Gloucester and London extension as far as Hitchin; appointed James Allport (qv) as first General Manager to complete extensions to London and Scotland (subsequent to his retirement)
Honours	MP for Leicester, 1848-52; Alderman for Borough of Leicester; JP for Leicestershire; offered Mayoralty of Leicester but refused on religious grounds

| *Died* | Belgrave, Leicester, 26 October 1862 |
| *Buried* | Leicester Public Cemetery |

If there would most likely have been no Midland Railway without George Hudson, then there equally would most likely have been only a financially crippled near-bankrupt line without John Ellis, in place of the major national transport concern that the Midland actually became. The upheavals that preceded and surrounded Hudson's downfall (qv) left the Midland in a state of acute financial embarrassment, with huge legal costs, maintenance severely underfunded and a rate of return on investment barely a quarter of what it had been at the time of the Hudson amalgamation. John Ellis (and later his son Edward) was the main reason that the line did not fulfil the accountants' predictions of doom, and go under.

Ellis came from Quaker farming stock in the northern part of Leicestershire. His own farm, at Beaumont Leys, which he ran from 1807 to 1847, was equally successful, and he also operated a corn-merchant's business in Leicester itself. In 1830, through his Quaker connections with the Pease family, he met George Stephenson, '[the] object being to see how the smoke and steam from Locomotive Engines would operate on passengers in the Tunnel'. He was 'delighted with the experiment we tried', and jointly with the colliery owner William Stenton (or Stinson) became a major backer of the Leicester & Swannington Railway, a 16-mile line promoted primarily to transport coal, stone and agricultural produce from north Leicestershire into Leicester itself. Resisting the temptation to headlong expansion and concentrating on its core business of goods traffic, the railway remained small but prosperous, and when it amalgamated with the Midland in 1845 Hudson had to exchange each £50 L&S share for a £100 share in the new concern, and Ellis became Hudson's Vice-Chairman.

Ellis shared Hudson's vision of an extensive railway network – he was largely responsible during this period for the Midland's acquisition of the Bristol & Gloucester Railway – but his Quaker background meant that he avoided Hudson's financial wheeling and dealing. When after Hudson's fall he took over as Chairman of the now impoverished Midland, he applied to the problem of rescuing it the same concepts of financial probity and concentration on core business that had been so successful on the little Leicester & Swannington. The Great Exhibition of 1851 (housed in the 'Crystal Palace' designed by Midland board member Joseph Paxton, it is said initially on his blotter during a dull Derby board meeting) had led to a major resurgence in industrial production and manufacturing, much of it located in the Midland's main catchment area. Ellis concentrated on capturing this business, building one line (along the Erewash Valley) especially for it, but eschewing other, less clearly profitable branch-line schemes.

In this he was successful, and his personal respectability, proven by his Quaker background and performance on the L&S, served to calm City financial fears until the Midland could show it was returning to profit. But the same Great Exhibition had demonstrated a key weakness in the Midland's position, which it was clear Ellis would also have to address – the fact that the major long-haul passenger flows from the area were to and from London, to which the Midland had no direct access. The same was increasingly true, Ellis also discovered, for the new traffic increases in both coal and manufactured goods (though the route taken by these latter was different, through Rugby rather than down the East Coast line). And – as I pointed out in *Dining At Speed* (Silver Link Publishing, 2004, 1-85794-211-6) – if you wanted a Victorian manufacturer to place his goods with you, you needed to offer him equivalent passenger services too.

Ellis's response to this problem was three-fold. First, he revived the 1847 scheme for a line from Leicester through Bedford to Hitchin, which already had Parliamentary approval, creating an end-on junction with the GNR with potential access to King's Cross (and incidentally exploiting the potential wealth of the Northamptonshire iron ore fields that it crossed). Second, he joined Mark Huish of the LNWR in negotiating a profit-sharing agreement for through traffic to London (and in the other direction to Scotland), the so-called 'octuple agreement' of 1851, to enable those lines that, like the Midland, 'lost' their through passengers or goods traffic to the East or West Coast routes, to claim a fixed proportion of the through receipts. And third – and perhaps the most significant of all – he appointed James Allport (qv) as the Midland's first General Manager, with a brief to complete both London and Scottish extensions, to enable the railway to compete on equal terms with its East and West Coast rivals.

The strategy worked. The Hitchin extension (still the Midland's London main line as far south as Bedford) was brought into use on 7 May 1857. The 'octuple agreement', while it lasted, paid 50% on through freight and 37% on through passengers. Allport completed the London extension and the new St Pancras station by 1867, and the Scottish extension ten years later. By the time Ellis retired, in 1858, Midland dividends were above £3 per share, and by 1860, with the line carrying 12% of all UK mineral traffic, would reach £6 per share. Ellis lived a further two years after this, dying in 1862, with his son also becoming Chairman ten years later.

Robert Fairlie
1830-85

Consultant Railway Engineer

Born	Glasgow, 5 April 1830, son of Archibald Fairlie, civil engineer, and his wife Margaret Taylor
Education	Apprenticeships at Crewe and Swindon
Married	Eliza Anne England, by special licence (possibly in Canterbury), 4 January 1862, without the consent of her father, George England; his Times obituary claims he had been married previously, but gives no details.
Best-known works	Double-bogie double-ended locomotives (mainly for narrow gauge) constructed to his patents from 1864 onwards, especially those for the Festiniog Railway; also designed single-ended locomotives (with one power bogie only) on the same principle, eg for Welsh Highland; major promoter of, and locomotive consultant to, narrow gauge railways worldwide; wrote *Locomotive Engines, What they are and What they ought to be* (1864), *Railways and their Management* (1868), *The Gauge for the Railways of the Future* (1870, see also below), *On the Gauge of Railways* (1871-72) and *Railways or No Railways* (1872)
Honours	Freemason, 1856; Member of Honourable Artillery Company,

1859; Member of Inst of Civil Engineers in or before 1867; Papers to British Assoc for Advancement of Science, 1870 and 1871; Gold Medal of Czar of Russia, 1871 (though it is unclear whether this may have been ultimately intended for, or to be shared jointly with, Charles Spooner of the Festiniog Railway)

Died   The Woodlands, Clapham Common, London, 31 July 1885

Buried   Highgate Cemetery, London

Robert Francis Fairlie is of course famous worldwide for his 'double Fairlie' locomotives, and in the UK is particularly associated with the Festiniog Railway, whose archives indeed hold the most detailed accounts of him. Notwithstanding, however, he remains another of the '50 famous railwaymen', like Thomas Clayton, large chunks of whose personal life seem to elude the researcher – in his case, not helped particularly by the incomplete and untrustworthy nature of the 1892 entry on him in the *DNB* (though a revised entry, which clarifies some of this elusiveness, is now posted on the new on-line Oxford *DNB*). Thus there seems to be no clear record of his first marriage; similarly, several details of his professional training are unclear – both *DNB* entries record him as training 'at Crewe and Swindon', but precisely when and under whom again seems not to be known (and apprenticeship at two such different locomotive works would be more than somewhat unusual).

We do, however, know something of the earlier stages of his career, though here again there are curious gaps. From 1852 to 1854 he was Locomotive Superintendent of the Londonderry & Coleraine Railway, which he seems to have left as a result of some sort of dispute; the *DNB* entry suggests that it might have been over money, as his next post was 'a more lucrative position', while Ransom suggests that a new manager was put in place over his head. There then seems to have followed a further hiatus, as we next find Fairlie employed in 1856 on the newly built Bombay & Baroda Railway (this was the more lucrative position the *DNB* entry reported). Once again he seems to have left after a short period, and certainly before 1861 – possibly as early as his HAC membership in 1859 – he was back in London, working as an independent consulting engineer from premises in Gracechurch Street. It was during this period that there occurred two of the key events of his career – his patenting of his double-bogie locomotive design (1864) and his meeting with George England.

George England (1812-78) was born in Newcastle-upon-Tyne, but trained in Deptford under John Penn, and lived most of his life in London, where he invented and patented the traversing screw jack in 1839. In 1840 he set up an engineering works in Pomeroy Street, New Cross Gate, to build traversing screw gear and light locomotives (steam railcars and small engines, especially for narrow gauge industrial and agricultural lines). His works, which was not connected to any main-line railway – locomotives were transported on the Victorian horse-drawn equivalent of a low-loader – had a fine reputation for precision engineering, but he was also a man capable of violent rages and physical assault.

How Fairlie came to make his acquaintance is not precisely clear, but by late 1860 he was a frequent visitor at England's premises, and on good terms with his son and particularly his daughter Eliza (Lizzie). In January 1861, when she was 17 and he was 30, he asked her father for her hand, but England asked him to 'hold off for two years'. However, a year later they eloped and married by special licence, resulting in a celebrated court case that only collapsed when it became clear that George England was not legally married to Lizzie's mother when she was born, so that technically his consent to her marriage was not needed. This somewhat 'Trial by Jury' episode does not seem to have soured Fairlie's relationship with the family in general. George England seems to have introduced Fairlie to the Spooners of the Festiniog Railway, where he had his most noteworthy UK successes, and when he retired in 1869 following a worsening of his periodic rages, his son George junior, Fairlie and the Great Western's J. S. Frazer – possibly a contact of Fairlie's from his Swindon days – leased the works jointly as the Fairlie Engine & Steam Carriage (later '& Rolling Stock') Company.

Fairlie's double-bogie locomotive, the design for which he is probably best known, was patented in 1864, from his Gracechurch Street works. The earliest locomotive actually built to the design, *Progress* for the Neath & Brecon Railway, was in fact for standard gauge, and subsequent locomotives were constructed for anything from 1ft 11⅓in gauge up to standard gauge and even beyond, though narrow gauges predominated. The classic 'double Fairlie' had two boilers and smokeboxes, facing outwards from a central firebox and driving position, the frames being articulated on two powered bogies, one at either end. *Progress* suffered from draughting problems caused by the alternate exhaust from the two smokeboxes, but the inclusion of a brick partition across the middle of the smokebox cured this and subsequent engines were highly successful There was also a later, lighter 'single Fairlie' variant, with a conventional single boiler and cab at one end, and one power bogie only, but once again on an articulated undercarriage.

These two key aspects of Fairlie's career came together when the Festiniog Railway, originally a horse-drawn line with gravity feed downhill for its loaded slate wagons, decided in 1861-62, under Charles

Spooner's aegis, to convert to steam locomotion. George England tendered for the locomotives – the smallest ever built for a public railway to that date – and after initial priming troubles they were a notable success, increasing traffic so much that by 1869 greater capacity was needed. The Festiniog obtained an Act permitting it to double the track, but this extremely expensive solution was avoided when Spooner instead authorised the purchase of the first narrow gauge 'double Fairlie' – once again built by George England, and one suspects very probably suggested by him to Spooner in the first place as a solution to the capacity problem. The locomotive, *Little Wonder*, delivered in 1869, was an instant success; it ran steadily on the diminutive track at 35mph, and hauled three times the weight of the previous 0-4-0STs. Press demonstrations, and international visits – including one from Russia, which led to orders for the Imperial Livny Railway and the gold medals referred to above – led to national and international fame.

From 1870 onwards, following the publication of *The Gauge for Railways of the Future*, Fairlie's prime interest shifted from simply designing and supplying articulated locomotives to the more general promotion of narrow gauge railways of various widths as a means of opening up difficult terrain, especially in undeveloped areas. His influence – though not in all cases his locomotives – figured large in the gauge choices of the New Zealand and South African systems, the Denver & Rio Grande in the USA, the Barbados Railway, and the Bolivar and La Guiara & Caracas lines in Venezuela, among others. It was during this Venezuelan expedition in 1873-74 that he contracted first sunstroke and then jungle fever, and although he managed to make a return to England, he was never fully fit again. He died in 1885.

Like George Stephenson (to whose *Rocket* his *Little*

Wonder has sometimes been compared), Fairlie's ideas on locomotive design were not individually original. Earlier double-ended locomotives had been built by Horatio Allen in the USA in 1833 and by Cockerill for the 1851 Semmering Trials, and Jean-Jacques Meyer had taken out an articulation patent in 1861 (though nothing was built under it until 1868). Where Fairlie's patent was truly original, however, was in bringing together these concepts to form a locomotive design that had total adhesion, could be driven equally easily in either direction without turning, could be easily lifted off its bogies for running repairs and thus had high-percentage availability, could negotiate sharp curves relative to its overall length, and was equally at home on very narrow and full-size gauges. If this description of the capabilities of the 'double Fairlie' reminds one of Bulleid's specifications a century later for his final 'Leader' design (qv), this should come as no surprise: Fairlie has indeed been recognised as the conceptual originator of the criteria both for that design and for the long line of double-ended diesel and electric locomotives that superseded steam both in the UK and elsewhere.

Sam Fay
1856-1953

Railway Manager

Born	Hamble-le-Rice, Hants, 30 December 1856, second son of farmer Joshua Fay
Education	Blenheim House School, Fareham, then at own request joined LSWR in 1872, age 15½
Married	Frances Anne Farbrother, Kingston-upon-Thames, 1883
Best-known works	Restored bankrupt MSWJR to solvency, 1892-97; as General Manager of Great Central, 1902-23, exploited opportunities for fast freight and up-market suburban traffic on new London Extension to build up run-down finances; devised Conciliation Boards to avoid strikes, 1906-08; developed Immingham Docks, 1912; after Grouping, became Chairman of Beyer Peacock, 1923-33
Honours	Knighthood, 1912 (by King George V at opening of Immingham Docks)
Died	Awbridge, Hants, 30 May 1953
Buried	All Saints, Awbridge, churchyard, in same tomb as his wife, who predeceased him in 1946

George Dow, in his history of the Great Central Railway, has called Sam Fay (christened Samuel but always known simply as Sam, even after receiving his knighthood) 'adventurous and publicity-minded ... one of the most enterprising and innovative of all railway General Managers'. This sounds high praise, but if one takes into account not only his career on the Great Central but his earlier work on the LSWR and the Midland & South Western Junction, it is if anything an understatement: his enterprise and flair for publicity were indeed enormous, but so was his ability to turn round financially ailing companies – the same flair for which his predecessor Edward Watkin had been hired, but in Fay's case with even more dramatic and lasting effect.

From a Huguenot family, Fay seems to have enjoyed a fairly up-market education, but – always fascinated by railways – he left school at 15½ and joined the London & South Western Railway as a junior clerk. By 1891 he had become Assistant Storekeeper at Nine Elms (a more imposing post than its title sounds, since 'stores' in railway parlance includes everything, even locomotives!), and had showed his flair for public relations as co-founder of the *South Western Gazette* in 1881, and author of the company's history *A Royal Road* in 1883. In 1892 he was head-hunted by the Midland & South Western Junction Railway – a line that always remained close to his heart – to attempt to restore it to solvency, which he successfully achieved by 1897. In 1899 the LSWR head-hunted him back again to be Superintendent of the Line, and in 1902 he was recruited by the imposingly named but financially weak Great Central, plagued by the cost and revenue problems of its recently completed London Extension, to fill Sir William Pollitt's place as General Manager upon Pollitt's elevation to the Board.

Ably assisted by J. G. Robinson (qv), Fay continued and extended the fast, frequent express services that had been devised by Pollitt, fitting water troughs to enable non-stop London-Sheffield running, improving timings, and improving the Manchester service connections with the part-GCR-owned Cheshire Lines Committee trains. He also exploited the Great Central's central position to introduce fast long-distance cross-country services with on-board catering, with routes such as Liverpool-Cromer and Newcastle-Bournemouth, the latter winning a special mention for its excellent catering in Brereton's review for *Transport* magazine almost as soon as it was introduced. Fay put his flair for publicity to work in a series of posters advertising both regular and excursion services, the most audacious probably being the football excursion poster that correctly predicted the winning goal of the 1904 Cup Final for which it was advertising train services – obviously, before the match! Fay even had the Great Central acquire its own travel agents, by buying out Dean & Dawson.

However, it was very soon clear that long-distance passenger services alone were not going to make the revenue projections come right: in fact, Robinson tabled a report to Fay in 1910 showing that express revenue was 2s 2d per mile, while expenses came to 3s 6d. Clearly the line had to depend on other sources than just the expresses for its funds, though they were essential for publicity and to pull in the business passengers who (it was hoped) would then consign their products via GC freight. Two other markets were possible, and Fay developed both of them energetically.

The first market was that for up-market outer-suburban services. John Bell had resigned as General Manager of the Metropolitan in 1901, and Fay and Charles Ellis, Bell's successor, got on well together. A 1903 scheme for shared season tickets was followed in 1905 by the Metropolitan & Great Central Railway Act, which put the management of the joint lines on a regular basis. Suburban services were provided both jointly with the Metropolitan, via Rickmansworth and Aylesbury, and jointly with the Great Western, via High Wycombe and Princes Risborough. Timings were very smart indeed, and the quality of the new carriage stock constructed for the lines was among the highest of any suburban system at the time. The services, as one would expect from Fay, were strenuously advertised, and there was a concerted drive by both Fay and the Metropolitan's R. H. Selbie (qv) to build up custom by promoting outer-suburban commuting, through adverts with slogans such as 'Live in the Country' or 'Great Central – the Line of Health' (Selbie's alternative was the famous 'Live in Metroland').

The other market – financially perhaps even more important – was express and cross-country freight, and this too Fay strenuously built up, capitalising on the central position of the line and its capacity for transfer freight not only north-south but also east-west via the Banbury link with the Great Western. Coal from Annesley went to London and Bristol alike. Fish from Grimsby (and later Immingham, which Fay developed as a port, earning himself a knighthood from King George V on the spot when it was opened in 1912) went by express freight to London, Swindon, Plymouth and Wales – with Welsh coal for the trawlers coming back the other way. Fast general merchandise trains ran from York to London, Cardiff and Bristol. Timings once again were very sharp – for the fitted freights even into the 1950s. This indeed was what earned the Great Central its money – though despite all Fay's efforts, never quite enough of it to overcome the initial 'dead weight' of the London Extension costs and the loss-making but politically essential express passenger services.

Fay was also noteworthy as an innovator both in management education and in management-union relations. In the former area he initiated support of railway administration courses offered at Manchester and the LSE, arranging for the company to pay half the fees of any employees attending. He also instituted competitive examinations among junior staff for management training apprenticeships involving duty in every department of the company in turn. In the field of labour relations, he is probably best known for having devised the 'conciliation boards' system for negotiating pay and conditions without resorting to industrial strife, the source of the railway employment term 'conciliation grade staff'. (The system was promoted as from Lloyd George, but Fay did all the essential donkey-work of its development.) The full version of the system as applied on the GCR in 1906-08 involved six Sectional Boards, one for each major railway 'trade', with equal representation by unions and management on each, with a Central Board in overall control.

Fay's later years in office were dominated first by the First World War, then by the 1923 Grouping. The war put the usual strains on the Great Central, much as it did on other railways – 'war bonus' wage inflation, the need to prioritise war freight, the need to manufacture war supplies in its shops, the need for ambulance trains, and the need to save fuel and steel and economise on maintenance.

However, there were also several differences, which directly related to Fay's position as General Manager of that line. In the first place, Fay made sure that the GCR recruited women to cover the manpower gap created by the 'rush to the colours' both more quickly and more extensively than most other lines. Second, partly through Fay's membership of the Railway Executive Committee and partly through recognition of its strategic central position on the rail network, the line was allowed to retain its fast express timings and many of its restaurant car services, while other lines were shorn of both. Fay himself served as Director of Movements at the War Office, with the notional rank of General (though he never wore uniform) from 1917, and from March 1918 as Director-General of Movements & Railways, which carried with it a seat on the Army Council.

Fay was not able to return to the Great Central until

May 1919, and the Railway Executive Committee continued to control British lines until the end of that year. Thus there were effectively only three years of independent operation left for the line before the enforced Grouping of 1923, when the Great Central became part of the LNER, Marylebone became the LNER's official registered offices, and Fay retired. He continued to be active in the railway world, however, as a Director of two Argentinean lines and as Chairman of Beyer Peacock, which had for many years been one of the GCR's favoured locomotive suppliers. Fay remained as Chairman for ten years, steering Beyer Peacock through the first part of the Great Depression, cutting costs at Gorton Works, promoting the sales of Beyer-Garratt locomotives worldwide, and bringing the agricultural steam engine works of Richard Garrett of Leiston (no relation to Herbert Garratt!) into the Beyer empire. He retired as Chairman and as a Director in 1933, aged 77, and returned to his Hampshire roots at Awbridge, where he lived for a further 20 years, dying at the ripe old age of 97.

Henry Fowler
1870-1938

Locomotive Engineer

Born	Port Street, Bengeworth, Evesham, 29 July 1870, son of a cabinet-maker
Education	Evesham Grammar School, 1879-85, then Mason's College, Birmingham, 1885-87; apprenticed under Aspinall (qv) at Horwich, 1887; awarded Whitworth Exhibition, 1891
Married	Emmie Needham Smith, 1895
Best-known works	Introduced standard locomotives on MR and LMS; began line production methods for locomotive repairs; introduced superheated compound 4-4-0s, 2-6-6-2 Beyer-Garratts for coal traffic, 'Royal Scot' and 'Patriot' 4-6-0s; authorised introduction of diesel shunters
Honours	Hon LLD, Birmingham University, and DSc, Manchester; President, Inst of Locomotive Engineers, 1912; Secretary, Assoc of Railway Locomotive Engineers, 1913; CBE for wartime services, 1917; knighthood, 1918; President, Inst of Automobile Engineers, 1920-21 and Inst of Mechanical Engineers, 1927; Council Member, Inst of Civil Engineers, 1928-34
Died	Spondon Hall, Derby, 16 October 1938
Buried	Nottingham Road Cemetery, Derby

According to Hamilton Ellis, Sir Henry Fowler is supposed to have once remarked to a dinner colleague, 'My dear fellow, I never designed a locomotive in my life!' The story may or may not be true – the notion behind it probably wasn't (see the comments on his large compound proposals, below) – but it remains true that Fowler's greatest strength, both as a young engineer and later as CME of first the Midland and then the LMS, lay in the academic and managerial aspects of locomotive engineering rather than straightforward design. This is evidenced as early as his time under Aspinall, when as an apprentice he won the prestigious Whitworth Exhibition, and later, at Horwich, when he first managed the Gas Department then, in 1899, undertook a series of complex tests on train resistance.

From Horwich he joined the Midland Railway in 1900, becoming Assistant Works Manager at Derby in 1907 and Works Manager in 1909. He took over as CME of the Midland in 1909, following Deeley's abrupt departure, and held the post till the Midland was merged into the LMS in 1923, when he became first Deputy CME to George Hughes, then succeeded him in September 1925.

In both his CME posts, Fowler found himself embroiled in problems with senior management colleagues. On the Midland he inherited the same set of struggles vis à vis the operating department under Paget that had eventually triggered Deeley's sudden resignation; on the LMS he found himself similarly embroiled with J. E. Anderson, the Chief of Motive Power, and J. H. Follows, the Vice-President to whom Anderson and he both reported. On the LMS, also, he had the additional problem of substantial antipathy between the staff of the various former locomotive departments, especially Derby and Crewe.

On the Midland Railway, Fowler continued the standardisation policy introduced under Deeley, with the addition of superheating (on which he published a paper in 1913/14) and increased power classifications

(Fowler's 0-6-0s were power class 4 rather than 2 or 3; his 0-6-0Ts were class 3 rather than 1). When, after a very brief interregnum under Hughes, he took over the larger territory of the entire LMS, he applied the same policy to that organisation, scrapping small non-standard classes wholesale, and continuing his own standard designs – which, by definition of course, were of Midland origin, and consequently not well liked at Crewe. He did, however, introduce one entirely new standard class – a 2-6-4T for suburban passenger workings across the system – which though not particularly glamorous is generally credited with being one of the best tank engine designs of the 20th century (unfortunately the smaller 2-6-2T that followed it was just about equally unsuccessful, being seriously under-boilered). He also attempted – not entirely successfully, given the internal warfare of the period – to standardise locomotive repair systems in the various works, introducing line-production methods in order to reduce overhaul time.

Fowler's 'Midland standardisation' policy, together with superheating, worked well for all locomotive stock up to and including power class 4, but where more powerful express passenger or heavy goods engines were called for, there was a problem. In these areas the Midland design models did not offer any solutions (except just possibly the SDJR 2-8-0s – but these seem never to have been considered), and, particularly for express passenger traffic, the early LMS was seriously short of large engines, since both the 'Claughtons' of the LNWR and Hughes's LYR 4-6-0s were indifferent performers as originally built. It was here, however, that the problems with Anderson and Follows became most acute, even though in the express passenger case the eventual solution (the 'Royal Scots') turned out famously.

Fowler, as we have seen, was a Midland man, and continued the Derby compound tradition for medium-powered passenger 4-4-0s, though with superheat added. As a research engineer, he was also very impressed with the compounds' efficiency and economy. His own thoughts for a large express passenger engine therefore inevitably turned to a bigger compound, and he outlined a three-cylinder 4-6-0 (with GWR-style 30-inch stroke) in 1924, while still deputy to Hughes, and followed it in 1926, after becoming CME, with a proposal for a four-cylinder compound 'Pacific' for express passenger work, and a similar 2-8-2 (with the same boiler on 5ft 3in wheels) for heavy freight. This was not merely a 'what if' project – it was researched both by a visit to France in October 1925 (with Bulleid from Doncaster accompanying the party, possibly as a technical interpreter!), and experimental tests involving converting Hughes 4-6-0 No 10456 to compound working; in addition, a design team making use of skills from all three main English LMS works was set up. There is some evidence that the 'Pacific' design in particular, if carried through, would have been a good performer.

Anderson and Follows, however, disliked these designs, partly on what appear to be fairly doctrinaire grounds of 'the least wheels for the job', and partly on the rather more serious grounds that both designs would require the enlargement of a substantial number of LMS turntables. In late 1926, following trials of GWR No 5000 *Launceston Castle* on the West Coast Main Line, they persuaded the LMS Board (apparently behind Fowler's back) to go instead for 50 locomotives of basically the GWR 'Castle' Class design, to be ready for the summer of 1927. When this proved impossible for various reasons (including loading gauge differences), Derby Works was then constrained to place an order with the North British Locomotive Company for a large-boilered three-cylinder 4-6-0 – Anderson preferred three cylinders to four – with high boiler pressure, long valve travel and high superheat.

The order was actioned at top speed. North British did most of the overall design, Derby Works supplied drawings of elements of its standard practice, and a set of 'Lord Nelson' drawings was borrowed from Maunsell of the Southern, though only the firebox and cab seem to have been actually used. The resultant express locos came out on time and were, as we all know, a great success. They were officially credited to Fowler; and in fact he went on to combine their chassis with his rebuilt larger 'Claughton' boiler to produce the equally successful 'Patriot' ('Baby Scot') 4-6-0s for slightly lighter duties – but they weren't his idea, and indeed not his design preference.

Anderson's interference in the heavy freight locomotive design had a less successful outcome. Hughes had begun thinking in terms of a Beyer-Garratt design for the heavy Toton-Brent coal traffic, which regularly had to be double-headed even by Fowler 4Fs. In May 1925 Beyer Peacock suggested a 2-6-2+2-6-2 design to him, making use of all their standard components, importantly including axle bearings. To their total surprise, however, in the very same month, Anderson, from his Derby base, also came up with a request to Beyer, this time for a 2-6-0+0-6-2 design with standard Derby goods loco 5ft 3in wheels. When Fowler took over as CME, the Hughes Garratt project was terminated (Fowler, as we know, was thinking of a 2-8-2 with a wider route availability than simply Toton-Brent), but amazingly Anderson persisted with his own order to Beyer behind Fowler's back, not even informing him of the contract's existence until after he succeeded Hughes as CME.

Anderson also insisted that Beyer replace their own standard wheels and axle bearings with traditional Midland designs, sending details up from Derby, even though Fowler himself had specified more up-to-date Horwich designs in the successful 2-6-4Ts. The result was that the LMS Garratts were flawed from the start, and required shopping for axle-box repairs twice as frequently as they should have. But the evil didn't stop there – Fowler had intended his 2-8-2 as a much more widely available heavy freight engine, and was now left requiring a second design. He elected to authorise a Midland-type 0-8-0 with a superheated Belpaire boiler pressed at 200psi – but here again the Anderson influence led to the final design authorisation making use of the wretched ex-Midland 'Class 4' axle bearings, with all the resultant frequent in-shoppings to repair running gear that followed. They were actually outlived, in the end, by the ex-LNWR 'G2' 0-8-0s they were intended to replace.

Though Fowler's sufferings under Anderson and Follows were in many ways a re-run of those of Deeley under Paget, he avoided the explosive end to them that had occurred in Deeley's case. In January 1931 he resigned as CME, succeeded as a temporary measure by his Carriage & Wagon Superintendent, E. J. H. Lemon, but he did not retire completely, instead moving 'upstairs' to become advisor to the LMS Vice-President for research. In this capacity he made one final innovation – he authorised in 1932 the purchase of the initial pair of 0-6-0 diesel-electric shunters, one each from Armstrong Whitworth and English Electric, the direct ancestors of the BR standard diesel shunter type. He finally retired in 1933, and died in 1938.

Daniel Gooch
1816-1889

Locomotive Engineer and Manager

Born	Bedlington, Northumberland, 24 August 1816, third son of John Gooch, cashier at Bedlington Ironworks and friend of George Stephenson
Education	Dame School at Bedlington (the Misses Robson) from age 4 (1820), then Mr Thompson's School at Crow Hall, Cramlington, followed by apprenticeships and pupillages at Tredegar Iron Works (where the family had moved), Robert Stephenson's Vulcan Foundry at Warrington, Dundee Foundry, and Robert Stephenson's at Newcastle, 1831-36
Married	(1) Margaret Tanner, Bishopwearmouth, Co Durham, 22 March 1838 (d 22 May 1868); (2) Emily Burder, Christ Church, Lancaster Gate, London, 17 September 1870
Best-known works	Locomotive Assistant to Brunel, GWR, 1837-64; laid out original Swindon Works, 1841; designed locomotives *Firefly* (1840), *Great Western* (1846) and heavy 4-4-0ST design for use west of Exeter; left GWR to supervise laying of Atlantic cable 1864, but returned 1865 as Chairman, remaining so till his death; oversaw initial stages of

Honours	liquidation of broad gauge, and supported project for Severn Tunnel Baronetcy, 1865, for work on Atlantic cable; MP for Cricklade, 1865-85; JP for Berkshire; Masonic honours of Grand Sword-bearer of England and Provincial Grand Master, Berks & Bucks
Died	Clever Park, Windsor, 15 October 1889
Buried	Clever Churchyard, under a memorial slab, alongside his first wife (his second wife, who survived him, was buried in a separate plot nearby)

Daniel Gooch, best known perhaps as the designer of the Great Western's famous 'Iron Duke' Class broad gauge 4-2-2 express locomotives, which lasted with rebuildings right up to the end of broad gauge in 1892, three years after his death, was yet another of the group of early and influential railwaymen who sprang from the Northumbrian coalmining and engineering environment. It is customary among some commentators to see the 'Stephenson' and 'Brunel' traditions of railway engineering as implacably opposed, but Gooch's career amply demonstrates that this was not so – together with Brunel's close personal friendship with and professional admiration for Stephenson's son Robert.

Both of Daniel Gooch's elder brothers were closely involved with early railway engineering – his eldest brother, Tom, as a civil engineer and senior assistant to Robert Stephenson, and his middle brother John as a locomotive engineer with the LSWR. Daniel's first choice of career appears to have been as manager of a locomotive building works. His apprenticeships and pupillage training were systematically organised (apparently by himself) to introduce him to as many varying aspects of civil and mechanical steam engineering (including marine engineering!) as practicable, and his famous letter of July 1837 applying to become Brunel's 'locomotive assistant' mentions that just such a position had at that immediate time fallen through, leaving him unemployed and dependent on work found for him by his brother Tom on the Manchester & Leeds Railway. It seems likely that Brunel already knew something of Daniel Gooch's ability through their common friendship with Robert Stephenson, for he appointed him virtually by return of post, and Gooch was at work on the GWR by 18 August – a line of employment from which, apart from one brief diversion in 1864/65, he never looked back.

To Brunel the young Gooch was invaluable, though there was periodic friction between the two men throughout the 1840s over Gooch's status as an independent locomotive superintendent. Brunel himself (qv) was a brilliant civil engineer but a poor locomotive man; his early attempts at locomotive specifications would not steam and were underpowered (and indeed at one point complaints about them almost cost Gooch his job with the directors). In response, Gooch first developed the 'Firefly' Class (from the *North Star* designed by Robert Stephenson), then in 1846, following his commissioning of Swindon Works, the 'colossal' (for the period) *Great Western* – like the 'Firefly' Class, a 2-2-2, but much more powerful. After conversion to a 4-2-2 it was effectively the origin of the 'Iron Duke' express locomotives, which, suitably rebuilt, continued to handle all the broad gauge express traffic of the GWR until its abolition in 1892. Other Gooch locomotives included the 'Lalla Rookh' Class of early 4-4-0s, constructed by Robert Stephenson and somewhat less successful (the leading wheels were not bogies and had a tendency to derail) and the heavy but remarkably successful 4-4-0STs for the steeply graded routes west of Exeter.

In 1864, after a decade of disunited leadership among his directors, Gooch resigned from his Locomotive Superintendent post at Swindon in order to take chief responsibility for laying the first Atlantic cable, using Brunel's *Great Eastern*, which he had recently purchased jointly with Thomas Brassey (see also under Locke) and William Barber – a task for which Queen Victoria created him a Knight Baronet the following year. In that year, also, he returned to the Great Western, but this time as Chairman of the Board. The company was passing through a severe depression and required strong and economical leadership if it was to avoid bankruptcy. This Gooch, in his newly elevated role, duly provided – possibly even in some ways a trifle too economically, with an effect on the company image – remaining at the helm until his death in 1889.

This final phase in Gooch's career indeed led to one of the major ironies of his life – that the very man who had so ably defended the broad gauge before the Gauge Commission in 1845-46, and designed some of its most spectacular express locomotives, should in his later years have presided over the main part of its eventual demise. But, as author Adrian Vaughan has pointed out, despite their common breath of vision and enthusiasm for hard work, Brunel and Gooch differed in that Brunel most desired fame, while Gooch was content with 'plain old-fashioned wealth'. He had a number of other business interests outside the GWR, and on his death left an estate worth £670,000.

Nigel Gresley
1876-1941

Locomotive & Carriage Engineer

Born	Herbert Nigel Gresley, Dublin St, Edinburgh, 19 June 1876 (the fifth child of the Rector of Netherseale, Derbyshire)
Education	Marlborough College, then premium apprenticeship under Webb (qv) at Crewe, 1893, followed by pupillage under Aspinall (qv) at Horwich, 1898
Married	Ethel Francis Fullagar, St Anne's, 1901
Best-known works	CME of GNR and LNER, 1911-1941; pioneer in UK of articulated coaches, buffet-cars, and streamlined locomotives; designer of *Great Northern*, *Flying Scotsman*, *Cock o' the North* and record-breaking *Mallard*, 'K3' 2-6-0s, 'O2' 2-8-0s, 'B17' ('Sandringham') 4-6-0s for East Anglia, and 'V2' (*Green Arrow*) mixed traffic 2-6-2s, all with three-cylinder propulsion and conjugated valve gear
Honours	CBE 1918; knighthood, Hon DSc Manchester University, President, Inst of Mechanical Engineers, President, ARLE, all 1936
Died	Watton House, Hertford, 5 April 1941, of heart failure
Buried	Netherseale churchyard; memorial service at Chelsea Old Church, London (later destroyed in Blitz)

Inevitably Gresley and Stanier invite comparisons as locomotive engineers. Between them they were probably the two great giants of British railway engineering during the period between the World Wars They were born in the same year (1876); both were public-school educated and took to locomotive apprenticeship out of love for railway engineering; and both were men of a careful and scientifically minded turn of design. But the situations in which they found themselves could scarcely have been more different – while Stanier, after long and patient service within the Swindon system, found himself head-hunted in 1935 as an emergency measure to a railway whose locomotive position was little short of disastrous, Gresley came early to his chieftaincy, in 1911, and, apart from the intrusion of the First World War (which saw him in charge of munitions and earned him a CBE), was able at length to explore and consolidate a series of designs that gave his line, the GNR, the best of the LNER constituent engines and formed the basis for consistently good locomotive and carriage practice on the LNER itself throughout the inter-war years.

Indeed, Ivatt had done his work so well that for the first few years of Gresley's tenure there was no call for new engines. As a result, having been Ivatt's Carriage & Wagon Superintendent before he became CME, Gresley was able to concentrate on carriage design, experimenting with articulated coaches, electric lighting and steam heating – all elements that featured large in his subsequent standard designs. When his new locomotives did start to emerge, prototype engines were carefully tested before production runs were set in motion, and subsequent batches of a given type were systematically improved. For example, in the case of the 2-6-0s, this was done by fitting larger and more powerful boilers, and all were superheated, a feature that Ivatt had only just begun to introduce before he retired. From 1918, also, Gresley began introducing what was in many ways to become his locomotive trademark – three-cylinder designs with conjugated valve gear (ie two sets operating all three cylinders).

Although it was first actually applied on a 2-8-0, this arrangement, which some found overly complex and which deteriorated under Second World War running conditions, originated in 1915 as the result of a search for a larger and more powerful express engine design. This ultimately found expression from 1922 onwards in the 'A1' (*Great Northern*), 'A3' (*Flying Scotsman*) and 'A4' (streamlined) 'Pacifics'. Gresley's wide-firebox 'Pacifics' were the logical successors to Ivatt's large 'Atlantics'. The latter were, of course, two-cylinder machines, but the larger design would necessarily require multiple cylinders to generate sufficient tractive force. Possibly influenced by Great Western thinking, Gresley at first schemed a four-cylinder 'Pacific', but before committing the GNR to building a prototype for testing, he rebuilt an Ivatt 'Atlantic' to the same four-cylinder layout. The rebuild proved seriously underboilered (and also, if it had actually been a 'Pacific', would have been seriously underpowered, though it was well enough powered for an 'Atlantic'). Gresley therefore began to work seriously on three-cylinder arrangements, initially for his proposed 'Pacific' design but eventually for most of his larger locomotives

The 'A1' 'Pacific' design came out in the very last year of the Great Northern Railway's separate existence. However, the formation of the LNER in the following year, and Gresley's appointment as CME of the newly enlarged company, added to the existing design partnership of Gresley and Bulleid (qv) one of the most important railway managerial partnerships and friendships of the Grouping years – that of Gresley and Sir Ralph Wedgwood (also qv). The synergistic combination of Gresley's careful design testing and Wedgwood's commercial flair led to such innovations as the famous buffet-cars (initially introduced at

Wedgwood's request for the King's Cross-Cambridge service, but subsequently extended first to the tourist stock sets, then to system-wide use on lighter loaded services), three successive stock upgrades, and corridor-tender working on the now non-stop 'Flying Scotsman'. It also led, most famously of all, to the 'streaks' – the 'A4' streamlined 'Pacifics', hauling specially designed stock on the streamlined 'Silver Jubilee', 'Coronation' and 'West Riding Limited' (and special streamlined 'B17s' for the not quite so prestigious 'East Anglian').

True to form, Gresley only produced enough 'A4s' in the initial batch – just four – to cover the 'Silver Jubilee' itself. Although prepared quickly, the designs were most carefully thought out, internal streamlining in the Chapelon fashion being as important as the spectacular external casing, with styling derived from Bugatti and special aerofoil wheel splashers by Bulleid. A year's testing on the new express showed both the design and the service to be successful, and Gresley produced the famous second ('Wildfowl') batch of 'A4s', including the record-breaking *Mallard*, while Wedgwood authorised the two new special streamliners mentioned above. Running at regular speeds of 90mph-plus, however, produced problems of braking time, requiring an empty block to be left ahead of the 'streaks' at all times, and it was in fact during the course of one of an extensive series of braking tests with 'A4s' to attempt to reduce braking time from these speeds that *Mallard* performed her record-breaking feat of 126mph.

The tests did lead to reduced braking times, but the problem of mixing high-speed and ordinary traffic was never completely solved. To help towards such a solution, and likewise as part of his 'continuous improvement' policy, Wedgwood wanted the heavier non-streamlined LNER expresses to be accelerated also, and in 1938 Gresley began work on a 4-8-2, using features from his experimental 'P2' *Cock o' the North* design (but avoiding the poppet valves of the first two members of that class, which had proved unsuccessful). But the Second World War intervened, and although Gresley's successors Thompson and Peppercorn toyed with a revival of the idea during 1946, nothing came of it. Gresley's last prototype – the 'V4' 2-6-2 *Bantam Cock*, a scaled-down version of his hugely successful 'V2' mixed traffic design for lighter duties – appeared under wartime conditions in February 1941, less than two months before his death from a heart attack at the age of 64.

Timothy Hackworth
1786-1850

Early Locomotive Engineer

Born	Wylam, 22 December 1786, eldest son of foreman blacksmith John Hackworth (d 1802)
Education	Wylam village school, then apprentice blacksmith, Wylam Colliery, 1800
Married	Jane Golightly, Ovingham Parish Church, December 1813
Best-known works	Resident Engineer, Stockton & Darlington Railway, 1824-40; developed Shildon locomotive works, 1833; developed blast-pipe and return flue; designed *Royal George* (1827, the world's first 0-6-0), *Sans Pareil* (1829), *Derwent* (1839 or 1845 – date uncertain)
Honours	Member, British Assoc for Advancement of Science; locomotives named after him on S&DR (1851), GWR (1865) and LBSCR (1897); 'Royal George' fountain in Shildon Park
Died	Soho Cottage, Shildon, 7 July 1850
Buried	Shildon Parish Church churchyard, beneath an elaborate monumental stone

Timothy Hackworth was one of the group of North Eastern engineers and collierymen working in and around Wylam, Northumberland, also including the two Stephensons (qv), William Hedley and Nicholas Wood, who jointly originated the practical working steam locomotive during the first three decades of the 19th century. As I have remarked in the entries on the Stephensons, many of the innovations that led to the classic 'Stephenson locomotive' design seem to have arisen semi-independently and been informally discussed jointly among the members of this group, so that it is hard to pin down exactly who was responsible for exactly which design innovation. Thus both the development of the blast-pipe and the use of a return-flue boiler, key elements of the 'Stephenson' locomotive to be found characteristically in Hackworth's work, appear to have been also invented separately by Richard Trevithick at the other end of the country, and incorporated into the 'Stephenson' design equally separately by George and Robert, while Hackworth was working for (or should it be 'with'?) them.

The phenomenon around that time of common multiple 'inventions' of the same basic design device is described by some writers as 'steam engine time', as if the overall intellectual climate was such as to lead any competent investigator into steam locomotives to come up with the same set of basic ideas. To some extent this may perhaps be true, but it probably has much more to do with the completely unstructured and informal nature of railway engineering as a profession at this early period, and the local personal 'networking' that went on between the colliery engineer-blacksmiths of the Grand Alliance pits, who (if one excepts Trevithick) were the prime movers in these developments. However, in addition to his share in these basic inventions (and his son John listed no fewer than 40 of them), one development clearly belongs to Hackworth alone as of right – the conception and development of the slow but powerful heavy freight locomotive, embodied first in his *Royal George* 0-6-0 of 1827.

Timothy Hackworth was born at Wylam in 1786, and

entered employment at the pit of that name in 1800 as an apprentice blacksmith. He was appointed foreman blacksmith to the colliery, his late father's former post, in 1807, aged 21, and in that capacity he helped William Hedley build the famous *Puffing Billy* and *Wylam Dilly* locomotives around 1813-15. In the latter year, now a Wesleyan preacher, he resigned over Sabbath working at Wylam, and took up a similar post at Walbottle. In 1824 George Stephenson head-hunted Hackworth from that post to supervise the new locomotive building works he was setting up in Newcastle under his son's name during Robert's absence abroad, and was so impressed with his performance that he offered him a partnership in the firm, which Hackworth turned down (possibly because the financial investment required was of the order of £800 per partner). George Stephenson, in his other capacity as official Engineer to the Stockton & Darlington Railway, then offered Hackworth the post of Resident Engineer on that line (Stephenson himself had many other schemes afoot at this time, and needed someone on site to deal with day-to-day management and engineering design), which Hackworth accepted.

Hackworth remained with the S&DR till 1840, and most of his key engineering innovation work was done during this period. The early S&DR locomotives (including Stephenson's *Locomotion*) were underpowered and prone both to slipping on gradients and to running short of steam, and it was to counter these problems that he designed the *Royal George* (1827), the world's first 0-6-0 freight engine, still with 'Killingworth' cylinders emerging vertically from the top of the firebox, but with a much bigger boiler incorporating a return flue, an effective blast-pipe, and all six wheels coupled. The blast-pipe and the return flue ensured adequate steam, and the greater adhesion overcame the problem of slipping, though the 'Killingworth' motion meant that high speeds could not be achieved.

This inability to achieve high speeds was also a contributory factor to the failure two years later of Hackworth's *Sans Pareil* to win the Rainhill Trials against Stephenson's *Rocket* (it also suffered on the days of the trials from feed pump and cylinder breakdown, which was a more cogent defect). But despite missing out at Rainhill, *Sans Pareil* subsequently proved to be a perfectly practical freight engine, working on the Leigh & Bolton Railway for several years. A fine later example of Hackworth's freight locomotive designs is *Derwent*, again an 0-6-0 but this time with direct drive from inclined cylinders, built for the S&DR by Alfred Kitching at dates variously recorded as 1839 (just before Hackworth's departure) and 1845, a year or two after.

Towards the end of his life, however, Hackworth produced a locomotive, the *Sanspareil No 2* (1849), that demonstrated that his work, had he lived longer, would have taken an entirely new direction. A 2-2-2 with outside slab frames, horizontal inside cylinders of 15in by 22in with 'passover' slide valves and pistons and rods in one piece, a welded boiler, a raised firebox and 6ft 6in driving wheels, it covered 45 miles with a 200-ton freight train at 28mph on tests, and the same distance hauling six carriages of the period at 42mph. It is commonly considered his magnum opus.

Hackworth's other major contribution to the development of railway engineering was the concept of the railway works (as distinct from a private locomotive builder such as Robert Stephenson's works in Newcastle or Hackworth's own Soho Works). He established the S&DR's Shildon Works (later part of the NER and LNER works systems) in 1833, the first railway works in the world, and continued to develop it during the remainder of his time with the S&DR, subsequently developing, with the company's permission, his own private locomotive works nearby at Soho. He died in Soho Cottage, Shildon (now a museum to him), in 1850.

George Hudson
1800-1871

Railway Entrepreneur and Investor

Born	Howsham, nr York, 10 March 1800
Education	Little is known of his initial education (his father died when he was 9, and he had to make his own way); apprenticed c1815 to York drapers Rebecca Bell and her brother Richard Nicholson; partner in firm February 1821
Married	Elizabeth Nicholson (sister of employers), Holy Trinity, Goodramgate, York, 17 July 1821
Best-known works	York & North Midland Railway, 1836; Newcastle & Darlington (later York, Newcastle & Berwick) Railway, 1844; Midland Railway (formed by takeover and amalgamation), 1844; takeover of Eastern Counties Railway, 1845
Honours	Lord Mayor of York (three times); MP for Sunderland, 1845; Deputy Lord Lieutenant for Durham, 1845; member of Carlton Club, January 1846; invited to Royal Society conversazione and introduced to Prince Consort, March 1846; presented to Queen Victoria, 1847; Freedom of Merchants' Company of York, 1847
Died	37 Churton Street, Pimlico, London, 14 December 1871
Buried	St Peter's, Scrayingham, Yorks (parish church for his native village of Howsham), near entrance to churchyard

The fifth son of a Yorkshire yeoman farmer, and early orphaned, George Hudson (aka 'The Railway King') rose from a lowly draper's assistant to become the first railway millionaire and an MP, owning a country estate and a London town house and controlling more than a quarter of the railway mileage of the country via his companies – then fell equally dramatically following revelations of financial mismanagement (never quite amounting to actual fraud by the accounting standards of the time, though it certainly would if carried out today) and bribery of members of Parliament.

His initial financial acquisition came from a bequest of his great-uncle Matthew Bottrill (who lived locally), who left him £30,000 (including his fine house in Monkgate) in 1827. Initially he became active simply in York municipal affairs, but after a local railway promotion group in York (initially for a horse-drawn line) elected him treasurer in 1833, a chance meeting with George Stephenson in Whitby the following year set him on a course of promoting steam railways on a national scale.

It is not certain whether Hudson's meteoric career – which coincided almost exactly with the first period of Victorian 'Railway Mania' – was fuelled solely by a mixture of financial greed and power mania, or whether he was also a genuine visionary (in this respect he somewhat resembles Edward Watkin (qv), though the latter had much greater financial probity). Certainly Stephenson had a passionate vision of a national system of railways, and he may well have communicated this to Hudson – though Hudson's vision of one great amalgamated national monopoly (with himself at its head, of course!) was not one that Stephenson shared – the latter much preferred a medley of local lines operating in open competition.

Hudson's method was a mixture of promoting new lines, amalgamating existing lines with his new ones to create larger entities, and acquiring controlling interests in other such lines and amalgamations. His initial promotions, in particular the York & North Midland (the germ of what later became the Midland Railway), appear to have been funded in a reasonably regular manner – for the time, at any rate – involving subscription publicity, appropriate 'name-dropping' (in this case that of George Stephenson) and lobbying parliamentary and similar vested interests. As Hudson's headlong rush from scheme to scheme progressed, however, it became more and more essential to ensure high returns on existing investments irrespective of actual performance (in order to attract inflow of new capital). Hudson achieved this by the simple (and at that time not actually forbidden!) expedient of paying the dividends on his existing lines to ensure capital inflow on the new ones, but paying them out of that very inflow as it came in. He also began increasingly to supplement lobbying for his new schemes with financial inducement in order to speed their parliamentary approval, particularly after becoming an MP himself in 1845.

Clearly, such a state of affairs could not last. It depended upon an ever-increasing inflow of capital for new schemes, and that in turn depended upon a continuing economic 'boom', which came to an abrupt end with the depression of 1848. It also depended upon his existing schemes, even if not making the promised profits, not actually making a loss, and by 1847 both the young Midland Railway and, more importantly, the Eastern Counties Railway, which he had acquired in 1845, were in a loss-making position sufficient to force Hudson to resort to some highly creative accounting – as author Hunter Davies puts it, 'desperately balancing the books, rewriting balance sheets, adding noughts to profits'. Investigations of Hudson's dealings began at a shareholders' meeting of the York & North Midland, and continued at meetings on his other lines, most especially the Eastern Counties, where he was found to have altered figures in the annual accounts, paid more than £200,000 worth of dividends out of capital, and apparently 'lost' thousands of pounds under a heading 'Secret Service', which Hudson maintained meant payments 'for parliamentary service'.

Hudson was officially charged with bribing MPs, called upon to explain himself to the house, and ejected. He was eventually shown to have embezzled at least £600,000 from his various companies. Effectively bankrupt (he was in fact briefly imprisoned for debt), he sold his country estate and town house, paid as many debtors as he could, left his wife in lodgings, and fled to Paris. He lived there in poverty till 1868 (meeting Dickens by chance in 1863), when a group of North Eastern worthies took pity on him and raised a subscription to buy him a modest annuity of £600 per annum to enable him to return home to England once imprisonment for debt had been repealed in 1870 (he still at that point owed the North Eastern Railway £170,000 including costs). He lived in a rented house in Pimlico, where he died in 1871.

Hudson's unbridled activities were not simply the result of his personal greed; they would not have been possible without the lax financial and economic regulatory régimes of the early Victorian period, and the 'get rich quick' philosophy of the time, embodied in works like Samuel Smiles's *Self Help*. A considerable number of individuals made a lot of money on his coat-tails – and an equally considerable number lost a lot at his fall. Despite it all, however, he does deserve the title of one of the '50 famous railwaymen' – he effectively created three of the country's principal pre-Grouping railways, the Midland, the North Eastern and the Great Eastern (successor to the Eastern Counties). Many of the lines he promoted exist to this day – most particularly the northern half of the East Coast Main Line to Scotland, and the Virgin Cross-Country route from York to Birmingham. They might well all have happened without him, but without him the process would have taken much longer and been considerably more piecemeal.

Henry Ivatt
1851-1923

Locomotive Engineer

Born	Coveney Rectory, Isle of Ely, 16 September 1851
Education	Liverpool College; apprenticed (1868) under Ramsbottom and subsequently Webb (qqv) at Crewe Works
Married	Margaret Campbell, Hampstead, 20 September 1876
Best-known works	CME of GNR, 1886-1911; introduced 'large engine' policy, culminating in first British 'Atlantics' ('C2' or '990' Class 4-4-2s) and large-boilered wide-firebox 4-4-2s ('C1' Class); patented water scoop and built-up crank-axle; oversaw introduction of 12-wheel bogie carriages with automatic couplings
Honours	Vice-President, Inst of Mechanical Engineers, 1922
Died	St Clair, Haywards Heath, 25 October 1923
Buried	Cuckfield Cemetery

Like his successor Gresley, Henry Alfred Ivatt was the son of a clergyman, and was trained at Crewe – in his case under Ramsbottom as well as Francis Webb. After completing his apprenticeship, he spent some time as a fireman, gaining a practical familiarity with locomotive operation the lessons of which never left him (and neither, for that matter, did his concern for engine staff welfare). Indeed, this concern with operating needs may well be regarded as the main wellspring of his locomotive designs, and the reason why they were so successful and long-lasting.

Ivatt's first post as a CME, in 1886, was with the Great Southern & Western Railway of Ireland, where he completed the 4-4-0 designs bequeathed to him by Aspinall (qv), then produced 0-6-0Ts and elegant (if a trifle small by later standards) 4-4-2Ts for passenger work. He also designed and patented the spring-loaded flap for carriage sash windows, a design that became a virtual UK standard for nearly all the earlier part of the 20th century, and produced an experimental compound 4-4-0 (which showed no major advantage over its simple equivalent, possibly because the 150psi boiler pressure – normal for the period – was rather too low for effective compounding). Life in Ireland was quiet, but Ivatt's fame was spreading. During 1895 he was head-hunted by Henry Oakley (qv) as a potential successor to Patrick Stirling (qv), then over 70 and showing no sign of being prepared to retire. When Stirling died the following year, Ivatt moved to the Great Northern at a salary – £2,500 per annum – of his own naming.

When he reached Doncaster, Ivatt found the GNR locomotive stock in a crisis in some way similar to that faced by Stanier on the LMS 40 years later. Both passenger and freight trains had vastly increased in size and weight (the former by introducing corridor and dining stock and the latter as a result of growing mineral traffic). And while the designs of his predecessor Patrick Stirling were consistent and excellently thought out, they were no longer powerful enough for the new loads imposed on them. Ivatt therefore embarked on his famous 'large engine' policy. First 4-4-0s then 4-4-2s (the famous Ivatt 'Atlantics') replaced the equally famous Stirling 'Single' 4-2-2s for fast passenger work – not without some objections, for the GNR had its 'small engine' faction at that point as well as the Midland – and sturdy 0-6-0s were followed in 1901 by the 'Long Tom' 0-8-0s for mineral traffic.

The 'Long Toms' had a considerably higher starting tractive effort than any of the 0-6-0s that preceded them (27,600lb in fact), but some laymen may find it curious that the tractive efforts of the large and small 'Atlantics' were exactly the same, and indeed both of them were in the same general range as the Stirling 4-2-2s they were intended to replace. (Indeed, even the pundits of British Railways were foxed by this fact, and accordingly classified the large ('C1') 'Atlantics' as 3P on the old LMS power scale, quite clearly the 'understatement of the decade'!) The point was that what Ivatt was after was not an increase in starting tractive effort, but an increase in running power under way, and, as he himself said, 'the measure of the power of a locomotive is the boiler' (and, he might well have added, the size of the firebox to supply the heat). Stirling's 'Singles' had just over 1,000sq ft of heating surface and around 20sq ft of grate area; Ivatt's first ('small') 'Atlantics' had 1,400sq ft of heating surface and 27sq ft of grate, and with the adoption of the wide Wooten firebox (which he had observed on a visit to America that also investigated automatic couplings), No 251, the first of the 'large Atlantics', had no less than 2500sq ft of heating surface and 31sq ft of grate.

More and larger locomotives require additional production and repair facilities, and with the help of his principal assistant, D. Earle Marsh, later CME of the Brighton line, he both refitted Doncaster Works with new machines and pneumatic tools, and between 1899 and 1901 oversaw the construction of a major new erecting and repair shop, the 'Crimpsall' (so called from its location by Crimpsall Road). He continued to experiment with compound traction, building two four-cylinder compound versions of his 'large Atlantic' design, one of which could also be worked in full-simple mode. However, despite the larger boilers involved, there were once again no clear power advantages over what must generally be reckoned to be one of the finest simple express locomotives ever built – and of course the mechanical complexity and initial construction costs of the compounds were greater. Late in his career (1908) he began to introduce superheating on the 'Long Toms' and the 'Atlantics', and designed a superheated 0-6-0.

Ivatt, unlike Stirling, was not prepared to die in harness. He retired in 1911, handing over to his protégé and successor Gresley through an amicable three-month period of double office. He lived long enough to see his successor become CME of the newly formed LNER in 1923.

Samuel Johnson
1831-1912

Locomotive Engineer

Born	Bramley, nr Leeds, 14 October 1831, son of James Johnson, later an engineer on the GNR under Sturrock
Education	Leeds Grammar School; apprenticed to James Fenton at E. B. Wilson's Locomotive Foundry, Leeds
Married	1881 Census gives wife's name as Emily; there were four children (all girls)
Best-known works	Locomotive Superintendent, Midland Railway, 1873-1903; oversaw major rebuilding of Derby Works (initiated just months before his appointment); pioneered high-level coal stages for quick refuelling, designed inside-cylinder, inside framed 0-6-0s, 2-4-0s, 0-6-0Ts and 0-4-4Ts, major range of 4-4-0s with increasingly large boilers culminating in '700' Class for Settle & Carlisle line and first three Midland compounds, both types with Belpaire fireboxes, and large 4-2-2 single-driver express engines
Honours	Gold Medal, Saltaire Exhibition, 1897; President, Inst of Mechanical Engineers, 1898; Grand Prix, Paris Exhibition, 1900; Commander, Order of Medjidieh and Officer, Order of Osmanieh (both Egyptian); JP for Nottingham
Died	Lenton House, Nottingham,

| | 15 January 1912, having been knocked down by a runaway horse and trap |
| *Buried* | St Peter's, Nottingham |

Samuel Waite Johnson was the son of a Leeds engineer. Following apprenticeship under James Fenton (builder of the famous 'Jenny Lind' locomotives) he served in various capacities on the Manchester, Sheffield & Lincolnshire, the Great Northern, the Edinburgh & Glasgow and the Great Eastern railways (the two last as Locomotive Superintendent), before coming to the Midland in that role in 1873 on the death of Matthew Kirtley (qv) as part of Allport's and Ellis's passenger comfort revolution.

On arrival at Derby he found a major rebuilding of the Works just initiated, and a line well on the way towards locomotive standardisation, with a locomotive fleet that was sturdy and generally reliable, albeit in some way old-fashioned (for example, in the use of double frames and well tanks). Carriages, of course, were no longer his responsibility – Clayton (qv) looked after those. Johnson saw through the Works rebuilding, and subsequently added additional engine sheds and turntables among various upgrades. He also planned a further Works modernisation just before his retirement, but these plans never came to fruition, partly because of a need to divert a nearby canal to accommodate them. (Instead, his successors Deeley and Fowler (qqv) undertook extensive reorganisation within the existing physical structure.)

On the locomotive side, Johnson continued the moves towards standardisation begun by Kirtley and also moved decisively towards modernisation, introducing inside frames in place of Kirtley's by now old-fashioned sandwich frames, and side tanks in place of well tanks, building even shunting engines with cabs rather than spectacle-plates, raising boiler pressures and steadily enlarging boiler sizes, culminating post-1900 in the introduction of really large boilers with Belpaire fireboxes for classes intended for use on the Settle-Carlisle line's heavy trains and steep gradients. He continued the traditional 0-6-0s for the Toton coal traffic and 0-6-0Ts for shunting, and built further 2-4-0s and 0-4-4Ts for second-string and local passenger work. However, his tours de force were the introduction of the 4-4-0 (including the two Belpaire designs referred to above, one of which was the initial Midland compound design, using Smith's principle) and – possibly his most celebrated and beautiful locomotives – the famous 4-2-2 Johnson 'Singles', produced from 1887 to 1900, and eventually numbering 95 in all. (One of the latter locomotives won a Gold Medal at the same Paris Exhibition where Clayton's carriage designs won Grand Prix.)

The genesis of these Johnson 'Singles', built like Patrick Stirling's famous 7ft 0in versions on the GNR virtually a generation after the old 2-2-2 single-driver locomotives had vanished from design history, is a matter worthy of some discussion. The advantage of single-driver locomotives (apart from the possibility of extra-large driving wheels for high-speed work) is that they are free-running and hence economical on fuel. The major disadvantage, and the thing that with increasing train weights eventually even ruled out Johnson's 4-2-2s from top-link express work, is the low proportion of the machine's total weight available for adhesion, leading to pronounced slipping and concomitant loss of time. This slipping can, however, be greatly reduced by a really efficient sanding gear, and it was two improvements in just such gear that led to Johnson reviving the 'single', albeit in 4-2-2 rather than 2-2-2 form, in 1887, 20 years after the last Kirtley 'single' had been turned out.

Neither improvement was by Johnson himself, though both were of Midland origin. It was Robert Weatherburn, the District Loco Superintendent at Leicester, who conceived the repositioning of both the boxes and the delivery pipes so as to ensure maximum sand was delivered to the wheels. He tried out his idea on an old Kirtley 'single' (officially condemned to stationary use) and 'informally' rostered it on Leicester-London express services, where to everyone's astonishment except perhaps his it kept excellent time and climbed hills splendidly. Johnson got to hear of it, called him to Derby, and after some admonition about keeping to official instructions, discussed the possibility of new 'singles' with him: it was actually Weatherburn, not Johnson, who suggested the 4-2-2 format.

The other major Midland contributor was Francis Holt, the Derby Works Manager, who invented a means of working the repositioned sandboxes first off the Westinghouse compressed air system, then, when the Westinghouse Corporation objected that this interfered with their brake compression, by steam. Even then, Johnson tested the idea by altering several of his 4-4-0s to run with driving wheels uncoupled (they did particularly well on gradients in this form) before actually committing himself to the succession of 95 4-2-2 'Singles' that eventually emerged from Derby, the final ten only three years before his retirement.

This story shows several important facets of Johnson's character as an engineer. To begin with it underlines his undoubted skills in team building and man management, his willingness to learn from others and to reward his subordinates' ideas. It also demonstrates his careful and painstaking commitment to detailed research in pursuit of engineering perfection; his locomotives were not only to be beautiful, but technically excellent, and few of his innovations, including the use of steel boilers on the 'Singles' and the later 0-6-0s, and the Smith compound system on his final batch of 4-4-0s, were introduced without extensive testing.

119

The Midland was of course well known for being a
'small-engine' line, and there was certainly a major
faction within its management that backed such a
policy. But despite his reversion to single-drivers for
express passenger work south of Nottingham, his
design record shows that Johnson was not in fact a
'small-engine' man. Throughout his tenure as
Locomotive Superintendent, his modernisations
moved to steadily increase boiler size, pressure, and
locomotive power. The 4-2-2s themselves, with tractive
efforts ranging from 12,945lb to 16,175lb, were the
power equivalent of 4-4-0s, and his final 'Midland
Compound' design was as powerful as any express
engine then running on the rival LNWR (and, indeed, as
powerful as Bowen Cooke's 'Prince of Wales' 4-6-0s that
came some time later!).

His two final designs before his retirement in
December 1903, ordered but never actually built,
perfectly demonstrate this move to large engines. They
were for a large but elegant 4-4-4T for passenger work,
with a tractive effort of 19,890lb – about 2,000lb greater
than the contemporary Whitelegg 'Tilbury' tanks – and
for ten 0-8-0s for the Toton coal traffic (by now much
too heavy for 0-6-0s to handle unaided), with 28,460lb
TE. But it seems that the 'small-engine' Mafia on his
Board scuppered both of them – certainly both orders
were subsequently cancelled, and not, so far as one
can tell, by his successor Deeley.

David Jones
1834-1906

Locomotive, Carriage and Wagon Engineer

Born	Manchester, 25 October 1834, son of an engineer
Education	Apprenticed under Ramsbottom at Longsight Works (Jones had left for Inverness by the time of Ramsbottom's move to Crewe)
Married	Mary Ann Snowie, Inverness, 16 September 1858 (died before 1881)
Best-known works	Locomotive Superintendent of the Highland Railway and consultant to various colonial railways; introduced the 4-6-0 to Britain; pioneered high power-to-weight ratios (in his later 4-4-0s) and louvred chimneys for improved draught; introduced first bogie sleeping-cars in Britain
Honours	Personal friend of Duke of Sutherland (for whom he built second *Dunrobin* tank engine and convertible saloon carriage complete with cocktail bar)
Died	Hampstead, 2 December 1906, following a motor car accident
Buried	Not known

David Jones was one of the more 'middle-class' of Victorian railway engineers in origin (he and Stroudley were known collectively during their time together on the Highland as 'The Gentleman-Engineers'). There do not seem to be any records surviving of his school education, but he was bound apprentice at only

13, and at least part of this time was served under Ramsbottom, then at the Longsight Works in Manchester. From there he went, in November 1855, to the newly opened Inverness & Nairn Railway, later to become part of the Highland line. By 1858 he was working as principal assistant to the Locomotive Superintendent Andrew Barclay, and on Barclay's resignation took over the Locomotive Superintendent's post in an acting capacity, only to be 'knocked back' to Running Superintendent when the Highland Board decided to appoint Stroudley (qv) to the senior position. In 1870, following the departure of both Stroudley and Dugald Drummond (qv) to Brighton, Jones finally became the Highland's Locomotive, Carriage & Wagon Superintendent, and held the post till his retirement, following a footplate scalding accident, in 1896.

His was a modest career on a relatively small, impecunious and remote railway, but Jones nonetheless made the most of it. The Highland, because of its gradients, was an early convert to the need for continuous braking systems, and Jones pioneered the use of continuous vacuum brakes on his stock and counter-pressure braking (making use of the power of the cylinders) on his locomotives. This same counter-pressure braking, together with long downhill 'idling' stretches and Scotland's windy climate, caused problems with draughting and exhaust smoke obscuring vision, and to counter these he introduced his famous louvred chimney design, the louvres facilitating airflow into and round the interior smokestack, helping to increase the draught and throw the smoke up and clear of the cab.

Counter-pressure braking also required more powerful cylinders, and that, together with the introduction of bogie sleepers on the through Anglo-Scottish services from Inverness – the first such sleepers in Britain – led to Jones's development on his express 4-4-0s of a systematically increased power-to-weight ratio. All had outside cylinders – Jones detested crank axles, needed for inside-cylinder designs, as liable to fracture – and initially his designs perpetuated the Allan 'Crewe'-type locomotives that he found running on the line on assuming office – even on his latest designs he continued to use the Allan straight-link motion. (Jones was not of course strictly a Crewe man by training, but apprenticeship under Ramsbottom at Longsight could hardly have left him unaware of the design developments in the more southerly of the LNWR works.)

The effect of this power increase can be easily demonstrated by comparing the tractive efforts of three Jones 4-4-0 classes. The 'Bruce' Class of 1886 weighed 43 tons and had 14,100lb TE; the 'Straths' of 1892 weighed 45 tons and had 16,786lb TE; and his final 'Loch' Class, built 1896, had 17,070lb TE, but still only weighed 49 tons. They were more powerful than the first series of McIntosh (qv) 'Dunalastairs', and more were added as late as 1917; they handled most of the Highland main-line express traffic for many years.

But David Jones's greatest claim to fame lies in being the first to introduce the 4-6-0 locomotive to Britain (a few 4-6-0Ts had been built by Sharp Stewart for India in about 1860, with double frames and part saddle/part pannier tanks, but they were so different from anything that came later, except in wheelbase notation, that they scarcely count!). This was of course his famous 'big goods' design of 1894, the most powerful locomotive in Britain at the time it entered service. It was technically a freight engine, as its nickname suggests, but because of its 5ft 3in coupled wheels it was in practice equally capable of handling heavy passenger traffic over the Highland gradients, and did so when required, right up to the 1930s.

The origins of the 'big goods' design are somewhat of a mystery. It has been suggested that Jones was motivated to produce it instead of the more probable freight 0-6-0 because of his dislike of crank axles, which all inside-cylinder (and therefore most 0-6-0) designs require. But it seems more likely that the basic 4-6-0 design concept goes back at least a further ten years, to a point in 1884 when Dübs & Co, together with a range of other Glasgow locomotive builders, was asked to supply a freight locomotive for Indian State Railways. The Dübs design, known as the 'L' Class, was available in both 'light' and 'heavy' versions; the 'heavy L' was about 10% more powerful, but otherwise the differences between them were only slight.

The 'L' Class was an inside-framed, outside-cylindered 4-6-0, with inclined cylinders, Allan straight-link valve motion (all typical Jones features), and 4ft 3in driving wheels. It proved ideal for Indian traffic, especially in the Punjab, which like the HR had long ruling gradients and a need for both high tractive effort and a light axle loading. It has never been precisely established who designed it, but evidence from both design style and Jones's own photographic collection strongly suggests it was his mind that oversaw the drawings, if not his hand that produced them. He was after all a consultant engineer to various colonial railways, including those of India, and certainly when the 'big goods' arrived ten years later, it looked very much like an enlarged 'heavy L', apart from those 5ft 3in drivers.

Jones also had in mind a heavy express 4-6-0, which eventually saw the light of day in 1900 as Peter Drummond's 'Castle' Class, and it is fair to credit him with this innovation too, since although the final product was 'Drummondised' in certain exterior details, the basic design was entirely that of his predecessor. The sole reason that Jones retired before it came out was the scalding accident referred to above, incurred on the footplate of one of his beloved 'big goods', which cost him the use of one leg. He retired in 1896 and moved to London, where he continued as an overseas locomotive consultant, though never thereafter in full health. He died ten years later, after a motor accident injured his sound leg.

Matthew Kirtley
1813-1873

Locomotive Engineer

Born	Tanfield, Co Durham, 6 February 1813, son of a colliery-owner
Education	Apprenticed under George and Robert Stephenson, and apparently, either as part of this apprenticeship or additionally, also trained under Timothy Hackworth at Shildon Works
Married	Ann (no further information available in sources)
Best-known works	First Locomotive Superintendent of Midland Railway; initiated use of brick arch and deflector plate in fireboxes; responsible for first enlargement of Derby Works following formation of MR; began provision of standard locomotive classes for new enlarged company – 2-2-2s and 2-4-0s for passenger work, 0-6-0s for freight, characteristically with inside cylinders and double frames
Honours	Founder member of Inst of Mechanical Engineers, 1847
Died	Litchurch Grange, 24 May 1873, after prolonged illness
Buried	Uttoxeter New Road Cemetery, Derby, beneath stone obelisk erected by subscription from Midland Railway staff

Although I have classified Matthew Kirtley as 'Locomotive Engineer', he was in some ways the archetypal early railwayman, able to turn his hand to almost anything to do with trains. Following his apprenticeships with the Stephensons and Hackworth, he became an engineman (ie driver) on the Liverpool & Manchester, Hull & Selby, and London & Birmingham lines; on the last he drove the first train to enter the newly completed Euston Station. He joined the little Birmingham & Derby Junction Railway in 1839 as a shed foreman, before becoming its Locomotive Superintendent in 1841, from whence he was employed in the same capacity by George Hudson's newly formed Midland Railway (which included the B&DJR) in 1844. He may well have owed his appointment to the Stephensons' recommendation and their friendship with Hudson, since he was neither the most senior of the superintendents on the three companies involved (one of whom was in fact his elder bother Tom) nor the one in charge of the largest stock.

Kirtley saw his old and new companies through a period of expansion that involved the locomotive stock in two major changes of scale. When the B&DJR amalgamated to form the Midland, it had just 12 locomotives; on the new Midland Railway of 1844 this jumped immediately to more than 100; and by Kirtley's death in 1873 the stock stood at 1,050. Kirtley rapidly grasped two key management factors about these changes of scale – first, that some attempt at standard classes was going to be essential, and second, that the North Midland works at Derby, the central works for the new railway, would need substantial enlargement and rearrangement if they were going to build the new standard locomotives he envisaged (instead of their being bought in from a motley range of contractors) as well as handle repairs.

Accordingly, Kirtley first embarked on a major expansion and redesign of the original Derby Works between 1844 and 1849, enthusiastically supported by George Hudson, meanwhile steadily increasing the scale and quality of repairs to the locomotives from the old companies, till even Robert Stephenson reported by mid-1849 that many were now 'fully equal to new engines'. Only after he had in place the facilities he needed did he commence building his own locomotives at Derby; the first one appeared in 1851 – characteristically, an 0-6-0 for freight work, with 5ft coupled wheels, inside cylinders, and a tractive effort of around 9,200lb.

Talk of 'standard classes' may at first seem to sit oddly with Kirtley's initial output, given the considerable variations in dimensions of his early locomotives. However, one has to realise that when he took office in 1844 not even the basic parameters of how many wheels a locomotive should have, and what wheel types should serve what purpose, had been settled. Kirtley had in his initial stock locomotives from various builders with both four and six wheels overall, and with various coupling arrangements. He rapidly concluded that six wheels, not four, was the minimum for effective traction (so *Rocket*-style 0-2-2s and Bury 0-4-0s were alike 'out'), and that the best wheel dispositions for different duties were 2-2-2 and 2-4-0 for passenger (the latter more important as trains grew heavier) and 0-6-0 for freight and – in well-tank form – for shunting. Typically, his locomotives had inside cylinders, usually of 24in stroke (22in on the 'Singles'), boilers with large steam domes capped by Salter spring balances, and double frames – initially straight, but curved on the later standard locomotives.

Kirtley's most important contribution to the development of the steam locomotive, however, was probably the insertion of a brick arch and a deflector plate into the firebox, thus permitting the locomotive to burn coal instead of the more expensive coke that had been standard on all early locomotives. This development, the result of a three-year series of experiments jointly with the Derby Works Outdoor

Locomotive Superintendent, Charles Markham, was first fitted to Kirtley's locomotives in 1859, and because of its simplicity and robustness rapidly became standard not only on the Midland but on all other lines too. His influence on carriage design was, however, much less forward-looking: his own carriages, even in the early 1870s, tended to be small four-wheeler affairs with luggage racks on the roof, and the Midland Board under James Allport (qv) had already taken the decision to authorise a separate carriage works under its own independent Carriage & Wagon Superintendent at the beginning of 1873.

The exponential growth of Midland locomotive stock under Kirtley meant inevitably that Derby Works once again needed further enlargement, and Kirtley's career with the Midland thus ended as it began, with a major rebuilding of Derby Works under way, including the separate carriage shop. Only the new paint shop had been fully completed, however, when Kirtley died, age 60, on 24 May 1873, after a prolonged illness. The remainder of the second expansion of Derby Works was completed by his successor, S. W. Johnson (qv).

The pioneers

George Stephenson, the 'father of railways', in his prime (c1825-35). In one of several portraits of this iconic personality, he is sitting, looking suitably authoritative and austere, holding what appears to be a pair of dividers – a figure radiating all the reverence of his middle years rather than the struggle of his early life. *Courtesy Science Museum Pictorial/Science & Society Picture Library*

An 1846 portrait of Robert Stephenson, George's son – and arguably the greater engineer of the two. *Courtesy Science Museum Pictorial/Science & Society Picture Library*

This portrait of Isambard Kingdom Brunel (for once, not the usual one with the hat and cigar!) is a steel engraving from a photograph probably taken in the last six years of his life. *Peter Townsend Collection, courtesy Silver Link Publishing*

A mid-19th-century oil painting of George Hudson, the 'Railway King' and one of the greatest of the early railway entrepreneurs, virtually single-handedly creating the 1840s 'railway mania' and with it much of the British main-line system. *Courtesy Science Museum Pictorial/Science & Society Picture Library*

This centenary bronze bust commemorating East Anglian railway engineer and entrepreneur Sir Samuel Morton Peto ('Baptist, Contractor, Politician and Philanthropist') can be seen on the concourse at Norwich Thorpe Station, which he built to form the terminus of his line from Yarmouth and Lowestoft. *Author*

George Pullman, inventor of the Pullman car – an early photograph dating from 1883, when Pullman was at the height of his career. *Courtesy Pullman Preservation Alliance*

iv

The engineers

Many nations have featured famous railwaymen and locomotives on their stamps, and several are featured here from Grenadines/St Vincent Bequia and Nevis. These two portray the Great Western Railway's Daniel Gooch and William Dean, with examples of their locomotives behind them. (For further information about the original stamps, contact Edward Beach of St Vincent Philatelic Services Ltd. at philatelic@vincysurf.com or Aviva Susman of IGPC at asusman@igpc.net.) *Courtesy Inter-Governmental Philatelic Corporation, New York, and St Vincent and Nevis Philatelic Services Ltd*

This oil painting of Francis William Webb dates from 1903, the year Webb retired from his post as Locomotive Superintendent of the LNWR. By now he was already suffering from the incurable illness that killed him three years later, and probably knew it – but none of this shows in his austere but imposing figure. *Courtesy Science Museum Pictorial/Science & Society Picture Library*

This rarely seen photograph shows the Midland's two most famous late Victorian designers, Tom Clayton of dining-car fame (left) and S. W. Johnson, designer of the famous 'Singles', posed probably in front of Johnson's house in Nottingham, with various female relatives. It is dated around 1899, when both men were 68. None of the female relatives are formally identified, but the group probably includes Johnson's wife (possibly the seated lady in the boater) and four daughters, and Clayton's second wife (possibly standing between the two men) and his daughter; the other younger woman may be one of his daughters-in-law. The identity of the two older women, seated front left, is not known. *Courtesy Science Museum Pictorial/Science & Society Picture Library*

This lithograph studio portrait of Dugald Drummond was published in *The Bailie*, the Glasgow engineering journal, on 11 June 1884. *Courtesy of the Mitchell Library, Cultural & Leisure Services, Glasgow City Council*

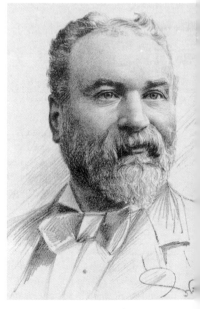

This portrait of J. F. McIntosh, also from the Mitchell Library's archives of *The Bailie*, dates from some 12 years later, May 1896, the same year as the first of his famous 'Dunalastair' 4-4-0s. *Courtesy of the Mitchell Library, Cultural & Leisure Services, Glasgow City Council*

This photograph of J. A. F. Aspinall in middle age comes from *The Railway Magazine*'s 'Illustrated Interview' No 36 of December 1900, when he was Vice-President of the Institution of Mechanical Engineers and LYR General Manager. *Author's collection*

A roundel portrait of J. G. Robinson from a group illustrating the chief officers of the Great Central Railway and accompanying an article on that railway published in *The Railway Magazine* in 1912. *Author's collection*

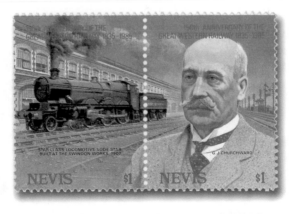

G. J. Churchward, pre-Grouping CME of the Great Western Railway, 1902-21. Behind him is 'Star' Class 4-6-0 *Lode Star*. *Courtesy Inter-Governmental Philatelic Corporation, New York, and St Vincent and Nevis Philatelic Services Ltd*

Four of the most famous Locomotive Superintendents of the 'Big Four' companies, portrayed on the same set of postage stamps referred to earlier. They are, clockwise from top left, The GWR's C. B. Collett, the LMS's William Stanier, himself

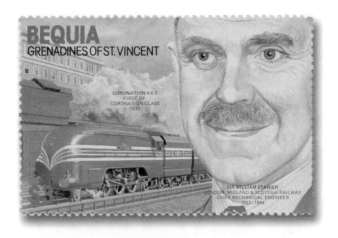

Swindon-trained, Nigel Gresley of the LNER, and the Southern Railway's O. V. S. Bulleid, who began his own career at Doncaster. *Courtesy Inter-Governmental Philatelic Corporation, New York, and St Vincent and Nevis Philatelic Services Ltd*

The managers

This oil painting is of railway entrepreneur and manager Sir Edward Watkin as he was in 1891, aged 72 – a mere ten years before his death, and just three years before the severe stroke that resulted in his retirement from his major railway Chairmanships. The subject's somewhat haunted expression speaks both of the driven character of the man, and of the strains of ill health and overwork that were to lead to the 1894 stroke. *Courtesy Science Museum Pictorial/Science & Society Picture Library*

Above Sir Sam Fay is seen here in another of *The Railway Magazine*'s biographical articles, this one from 1912 celebrating his knighthood at the opening of the GCR's Immingham Docks in that year. *Author's collection*

Right The opening of the Great Central's London Extension in 1899 was marked by another *RM* 'Illustrated Interview', this time with the company's General Manager William Pollitt, who was knighted in that same year. This portrait accompanied the interview. *Author's collection*

This oil painting of Sir Richard Moon, the LNWR's greatest Chairman, by William Carter, was made in 1900, the year following his death, but shows him as he was in 1890, his last year as Chairman. *Courtesy Science Museum Pictorial/Science & Society Picture Library*

A studio portrait of Henry Villard, the German-American railway entrepreneur who completed the Northern Pacific transcontinental link and revolutioniocd on train dining in the American West; it is one of the few known photographs of him. *Courtesy California State Railroad Museum*

This photograph of Robert Hope Selbie was taken to commemorate his appointment as General Manager of the Metropolitan Railway in 1908, and appeared in *The Railway Magazine*'s 'Portrait Gallery' feature for that year. *Author's collection*

Joseph Locke
1805-60

Early Railway Engineer

Born	Attercliffe, Sheffield, 9 August 1805, son of William Locke, fellow-worker and friend of George Stephenson at Walbottle Colliery, but by this time a colliery manager in the Barnsley area
Education	Barnsley Grammar School, 1812-18, then articled to William Stokes, Pelaw Colliery, 1818-20, and George Stephenson, 1823-26
Married	Phoebe McCreery, Liverpool, 1834
Best-known works	Grand Junction Railway, 1835; London & Southampton Railway, 1837; Sheffield, Ashton & Manchester Railway, 1839; laid out Crewe town and Works, 1843; eventually responsible for most of West Coast Anglo-Scottish route; also responsible for many overseas railways, including Paris-Le Havre, 1841
Honours	MP for Honiton, 1847-60; President, Inst of Civil Engineers, 1858-59; commemorative statue and park in Barnsley, and window in Westminster Abbey
Died	Moffat, Dumfriesshire, 18 September 1860, of 'internal inflammation' while on shooting holiday
Buried	Kensal Green Cemetery, London

Joseph Locke has been described as one of the three greatest early railway engineers, alongside the more famous duo of Brunel and Robert Stephenson (qqv). Born in 1805, he was the son of the Walbottle Colliery manager and friend of George Stephenson, William Locke, who later became a colliery manager in the Barnsley area, where Joseph spent much of his youth (and where he is still remembered by a statue and a memorial park in the town). In 1823 his father articled him to George Stephenson, and initially the young Locke was one of the Stephenson 'railway family' (see under Robert Stephenson), working with the two Stephensons and other pupils on a variety of railway engineering projects.

Locke's special skills were as a very precise and detailed civil engineer rather than as a locomotive man. He shared with Brunel a far-seeing vision and an ability to get through an immense amount of work. But unlike both Brunel and the elder Stephenson he combined with this an intense attention to detail and a flair for precise and accurate financial management of his contractors. The first of these characteristics meant that he could and did discover errors in his colleagues' surveys and designs (including those of George Stephenson on the Liverpool & Manchester Railway, which caused considerable estrangement between the two men). The second characteristic meant that, unlike many early railway engineers, including Brunel, his schemes acquired a reputation for coming in on time and on budget. As a result he built a substantial part of his early career on taking over as project engineer from other men, and correcting and completing their work. 'Send for Joseph Locke' almost became something of a catchword in early railway projects where it was feared things might go amiss.

Ironically, on one early occasion in his career this very ability to visualise exact detail backfired on Locke, with tragic consequences. He was in charge of the opening ceremony arrangements for the Liverpool

& Manchester Railway in 1830, and typically had organised all the arrangements, times, stops and arrivals down to the last detail, including dividing the VIPs between different trains, so that Wellington (the Prime Minister) was on the first train, and William Huskisson (MP for Liverpool) on the second. Locke was himself driving Stephenson's *Rocket*, heading the fourth train. What he had not foreseen, however, was that human beings are prone not to do as they are told, and also prone to panic – and also that human impatience and political attitudes play a large part in colouring crowd response.

All went well until the Parkside stop to take on water, when Huskisson decided he wanted to pay his respects to Wellington following a temporary rift between them, and strictly unofficially got down off the train to do so, accompanied by several other passengers, just as *Rocket* was approaching on the intervening track. (This was before the invention of either the steam brake or the locomotive whistle.) Locke tried to brake, but couldn't stop in time. The crowd scrambled furiously out of the way – except for Huskisson, who panicked and did a fair imitation of a scared pheasant. The rest, alas, is history – though *Rocket* managed 30mph on the race to get him to hospital. And Wellington's consequent late arrival at Liverpool (where he wasn't liked politically) was greeted with a near riot of catcalls and brickbats.

Despite this tragic incident, though, Locke very soon found himself making his name on three replacement schemes of the 'Send for Joseph Locke' kind: the Grand Junction Railway (Manchester-Birmingham, 1835), where he took over from Stephenson, and for which he subsequently laid out Crewe town and Works; the London & Southampton (1837), taken over from Francis Giles; and the Sheffield, Ashton & Manchester (ancestor of the Great Central), where he took over in 1839 from one of the other major civil engineering names of the day, C. B. Vignoles. It was during this period that he built up his connection with two major early railway engineering contractors, Thomas Brassey and William Mackenzie (themselves a partnership), who shared both his energy and his ability for detailed organisation. As a trio, Locke, Brassey and Mackenzie built the Paris-Le Havre railway in 1841, then in 1843, jointly with John Stephenson, the Lancaster & Carlisle line. Many other lines followed, both in the UK and on the European mainland.

Locke may have become estranged from George Stephenson, but he inherited the latter's vision of a national railway network, concentrating especially on railways in the North and North West. After the Grand Junction and the Lancaster & Carlisle came the Caledonian lines to Perth and Aberdeen, so that Locke was in the end single-handedly responsible as engineer for most of what is now the West Coast Main Line. Curiously, he seems to have been much less interested in the East Coast route, actually resigning from the post of engineer-in-chief to the London & York (ancestor to the Great Northern) shortly after having been appointed in 1844. One explanation is that he belatedly realised that the Rouen Railway, on which he was also engaged, would generate too much work to enable him to take on both – but he equally may have wished to avoid tangling with the redoubtable George Hudson (who opposed the scheme), and may also have felt a little shy about a project that would take him close to the heartland of his old mentor Stephenson.

Locke's economical engineering characteristically involved much less in the way of expensive earthworks and tunnelling than the schemes of his rivals. This in turn meant that he was willing to accept gradient profiles much heavier than on other lines (think of Shap and Beattock summits, both Locke works). This made for lower start-up costs, but engendered higher running costs in terms of the locomotive power required. In the event, however, both sides of the equation worked to the advantage of railway development: Locke's willingness to 'make trains go up hill' enlarged the received public vision of where it was possible for railways to go and what it was possible for them to do, while the effects of his civil works on locomotive design forced engineers to begin the road to increased size and power that led to the classic steam train of the 20th century.

John McIntosh
1846-1918

Locomotive Engineer

Born	Haugh of Kinnaird, 28 February 1846, son of a farm and railway labourer
Education	Apprenticed at Arbroath Workshops, Scottish North Eastern Railway, 1860 (merged with Caledonian Railway in 1865); passed fireman, 1865, driver, 1867
Married	Jeanie Fleming Logan, date not found but must have been after 1881, in which Census he is listed as bachelor
Best-known works	Locomotive Superintendent, Caledonian Railway, 1895-1914; patented gauge glass protector, spark arrester, self-adjusting sandpipe nozzle; designed 'Dunalastair' series of 4-4-0s (later series superheated), large inside-cylinder 4-6-0s (especially 'Cardean'), 0-4-4T series, 0-6-0s (some with the 'Dunalastair' boiler), the first Scottish 2-6-0s and the only Scottish 0-8-0 classes (one tender, one tank) for freight work
Honours	President, Assoc of Railway Locomotive Engineers, 1911; MVO 1913 (awarded personally by King George V)
Died	38 Dalziel Drive, Pollockshields, Glasgow, 6 February 1918
Buried	Privately (there is no record of his

grave in either of his two
neighbourhood Glasgow
cemeteries)

John Farquharson McIntosh, like David Jones, was an example of the 'second' Scottish engineering success story, that of the engineer who remained with one company for life but had influence way beyond either his railway or his native land (the 'first' Scottish engineering success story, typified by Dugald Drummond, is of course that of the 'rolling stone' engineer who moves from company to company and eventually leaves Scotland altogether to influence the broader world stage.) He was also, like the Stephensons, a classic example of the Victorian model of self-improvement: born into a humble labouring family on the Southesk estate, he rose by sheer hard work to become a leading locomotive designer with even more of his engines running on the Belgian State Railways than on his own Caledonian. He also walked with Royalty (as indeed did Jones, thanks to his friendship with the Duke of Sutherland (qv)).

In one way, however, he was most unusual. He was one of the very few Locomotive Superintendents to rise to the post not through the works and design side of railway engineering, but through the footplate and running operations side, successively as driver, Locomotive Inspector (around this time, 1876-77, he lost his right hand in an accident), Chief Inspector, and Locomotive Running Superintendent. Much earlier, in the days when railways were just beginning, both Locke and Kirtley drove engines among their many other activities, and much later Riddles was to have a predilection for engine-driving whenever he could (which was nowhere near as often as he would have liked). But McIntosh seems to have been the only regularly working engine driver to rise to a Superintendency, and it gave his designs a very special flavour.

The unusual nature of McIntosh's appointment was reflected in the initial misgivings of the Board: he was appointed on six months' probation and at less than half the starting salary of his predecessor Dugald Drummond. The Board needn't have worried, however; it rapidly became clear that McIntosh's engines were every bit as good as those of either Drummond or his immediate predecessor Lambie, especially the famous four 'Dunalastair' series of 4-4-0s, of ever-increasing size and power. Indeed, these locos, which were in many ways initially based on Drummond's own earlier 4-4-0 designs, stood direct comparison with Drummond's own later work on the LSWR (qv). The 'Dunalastair' boiler, in particular, has been described as 'made for generating steam' and 'one of the major advances in British locomotive engineering'; it was fitted a good deal more widely than just on the 'Dunalastairs' themselves – notably on the standard mixed traffic '812' Class 0-6-0s, one of which still survives under restoration, and on a total of 720 McIntosh-designed locos built for the Belgian State Railways by both Scots and Belgian builders, including both 4-4-0s, 0-6-0s and a series of 4-4-2Ts with no precise counterpart back on the 'Caley'.

As a former footplate man, McIntosh was particularly concerned with ensuring adequate power and free steaming. It is indeed sometimes said that in his designs he gave steam generation priority over fuel consumption (though one has to remember that in pre-1914 Scotland good coal was both cheap and plentiful). He adopted the superheater around 1910, fitting both Schmidt and Robinson (qv) versions; the extra weight of the superheater in some later 0-6-0s made it necessary to convert them to a 2-6-0 design, the first in Scotland, though they retained inside cylinders. His patents were also those that one might expect from a footplate man – in particular the gauge glass protector and the self-adjusting sandpipe nozzle (to overcome slipping). He also paid considerable attention to his hauled rolling-stock, pioneering both 12-wheel bogie coaches for the Anglo-Scottish express traffic and high-capacity mineral wagons. This in turn led to several famous 'firsts' in locomotive design – Scotland's only 0-8-0 class in 1901, to haul the mineral wagons, a remarkably handsome class of 0-8-0Ts two years later (1903), to shunt them, and the most powerful express passenger 4-6-0 in Britain (at the time it was built) in the *Sir James Thompson*, also of 1903.

Thus McIntosh's locomotive designs steered a middle course between standardisation (eg in the 'Dunalastairs', the standard 0-6-0s and his ubiquitous suburban and branch-line 0-4-4Ts) and a more 'horses for courses' philosophy, in small classes of heavy express and fast freight 4-6-0s, mineral 0-8-0s and heavy shunting tanks – though the smaller classes may have been a result of financial constraints rather than basic principle. His largest 4-6-0s, such as *Sir James Thompson* and the later and larger-boilered *Cardean*, did not have the runaway success of his 'Dunalastairs' (they couldn't, for example, really stand comparison with contemporary designs by Churchward in the way that his 4-4-0s could with Drummond's), but they were still a cut above most other 4-6-0s of the time. Their one problem was their length: Carlisle turntable could only accommodate them with the tender removed, but that was the LNWR's problem, not that of the 'Caley'. Perhaps his career was best summed up in his retirement notice in *Railway and Travel Monthly* for June 1914:

'It is noteworthy that Mr McIntosh, unlike many other great locomotive engineers, produced no failures; it is true he had no taste for daring and ingenious novelties, but stuck to sound practical methods.'

Richard Maunsell
1868-1944
Locomotive and Carriage Engineer

Born	Raheny, Co Dublin, 26 May 1868, son of John Maunsell, a leading Dublin solicitor with GS&WR connections
Education	Ardnagh Royal School; Trinity College Dublin, 1886-88 (initially reading law); apprenticed under H. A. Ivatt (qv), Inchicore (GS&WR), 1888-91, and Trinity College BA in engineering; pupil under J. A. F. Aspinall (qv), Horwich (LYR), 1891-94
Married	Edith Annie Pearson, of Bolton, Lancs, at St. Jude's Church, Kensington, London, 15 June 1896
Best-known works	CME of SECR, 1913-22, and Southern Railway, 1923-37; introduced modern line-production methods to Ashford and Eastleigh Works, and standardised previously diverse locomotive stock, designed 'N', 'N1', 'U' and 'U1' 2-6-0s, 'King Arthur' and 'Lord Nelson' 4-6-0s, 'Schools' 4-4-0s; oversaw, with principal carriage assistant Lionel Lynes, large-scale introduction of electric stock between the wars.
Honours	CBE, 1918
Died	Northbrooke House, Ashford, 7 March 1944
Buried	Bybrook Cemetery, Ashford

As the son of a leading Dublin solicitor, Richard Edward Lloyd Maunsell was originally destined (like

Bulleid after him!) for the legal profession. However, unlike Bulleid, he evinced such an attraction to railway engineering from quite an early age that his family agreed that, provided he finished his Trinity College, Dublin, degree, he could become a premium apprentice under Ivatt (qv) at Inchicore. Following pupillage under Aspinall (qv) at Horwich, he joined the East Indian Railway in 1894 as Assistant Locomotive Superintendent, returning, however, to Inchicore in 1896 as Works Manager under Coey, and in 1911 becoming Locomotive Superintendent on Coey's retirement. He was appointed CME of the South Eastern & Chatham Railway in 1913, and subsequently of the Southern in 1923, where he then remained until retirement in 1937.

Though a competent engineer, Maunsell was by temperament more of an administrator than a designer – a feature he shared with one of Aspinall's other pupils, Sir Henry Fowler. Like Gresley (also a pupil of Aspinall) he surrounded himself with an excellent design team, including James Clayton from Derby and Holcroft from Swindon (which may explain the somewhat 'Western' look of his 'N' Class 2-6-0s, Holcroft having been instrumental in 'nagging' Churchward into producing the GWR's '4300' Class 'Moguls'), and Lynes for carriage design. Clayton's inclusion in the team is perhaps of particular interest later, in the context of Bulleid's 'Leaders' (qv) – he brought much design material with him from Derby, and had worked on the notorious 2-6-2 Paget locomotive, a multi-cylinder design in some ways not unlike the 'Leader'; although he was ill during most of his 'overlap' with Bulleid (1937-38), some sources suggest he may well have had copies of some of the Paget drawings on file.

On the SECR Maunsell inherited a mixed and dubious stock of locomotives to highly varying designs from the two conjoined struggling predecessor companies, and an antiquated works at Ashford. He also inherited the problem of some of the tightest loading gauge clearances of any main-line British railway. These problems were if anything exacerbated in 1923, when the new Southern Railway took over an even more mixed bag of rolling-stock (some excellent but much antiquated), a totally different (though mercifully less tight) set of clearances, and three more works, at Eastleigh, Brighton and Lancing, all in need of modernisation. In addition, from 1926 was added the problem of coping with remaining steam services – some both heavy and prestigious – against the onward march and cost of the Southern's rolling electrification programme.

Maunsell's response to his problems on the SECR had been to modernise, standardise, and – where those were not viable options – to rebuild (with the better SECR 4-4-0s, for example). This policy, writ somewhat larger, was to continue post-Grouping (and indeed post-Maunsell too, with Bulleid's 'light Pacifics' especially). Ashford and Eastleigh Works were both modernised to make use of line-production methods, and production was concentrated there, while Brighton and Lancing were steadily run down (till, again post-Maunsell, wartime conditions required their return to full use). Beginning with the 'N' Class 2-6-0s on the SECR, expanded in both two- and three-cylinder versions across the Southern after 1923, new locomotive and carriage designs were so arranged that, broadly, they could run anywhere on the system (though there were some 'horses for courses', the most famous being the 'Brighton Belle' Pullman electrics and the 'Schools' Class 4-4-0s). Also, the rebuild of the SECR 4-4-0s was repeated on a larger scale with the under-performing 'N15' express 4-6-0s of the old LSWR, which became the 'King Arthur' Class and performed so well as rebuilt that Maunsell added additional new locomotives to the same design.

As electrification progressed, further rebuilds followed, as a means of conserving money by rendering locomotives displaced by 'the juice' suitable for operation further afield. This particularly affected ex-Brighton locomotives: in 1927, ten of Stroudley's old but valiant 'E1' Class 0-6-0Ts, superannuated from their work on London suburban trains, were rebuilt with larger bunkers as 'E1/R' 0-6-2Ts for use elsewhere on the system, especially the Torrington-Halwill branch. Likewise, in 1934 Billinton's 'L' Class 'Remembrance' 4-6-4Ts, relieved of their duties on the now-electrified 'Brighton Belle', became 'N15X' 4-6-0s for use on the main West of England line (as the class designation shows, they were thought of as honorary 'Arthurs'). All the rebuilds, as the saying goes, lived long and prospered.

Maunsell's best locomotive designs were probably the original 'Ns', with which he made his name, the rebuilt 'N15s' and the incomparable 'Schools' Class 4-4-0s, which have been called 'the finest 4-4-0s ever built'. Some of his other locomotives were less successful – the flagship 'Lord Nelsons', as we saw above, gave less than full performance until rebuilt by Bulleid (qv); the 'River' Class 2-6-4Ts were rough riders and were rebuilt as 'U' and 'U1' 2-6-0s following the 1927 Sevenoaks derailment (though the major culprit was the poor state of the trackbed); and the 'Q' Class 0-6-0s, though reasonably powerful, were unreliable steamers.

On the carriage side, Maunsell contributed, with help from Lynes, to both suburban and main-line electric stock. The suburban stock was mainly composed of older carriages rebuilt on new steel underframes, but the 1932 main-line stock for the Brighton electrification was almost entirely new. It comprised among other things several varieties of six-coach multiple units, through-gangwayed within the unit but not between units. Some had a single Pullman coach to provide refreshments, others had a SR pantry car where the Pullman would have been. There were also the special 'Brighton Belle' all-Pullman units. Maunsell's steam carriage stock included a major build of restaurant cars, sufficient to equip every conceivable combination of the multifarious Saturday variants of the 'Atlantic Coast Express' in competition with the Great Western's West of England services. (Catering was by Frederick Hotels – the Southern had no restaurant car department of its own.)

From 1935, however, Maunsell's energy began to flag, and he was really quite ill by the time he retired in 1937 (which may explain why the 'Q' Class, his last design, wasn't better). He retired at the end of October 1937, and died in 1944.

Richard Moon
1814-99

Director and Chairman

Born	Liverpool, 23 February 1814
Education	St Andrews University, Scotland
Married	Eleanor Brocklebank, Hazelholme, Cumberland, 1840 (d 31 January 1891)
Best-known works	Director of LNWR, 1851; Chair of Stores Committee, 1852; Chair of Committee of Investigation, 1855; Chair of Locomotive Expenditure Committee, 1858; Deputy Chairman of LNWR, 1861, then Chairman, 1861-91
Honours	Knight Baronet, 1887, in Jubilee Honours List
Died	Copsewood Grange, Coventry, 17 November 1899
Buried	Stoke Churchyard, Coventry

Richard Moon originally intended to enter the church, but opposition from his Liverpool merchant family (he was the eldest son) meant that after study at St Andrews he joined the family business instead, where he first evinced the financial and management flair that made him famous with the LNWR, of which he was elected a shareholder-director in 1851 (by this time he had retired from active participation in the family business). Formed by amalgamation in 1847, by 1851 the LNWR was encountering difficult financial circumstances caused by over-fast expansion (though its basic business position was sound). In the years that followed, Moon took what was at the time a 'reformist' position, chairing the Stores Expenditure

143

Committee from 1852 (with remit enlarged, significantly, also to cover locomotive expenditure in 1858), and an investigative committee in 1855 that called for more board members to be involved in executive 'hands-on' management. By 1861 he was Deputy Chairman of the Board under Moorsom, and when the latter died the same year, he replaced him, serving continuously till 1891, the longest-serving Chairman of any UK railway Board, except for Edward Watkin (qv).

Moon's contribution to railway management thinking can be summed up in a few short phrases (not necessarily of his own coining). One is 'executive responsibility' (ie hands-on management by the directors); another is 'functional management' – a single Locomotive Superintendent, a single main carriage works, a single Wagon Superintendent, and so on, rather than the separate Northern and Southern Division works and management that had come with the 1847 amalgamation. A third concept is 'standardisation': for example, Moon actively backed the development by Ramsbottom (qv) of the first mass-produced steam locomotive, the 'DX' Class 0-6-0, which eventually numbered 857 examples. All of these were, however, essentially tactical aids to an underlying strategic objective, defined by Moon himself in his remit to Francis Webb (qv) on his appointment as successor to Ramsbottom – 'to provide the best possible equipment and services at minimum cost'.

This objective led Moon to subject virtually every function of the LNWR's management to intense financial scrutiny (which may have contributed to his fearsome personal reputation). The company was during his Chairmanship the largest business operation in the world, and in managing an organisation of this size economically Moon was truly entering uncharted waters. One area in which he did not begrudge money, however, was in the salaries of his nucleus of senior officers, provided they were of sufficient quality; he hired good men, gave them massive functional responsibilities, worked them very hard, paid them very well – and they stayed with him. (This, incidentally, should tell us something about the real value to the LNWR of Webb, one of that nucleus of senior men, who ended up with a salary from Moon of £7,000 a year). In both these respects – asserting 'ownership' of the business, and powerful team-building – his management practices were significantly forward-looking.

Sometimes, however, Moon's overriding concern with what Sir Ralph Wedgwood (qv) was later to call 'continuous economy' led him (and his Board, which he dominated both professionally and personally) into decisions that were curiously conservative. Three examples make the point sufficiently well: he resisted throughout his Chairmanship the abolition of 2nd Class begun by Allport (qv) on the Midland (even when the Caledonian, the LNWR's West Coast partner, embraced it); he resisted until 1888 the adoption of the automatic Westinghouse brake (though the existence of Francis Webb's patented rival system may have had something to do with that, as well as cost); and he opposed, with some effectiveness, the dilution of operating ratios by the additional costs resulting from increases in train weight brought about by passenger demand for greater comfort and speed. This last had a curious knock-on effect, in that it seems to have been the principal reason why Moon backed Webb's compound locomotives, which did in fact save fuel and water costs, though incurring opportunity costs over uneven performance.

Moon was a dominant managerial figure, and a somewhat reserved man. His fearsome reputation as an autocrat may not have been totally justified, though it took people of Webb's calibre to stand up to him (and even then not always successfully). Certainly, even though his marriage into the Brocklebank family may have been partly dynastic, he relied personally very strongly on the support of his wife, and her death in January 1891 may well have precipitated his resignation from the Chairmanship in the following month. He left the LNWR in a dominant financial and competitive position among UK railways, to the extent that *The Times* printed a leader on the following day eulogising his contribution. He continued to raise matters in shareholders' meetings till at least 1893, but became ill in 1897, and died finally in November 1899. He has no official memorial – it seems, at his own request.

Georges Nagelmackers
1845-1905

Rail Travel Entrepreneur

Born	Liège, Belgium, 24 June 1845
Education	École des Mines, Liège; also trained in international banking (with special interest in railway matters) within the Nagelmackers family banking business
Married	Marguerite Hermet
Best-known works	Founded CIWL (Wagons-Lits company), 1876, after false start in 1870 cut short by Franco-Prussian War; introduced 'Indian Mail' express ([London]-Calais-Brindisi) as joint enterprise with P&O steamship line, 1879; introduced first Wagons-Lits dining-car, 1881; introduced 'Orient Express', 1883; numerous other 'trains de luxe'
Honours	Commander of Legion D'Honneur, 1900; also various Belgian and other continental decorations; personal (family) friend of King Leopold II of Belgium
Died	Chateau de Villepreux, 10 July 1905
Buried	D'Angleur cemetery, near Liège

Georges Nagelmackers was born into one of Belgium's foremost banking families, with connections at the very highest level of mainland European society. The Nagelmackers bank had been closely involved in the creation of the Belgian railway system, but Georges himself grew up with an even greater interest in international railway operation (at this point virtually unknown in Europe) than in international railway finance. In the course of a fact-finding visit to the USA in 1868-69, undertaken in the wake of a love affair with his first cousin unacceptable to his family, he met George Pullman (qv) and discussed the provision of luxury train services.

On return to Belgium in 1870 he proposed to his family's banking firm a scheme for building and operating, à la Pullman, a luxury international train service (initially to have been Ostend-Cologne-Berlin), but worsening political conditions, culminating in the Franco-Prussian War (1870-71), meant that the project never really got off the ground, and the Nagelmackers bank was unwilling to offer more than limited support.

Following the War, Nagelmackers resumed his proposals, this time with the financial support of a somewhat shady US business partner, Colonel William D'Alton Mann, whose compartment-based 'boudoir cars' he had opted to use as an initial standard design for luxury day/sleeper convertibles, rather than the Pullman saloon cars, whose open plan was less liked in privacy-minded Europe. (It was deemed 'immoral', among other things.) He also obtained the official personal support of King Leopold II, for whose affair with Cléo de Merode Mann was – ironically in view of his criticism of Pullman's saloon coaches – to supply a private 'boudoir car'. Initial short-term contracts to include Wagons-Lits cars on the Calais-Paris-Berlin and Paris-Vienna routes were followed in 1874 by a notable publicity coup – the provision for the Prince of Wales (later King Edward VII) of a day/sleeping 'boudoir car' for use from Calais to the Russian border break-of-gauge on a journey to attend a Russian Imperial wedding in St Petersburg.

Mann's own business practices, however, were becoming increasingly suspect (he had a large element of the confidence trickster in his make-up) and in 1876 Nagelmackers bought him out and the Wagons-Lits

Company as we now know it was finally born. A contract with the P&O steamship line established the 'Indian Mail' service from Calais (for London) to Brindisi in 1879; after initial experiments with temporary diners in Germany in 1880, Nagelmackers introduced a dining-car on the Nice-Marseilles service in late 1881, and followed it with a special dining/sleeping run of his Paris-Vienna service in 1882. Following the success of this, his grandest and most elaborate luxury express of all, the 'Orient Express', started operation on 4 October 1883. Other luxury trains followed, including among many the 'Train Bleu', the 'Nord Express', the 'Rome Express' in 1897, and the (original, pre-revolutionary) 'Trans-Siberian Express' in the following year.

Nagelmackers created a unique management structure for this international enterprise. Under an overall 'Direction-General', headed by himself and located in Paris, the company's operations were controlled by separate 'Directions' for each of the countries through which the trains passed, with offices located in each case in the appropriate capital city and under an appropriate national 'Directeur'. This ensured that no nation (or national railway company) felt that its Wagons-Lits trains were being run by a foreign power. The degree of decentralisation involved also meant that in the event of war or other international emergency Wagons-Lits operations were able to continue in those parts not directly affected by the crisis. The national 'Directeur' was also always a qualified engineer, to ensure that any special problems (for example, the intense winter cold in the Russian 'Direction') were tackled expertly and on the spot.

Some of these 'Directions' were particularly important. Austria, for example, was a key strategic location for many of Nagelmackers's routes, so the Austrian 'Direction' was among the most important after that located in Paris, and many early Wagons-Lits carriages were ordered from Austrian works. Following passenger complaints about hotel provision at Wagons-Lits destinations, a separate 'Direction' was also created that purchased, built and operated hotels in such diverse places as Paris, Istanbul, Madrid and Cairo; station buffet and refreshment room contracts were added to this 'Direction' shortly afterwards.

Although this structure gave Wagons-Lits a great deal of organisational flexibility, all the initial detailed route research – often under difficult conditions – and diplomatic negotiation were conducted by Nagelmackers personally, and the workload this engendered was a major contributing factor to his early death in 1905.

Henry Oakley
1823-1912

Railway Manager

Born	November 1823
Education	Not known
Married	Emma Thompson, 1863
Best-known works	Company Secretary, GNR, 1858-70; General Manager, 1870-98; Director 1897-1912; oversaw introduction of range of improvements (dining-cars, sleepers, corridor stock with lavatories) in response to competition from Midland, MSLR and LNWR; head-hunted Ivatt as replacement for Stirling to promote larger locomotive policy to cope with improved (and thus heavier) trains
Honours	Knighthood, 1891; Légion D'Honneur
Died	37 Chester Terrace, Regents Park, London, 8 February 1912
Buried	Brompton Cemetery

Henry Oakley spent almost his entire working life on the administrative side of the Great Northern Railway. Born in 1823, he first joined the GNR in 1849, only three years after the line had been sanctioned and a year before through services from London to York became a possibility. Aged 26 and so far unmarried (he did not marry till he was 40), his initial post was that of a humble junior clerk, but from then onwards his career blossomed in much the same way as his almost contemporary fictional character, the First Sea Lord in Gilbert and Sullivan's *HMS Pinafore*:

'As a junior clerk I made such a name
That an articled clerk I soon became:
I wore clean collars and a brand new suit
For the Pass Examination at the Institute.
That Pass Examination did so well for me
That now I am the ruler of the Queen's Nav-ee.'

From junior clerk in 1849 he became chief clerk to the Company Secretary, then Company Secretary himself in 1858, a post he held until becoming General Manager in 1870. He remained in that post until 1898, when he retired (age 75!) after having been made a Director of the line towards the end of the previous year. He continued to serve as a Director until his death in 1912.

Although he did not really partake of the futuristic strategic vision of his great contemporary James Allport (qv) on the Midland, Oakley combined meticulous attention to planning detail with a considerable degree of political skill and commercial guile in warding off the competitive moves of his rivals (In this case both the Midland and the MSLR, later to become the Great Central), coupled with an eye for what nowadays we should call market research. Under his régime, the Great Northern operated a more intensive express service than any of the other lines from London to the North, with a corresponding increase in income receipts and – until 1873 – steadily increasing profitability.

From that year onwards, however, the GNR under Oakley became for a time to some extent the victim of its own success. The more intensive services introduced by his superintendent F. P. Cockshott meant that Oakley had to provide improved block and interlocking signalling and introduce improvements to stations and goods yards, and between 1875 and 1880 revenue barely kept pace with investment expenditure. The worst year was probably 1877, when traffic receipts for the first half-year decreased by £14,000 and running expenses increased by £34,000. A similar problem occurred in the mid-1890s, when the East Coast Main Line had to be re-laid with heavier rail to take the growing weight of the Anglo-Scottish expresses. However, in the end Oakley solved the revenue problem by a combination of careful control of expenditures – hence Stirling's (qv) tendency to build locos just a few at a time – and negotiation of various deals with other companies to gain access to potential areas of traffic importance, ranging from the Norfolk holiday coast (via the M&GNR) to Manchester (via the MSLR) and Burton-upon-Trent. He was assisted in this activity by acting as Secretary to the Railway Companies' Association during much of the 1880s, which may have contributed to his knighthood in 1891.

Oakley's use of market research (and his control of finances) can best be seen in his improvements to on-train services for main-line passengers across his period of office, in particular his moves to introduce dining- and sleeping-cars. The ground-breaking 'Prince of Wales' Pullman dining-car on the 1879 Leeds-London business service was carefully monitored, even though any direct revenue shortfall for its use would be absorbed by the Pullman Company, because the GNR still incurred incidental costs in hauling such a heavy vehicle. In the Summer 1880 timetable, the original service (which had connections for Hull and North Yorkshire as well as Leeds) was split, the dining-car running on the Leeds portion only: Oakley notes that 'when we separated the West Yorkshire connection … there were not sufficient passengers to justify the haulage of so heavy a vehicle', and for the Winter timetable the joint service was restored.

With a similar eye to maximising customer usage, he asked Cockshott in 1886 to investigate customer attitudes to replacing the 20-minute refreshment stop at York on the Anglo-Scottish services with dining-cars. Cockshott duly canvassed customer opinion by direct interview and reported that passengers still appeared to find the York break preferable, '...especially for ladies, and in conversation with gentlemen ... I have been told they prefer to have the luncheon at York, with the opportunity of washing, to a meal in a dining-car.'

Dining-car introduction on the Scottish route was as a result delayed till 1893-94 (and the 'Flying Scotsman' itself didn't receive them till after Oakley's retirement, though when they did finally appear in 1900 the saving of half an hour on the journey time that resulted soon won over the waverers). The new 'transverse' design of sleeping-cars (first introduced on the GWR by William Dean (qv)) was much better received, however, and by January 1896 Oakley was noting that '...the new sleeping-car appears to be very popular with passengers. All reports have been much in its favour ... we are recommending that four more transverse cars be built by the NER.' (Typically financially canny, that last phrase!)

As noted above, Oakley retired as General Manager at the start of 1898, but continued as a Director till his death in 1912. His last Board meeting was indeed only days before he died on 8 February.

Samuel Peto
1809-89

Civil Engineer and Entrepreneur

Born	Woking, Surrey, 4 August 1809, eldest child of William Peto and Sophia Alloway (m 28 October 1808)
Education	Cobham village school, then Field's School, Marlow, and Jardine's School, Brixton; apprenticed 1823 to his uncle Henry Peto, a London builder, as carpenter, bricklayer and mason
Married	(1) Mary Grissell (sister of his partner Thomas Grissell), London (probably Lambeth), 18 May 1831 (d 20 May 1842); (2) Sarah Ainsworth Kelsall, daughter of Henry Kelsall of Rochdale, 12 July 1843
Best-known works	Pre-railway phase (with Thomas Grissell) 1830-46: Nelson's Column, Houses of Parliament, Reform Club, Lyceum Theatre, London brick sewer, Somerleyton Hall, nr Lowestoft (rebuilt 1844-51 for his own residence) Railway phase (with Edward Betts, 1846-55, and Brassey and Crampton, variously 1855-68): Lowestoft Docks; Lowestoft-Norwich line via Reedham Junction; South Eastern Railway; London, Chatham & Dover Railway; London Tilbury & Southend Railway; GNR Peterborough-Boston-Lincoln loop; Oxford Worcester & Wolverhampton Railway; GWR

	Oxford-Birmingham line; Grand Trunk Railway of Canada; various lines in Australia, Argentina, Denmark and Norway; Sebastopol-Balaclava Railway for Allies during Crimean War
Honours	Liberal MP for Norwich (1847-55), Finsbury (1859-65), Bristol (1865-68); Order of the Danneburg (Denmark), 1854; baronetcy, 1855, for services in Crimea (see above); JP for Uxbridge, 1877-84; Deputy Lieutenant for Suffolk; centenary commemorative bust and plaque erected on Norwich Thorpe station, 1989
Died	Blackhurst, Tunbridge Wells, 13 November 1889
Buried	Pembury parish churchyard

Samuel Peto's career – once again an epitome of both the triumphs and perils of Victorian 'self-help' – at first sight bears many parallels with that of George Hudson (qv). Like Hudson, he began in a small way (in his case as apprentice to his uncle, a London jobbing builder). Like Hudson, he had already begun on a career of civic wealth and fame – in his case in London rather than York – before becoming interested in railway construction. Like Hudson, at his zenith he dominated the railway scene, possibly even more than Hudson had done, since Peto's activities were international. Like Hudson, he became a millionaire and purchased a country estate. Like Hudson (and also his contemporary Sir Edward Watkin (qv)) he was for many years an MP – and, like Hudson, he went bankrupt.

However, 'Comparisons' – as Mrs Malaprop said – 'are odorous', and in this case the odours of the two men were very, very different. If Hudson didn't quite stink, financially, at times he came pretty close to it; and if Peto wasn't quite in the 'odour of sanctity', his upright Baptist philanthropy is still remembered in many places with affection, especially in his adopted home territory of the Norfolk-Suffolk border. Furthermore, while Hudson simply owned railways, Peto and his partner construction engineers actually built them (and as the list above shows, lots of other important works too).

Even their bankruptcies were utterly unlike. Hudson's downfall was as a result of shady if creative accounting, at times approaching, if never quite reaching, actual fraud. By contrast, Peto's 1868 financial crash came as a result of a major financial crisis (the Gurney Overend bank failure of 1866), which bankrupted the two major finance houses supporting him and various other railway contractors, and also left him with about £1 million of outstanding unpaid bills owed to him by debtors – though admittedly he was himself overstretched at the time, as witness his already having sold his beloved Somerleyton Hall in 1863. Peto's predicament evinced a good deal more sympathy than Hudson's had done two decades earlier; the Gurney crisis affected very many railway interests (Watkin chaired the Parliamentary committee that drafted new limited liability regulations as a result), and both Disraeli and Gladstone expressed sympathy and support for him, though he still had to resign his seat.

One of the most interesting aspects of Peto's career, perhaps, is that – unlike, for example, Robert Stephenson – he didn't start out as a railway engineer at all. He began, quite simply, as a builder. On his uncle's death in 1830, he went into partnership with his cousin to found the building firm of Peto & Grissell, at a time when London abounded in opportunities for prestigious projects. By a mixture of hard work and good luck, the young firm won the building contracts for several of them, including such spectacular examples as Nelson's Column, the Lyceum and the Houses of Parliament. Only towards the end of this phase did Peto's attention turn to the sort of civil engineering project that we would today describe as 'infrastructure' and would lead naturally on to the worlds of railway construction, with the London & Birmingham Railway's Curzon Street station in Birmingham, the London sewers and the Victoria Docks (and – a curiosity – the first ever ladies' public loo – in Bedford Street – initially costing twopence a 'go', but later reduced to one penny after much protest).

By the time the partnership with Grissell was dissolved in 1846, Peto was the largest employer of labour not merely in Britain but in the world. At the height of the first 'railway mania' it was perhaps inevitable that he would turn his developing interest in infrastructure to the growing and obviously remunerative field of railway construction and entrepreneurship – after all, many others, including Thomas Brassey, with whom he was to build various lines both at home and abroad, were doing just that, and Peto himself was closely involved with the initial Eastern Counties Railway line from London to Norwich via Ely from 1840 onwards. But the strongest stimulus to make this change seems to have come from a slightly unlikely source – his second marriage in 1843 and the purchase of Somerleyton Hall for his family home in the following year.

Peto took his new responsibilities as Lord of the Manor to his estate workers and the surrounding neighbourhood very seriously, and in addition to rebuilding the Hall he also both rebuilt the estate village and caused new docks to be constructed at the nearby fishing port of Lowestoft, where he also purchased 'barren land near to the town' to build a new esplanade and several hotels. To promote this enterprise, he built, also commencing in 1844, the Yarmouth-Norwich line, with a link from Lowestoft joining it at Reedham Junction completed by 1847. The avowed intent of this line, apart from encouraging tourists to his hotels, was to permit fresh fish to be transported quickly enough, with the help of packed ice, 'to get through to Manchester in time for high tea', as he himself put it in a speech in 1843. (One current version on a Lowestoft website even suggests that some fish were sent live!)

Significantly, it was during this very construction period that the Peto and Grissell building partnership was dissolved, and Peto & Betts was set up as a railway building contracting firm, later to be joined in several of the major works specified in the list above by Thomas Brassey and also by Thomas Crampton, who was both a civil and a locomotive engineer. Several of these lines were speculative 'contractors' lines', ie both built and financed by the contractors, with the hope of regaining their outlay from operating profit. Thus Peto features as a Director of several of his railways, or subsidiaries of larger lines, as well as their contractor, the most notable perhaps being the London, Chatham & Dover. This also explains how the firm of Peto, Betts & Crampton (as it was by this time) came to be so vulnerable to the Gurney Overend bank failure of 1866. It also explains how Peto came to be awarded a baronetcy for services during the Crimean War: he built the Sebastopol-Balaclava line as a 'contractors' line', but only charged the Government actual at-cost expenses – patriotism (or hope of honours?) replacing hope of return on capital.

Peto & Betts did not directly control all of the enormous workforce that built their 'contractors' lines', of course; many were recruited by individual sub-contractors working for them on various projects, often from the ranks of the free-wandering 'navvies' who tramped the land selling their labour to the highest (railway) bidder. This indirect control, however, could still be used, if need be, in quite fearsome displays of force, particularly to 'see off' a rival railway project or to gain physical control of works being undertaken by an opponent in a current Boardroom battle. One of these conflagrations, the 'alarming riot at Mickleton', involving a physical struggle to replace a sacked contractor on the Oxford, Worcester & Wolverhampton Railway, went on for 11 days during July 1851, included navvy gangs brought in from other Peto & Betts locations, and even embroiled no less a person than Isambard Kingdom Brunel.

However, Peto, in his parliamentary capacity, worked also by more peaceful means for the promotion of railway interests both abroad and at home. For example, in 1857 he promoted a bill to remove all tollgates within a 4-mile radius of Charing Cross, and in 1865 he and his wife sponsored a diplomatic reception at Richmond for the promotion of the Grand Trunk Railway of Canada. Also in that year he paid a further visit to North America, this time to the USA, partly general fact-finding as a MP but possibly also partly in connection with the building of the Atlantic & Western Railroad, of which he was a leading British supporter.

But all sides of his career, whether as contractor or MP, came to an abrupt and dismal end with his 1868 bankruptcy (even though that was more technical than absolute). He lived on for a further two decades in relative obscurity, partly abroad in Hungary and partly first in the West Country, then Pinner (where he served as a JP) and finally at Tunbridge Wells. He died in 1889.

William Pollitt
1842-1908

Railway Manager

Born	Ashton-under-Lyne, 24 February 1842
Education	Privately, then joined MSLR (later Great Central Railway), 1857, aged 15
Married	Esther Compton, Ashton-under-Lyne, 1862
Best-known works	General Manager of MSLR/GCR under Watkin (qv) and during building of London Extension; steered company through two changes of Chairman following Watkin's retirement; devised 'frequent light fast train' policy for London Extension, with refreshment vehicles on all trains; Board member from 1902
Honours	Knighthood, 1899, in Queen Victoria's 80th Birthday Honours List; JP; Colonel in Engineer & Volunteer Staff Corps; Officer of Order of Leopold, Belgium; High Sheriff of Cheshire
Died	Bowdon, Cheshire, 16 October 1908
Buried	Altrincham Cemetery

Like Henry Oakley (qv) on the Great Northern, William Pollitt was a life-long servant of a single railway company – in his case, the Manchester, Sheffield & Lincolnshire, later to become the Great Central. From a humble lad joining at just over 15 in June 1857, he rose to become Chief Clerk to the

Accountant, Robert Williams, by January 1868, then Accountant himself in 1869, following Williams's death. In this capacity, among other things, he was instrumental in 1878 in showing that it would pay the company to reduce 3rd Class fares to 1d per mile (at which point they ceased to be liable for Passenger Duty) because the loss of revenue would actually be less than the amount of duty payable on the existing fares. In January 1885 he became Assistant General Manager, and was General Manager from 1886 to 1902, when he retired and was elevated to the Board.

During his term as General Manager Pollitt faced both administrative and developmental challenges with considerable aplomb. On the administrative level, his diplomatic skills – which were substantial – were severely tested in coping with the policies and doings of his mercurial and combative Chairman, perhaps the most noteworthy examples being his making peace with the rival GNR, on whose co-operation much of the economic well-being of the MSLR depended, and later his negotiations with the Great Western in the hope of finding a way round the implacable enmity towards the London Extension of Watkin's successor as Chairman of the Metropolitan, John Bell. Also, later in his career he had the task of steering the Great Central (as it became) through two changes of Chairman within five years following Watkin's retirement from that post – first Lord Wharncliffe in 1894, then in 1899 (when Wharncliffe was clearly ailing, and indeed only lived a few days longer) Alexander Henderson, the line's final Chairman.

On the developmental front, Pollitt was responsible for two major projects. The first was a major redevelopment and extension of the fish docks in the port of Grimsby, carried out during 1890-95. Grimsby Port had originated as one of Watkin's pet projects, under Pollitt's predecessor Underdown, and a great deal of the MSLR's goods trade depended on it, especially grain, fish and coal. It had been opened by the Prince of Wales (later King Edward VII) in 1879, and the new dock was named after Princess (later Queen) Alexandra. Pollitt's 1890-95 extensions covered a further 5 acres and cost £115,000.

By far and away Pollitt's largest development project, however, was the London Extension. Although the initial vision for this project had come from Watkin, Pollitt was responsible for the detailed implementation at almost every stage. He had drawn up both the projected construction budget and the projected revenue income – the latter not entirely successfully, because in the absence of any direct data for the new line, he based his revenue projections on the pence per mile returns of the existing MSLR system, which later proved to be something of an error. He successfully filled the role of chief Parliamentary witness for the Great Central's proposals and it was he who set about the delicate business of raising the capital (as matters transpired, a further £2 million was eventually required over the £6 million that his original estimates had called for, so this was no easy task). During the construction stages of the project he assumed the role that today would be described as overall project manager; and in addition his diplomatic skills were tested to the utmost by two key sets of negotiations with other companies.

The first of these was with John Bell, who in 1894 had succeeded Watkin as Chairman of the Metropolitan Railway. To Bell, the shared line with the Great Central southwards from Verney Junction through Aylesbury, which in Watkin's and Pollitt's original scheme formed the key approach to the new terminus at Marylebone, smacked more of competition than co-operation. He wanted to build on from Quainton Road (the proposed start of the joint line) to Moreton Pinkney on behalf of the MSLR, before they had any end-on connection, in the hope of connecting the Metropolitan with the East

& West Junction Railway; when Pollitt denied him the opportunity by means of a counter-offer, then subsequently proposed a deviation for the widened joint line that met Bell's initial objections but would have involved demolishing the Metropolitan's West Hampstead station, Bell's resultant enmity and continuing delaying tactics eventually forced Pollitt to consider the option of an alternative line into London – the joint line with the Great Western through Princes Risborough. This time Pollitt's negotiations were more successful, but even here he had to resist attempts to define a western frontier beyond which the Great Central could not build.

Finally, once the London Extension was complete, it fell to Pollitt to organise rolling-stock and services – assisted by his son Harry, previously Works Manager at Gorton, who was Locomotive Engineer from 1894 to 1900. Bearing in mind the competitive nature of the line, Pollitt plumped for a service of short, light, fast Manchester-London expresses, with no stops closer to London than Aylesbury, refreshment services on all trains, and dining-cars on most (with at-seat service in some cases). There was also the Great Central's 'secret weapon', the first true buffet-cars, on the earliest and latest trains and those that ran between meal times. Palatial new stock, including the dining- and buffet-cars, was ordered for the new services, which started operation on 15 March 1899, together with 109 new locomotives – 4-4-0s and 4-2-2s for express work, and 0-6-0s for freight – to Harry Pollitt's design, and 536 covered vans for the fast fish trains, which started on 10 April. Indeed, the total outlay was so great that Pollitt had to set up an intermediate company, the Railway Rolling Stock Trust, to raise money for the new stock, buy it, and lease it to the Great Central by a hire-purchase agreement until the GCR could pay for it.

Pollitt continued to build up his express services – he needed to, to come anywhere near his revenue projections! From May 1900 he introduced through trains to Huddersfield, Halifax and Bradford, as well as the existing Manchester and Sheffield services. Perhaps finally accepting a sort of defeat by John Bell, however, he made no attempt initially to offer outer-suburban London commuter services, which he left to the Metropolitan. It was only after he had been elevated to the Board in 1902, six years before his death, that these began to be offered by his successor, Sam Fay (qv).

George Mortimer Pullman
1831-97

Entrepreneur and Carriage Designer

Born	Brocton, New York State, USA, 3 March 1831
Education	Grade School to age 14; subsequently apprenticed to his cabinet-maker brother in the family business at Albion, NY
Married	Harriet Amelia ('Hattie') Sanger, Chicago, 13 June 1867
Best-known works	Luxury convertible day/sleeping-cars with 'Pullman section' hanging berths (patented); 'hotel' sleeping/dining-cars; 'parlour' and dining-cars to exceptional standards; created Pullman Palace Car Co to both build and operate these vehicles; vestibule corridor connection between cars (patented)
Honours	Car *Pioneer* used as formal funeral train car for President Lincoln; personal friend of President Grant
Died	Chicago, 19 March 1897, of heart attack following stress of a strike at his works
Buried	Graceland Cemetery, Chicago; coffin encased in concrete block to avoid possible revenge desecration by ex-strikers

The third son of a general mechanic in up-state New York, George Mortimer Pullman left school at 14 to help support the growing family (which eventually totalled ten children) by acting as counter clerk in a local farm supplies store. At the age of 17 he moved to Albion, working for an elder brother in the family's cabinet-making business, first as an apprentice then as a travelling salesman. In the latter capacity he travelled, aged 22, overnight from Buffalo NY to Westfield in the winter of 1853 in an extremely uncomfortable early sleeping-car – a trip that most biographers agree awakened in him a lifelong passion for improving rail travel comfort.

Early in 1854 he left his brother's firm and moved to Chicago, setting himself up in business as a building contractor specialising in the jacking-up and moving of entire 'frame' buildings without interfering with the activities going on inside them (a technique originally developed by his father Lewis Pullman), culminating in the removal of the entire four-storey Tremont Hotel from its original swampy location to nearby firmer ground. Armed with the standing as an engineering contractor given him by this feat, he approached the Chicago & Alton RR in 1858 with a proposal to remodel two of its old cars to a more luxurious convertible day/sleeping format, with fold-down 'Pullman section' curtained bunks (to his own patent), proper pillows and bed linen, washrooms at each end of the car, oil lighting and heating from box stoves, and an attendant conductor.

The remodelled cars entered service in September 1859, and Pullman charged a supplement of $2 per berth (as against the $1.50 charged by the C&A for berths in the old primitive cars), which the public were more than willing to pay for the added comfort. This appears to have been the origin of the standard 'Pullman contract', which operated on his cars both in the USA and in Britain and Europe: Pullman supplied the cars and maintained them from the floor up, while the railway ran them and maintained them from floor down to rail level. The operating railway charged passengers the appropriate train fare, while the

Pullman organisation charged a per capita supplement for use of the particular facilities, plus a charge for whatever additional services, such as meals and drinks, were provided. (In the UK this arrangement continued until the end of the Pullman company as a private organisation in 1967, long after Pullman's own death.)

After a hiatus caused by the US Civil War, Pullman resumed work on de luxe carriage building with the new car *Pioneer*, the most luxurious and expensive railroad car yet seen in the USA. Unfortunately it was also out of gauge for the C&A, and languished unused until Abraham Lincoln's widow accepted his offer of it for the President's 1865 funeral train (whereupon the C&A altered those of their lineside structures it had been likely to foul). As a result Pullman became a household name, the C&A hired *Pioneer*, and by the end of 1866 Pullman had a total of 49 sleeping-cars in service on various US and Canadian roads. In February 1867 the Pullman Palace Car Co was incorporated, with works originally at Detroit and subsequently at Chicago. In 1868 Andrew Carnegie invested $100,000 in the company, and by mid-1869 Pullman was a millionaire.

Also in 1867 Pullman began to operate dining-cars as well as sleepers, to replace the much-dreaded 'refreshment stops', derived from coaching practice, which had previously dominated long-distance train catering. Initially these were 'hotel cars', with day travel, sleeping and dining (with food supplied from an end kitchen) all taking place in the same vehicle. However, patrons objected to the claustrophobic (and somewhat smelly!) nature of such journeys, and in the following year Pullman produced his first specially dedicated dining-car, named *Delmonico* after the New York restaurant of the same name. It was an immediate success, and within five years 700 Pullman cars of varying types were in operation on 150 railroads.

A dedicated dining-car implies a means whereby passengers in other cars can reach the diner, and this caused Pullman two problems. One was technical – how could they get there while the train was still moving? – and Pullman solved this by substituting a connecting 'vestibule' for the traditional American open end platform, an invention still in use to this day between coaches all over the world, and one that he patented. The other problem was financial and legal – the 'Pullman contract' involved passengers paying a supplement for Pullman service at-seat (or at-berth) throughout the journey, and clearly this could not apply to the dining-car proper if it was to offer a 'walk-up' service. (In Britain, all Pullman services were at-seat, so this problem did not arise.) Pullman solved this problem by developing a contract with the railroad companies that provided dining services on a 'cost-plus' basis, effectively passing any risk of loss through low take-up from his company to the railroad concerned.

Pullman's fame rapidly spread beyond the USA. Georges Nagelmackers (qv) visited him in 1869 and James Allport of the Midland Railway in 1872. As a result Pullman began operating sleeping-cars in Britain in 1874, and diners in 1879; Italian contracts followed in 1875, and a separate company was set up to run the British/European operation, with works at Derby. The first few British cars were shipped over from the USA in kit form and merely assembled at Derby, but thereafter most UK and European Pullmans were built on this side of the Atlantic. (It was this British company that Davison Dalziel (qv) bought after Pullman's death in 1897.)

Pullman's enterprises embodied the highest standards of both carriage design and business service. An early exponent of what today would be called TQM, he coined the company slogan 'Improvement is our Watchword', possibly even as early as 1867. He also provided the first genuine career advancement structure for black Americans, through his use, starting in the same year, of emancipated ex-house-slaves as 'porters' (ie conductors and waiters) on his sleeping- and dining-cars in both front-of-house and line-management grades (though, unfortunately, this enterprise also had the – probably unintended – effect of offering a stereotype of the black man as the white man's servant, especially when other companies took it up without the career structure element that Pullman had included). Like many 19th-century American (and other) business magnates, he was both a ruthless businessman and a devout Christian, building a model town (with no bars!) for his employees, leaving money in his will to churches, and founding seminaries.

John Ramsbottom
1814-97

Locomotive Engineer

Born	Todmorden, Lancs, 11 September 1814, son of local mill-owner (only steam-driven mill in the area)
Education	Local schoolmasters and Baptist ministers; apprenticeship in father's mill; Todmorden Mechanics Institute
Married	1881 Census gives wife's name as Mary (date of marriage not recorded)
Best-known works	Amalgamated various LNWR Divisional locomotive works into one organisation based on Crewe; developed modern piston-ring, tamper-proof safety-valve, wheel and screw reversing gear, water trough for taking on water at speed; introduced standardisation and mass-production of locomotives, in particular the 'DX' mixed traffic 0-6-0; later, consultant to development of LYR Horwich Works
Honours	Founder member of the Inst of Mechanical Engineers, 1847, President, 1870-71; Hon MEng, Dublin, 1868; Governor of Owens College, Manchester, where he founded scholarship for LNWR employees; silver plate given on retirement, 1871; Street named after him in Crewe, 1872; memorial window in Christ Church, Crewe

Died   Alderley Edge, 20 May 1897
Buried   Macclesfield Cemetery

Ramsbottom has been described (by O. S. Nock) as 'perhaps the greatest locomotive man of mid-Victorian times', and it is certainly true that if any single figure bridges the gap between the early small-scale railways and one-off locomotive practice of the opening railway years and the large-scale line-managed organisations of the 20th century, with their standard locomotive classes and interchangeable boilers and other accessories, it is he. Born in the days before any formal locomotive engineering training, even by apprenticeship – as a youth of 16 he walked from Todmorden to Manchester to witness the opening of the Liverpool & Manchester Railway – he nevertheless became not only an outstanding engineer and manager but a locomotive theoretician of sufficient magnitude to have a major scientific effect named after him – the 'Ramsbottom effect'. This was the condensation of leaky steam behind the piston, which he solved by developing the modern piston-ring. (The term was still in use in mainland Europe as late as the 1970s to describe, among other things, similar back-condensation in steam turbines.)

In 1839 Ramsbottom joined the locomotive building firm of Sharp Roberts & Co in Manchester, but his main career in locomotive engineering began with his appointment in 1842, on the recommendation of Charles Beyer of Sharp Roberts, as Locomotive Superintendent to the Manchester & Birmingham Railway. In 1846 this became one of the three main constituents of the LNWR, and Ramsbottom became Locomotive Superintendent of that railway's North Eastern Division. He then became Superintendent of the entire Northern Division following Richard Trevithick's 'golden handshake' of 1857, and took over locomotive responsibility for the entire line in 1862, following McConnell's resignation as Superintendent of the Southern Division (as a result of a critical Board report on the lack of cost-effectiveness of his locomotives).

It is difficult not to see Moon's (qv) hand in this sequence of events, particularly given that he and Ramsbottom shared a passion for management standardisation and economy. Ramsbottom had already invented the spring piston ring in 1852 and the tamper-proof safety valve in 1856, both prior to his preference over Richard Trevithick, and within a year of taking over at Crewe, in 1858, had initiated the construction of the famous 'DX' mixed traffic 0-6-0, cheaper, more standardised and easier to build than its predecessor, the 2-4-0 'Crewe Goods'. The 'DX' was the first genuinely mass-produced locomotive anywhere in the world, with almost 800 in service by the time Ramsbottom retired in 1871. Webb's (qv) additional build brought the 1874 LNWR total to 852, and 86 built additionally for the LYR, plus a few overseas sales, made up a total of 943, all to the same drawings. Ramsbottom perforce re-organised Crewe Works to make such a programme possible, and by the end of his time there the works were capable of turning out one locomotive every 2½ working days – more than 100 new locos a year. His two express 2-4-0 classes, the 'Samsons' and the 'Newtons', though less numerous, each eventually reached 90-plus.

Ramsbottom's other inventions or innovations included replacing the clumsy reversing lever used on all early locomotives with the subsequently standard screw reversing gear, adopting the injector for LNWR locomotive water feeds, and the installation of the first water troughs, on the Holyhead line at Mochdre, in the autumn of 1860. Although Ramsbottom is sometimes credited with inventing the water trough, the actual concept was proposed by one of his draughtsmen, in response to the problem of running the 'Irish Mail' from Euston to Holyhead in 6hr 40min to fulfil new Post Office contractual requirements; however, it was undoubtedly Ramsbottom who both pushed the idea through, and carried out the tests to make it practicable.

Ramsbottom retired from the LNWR in 1871, officially on grounds of ill health but actually – and somewhat ironically – as a result of a salary dispute with Sir Richard Moon. In retirement he continued his interest in railway engineering, becoming a Director of the Lancashire & Yorkshire Railway, where he was involved in the development of Horwich Works (completed by his former pupil Aspinall (qv), and of Beyer Peacock. He died in 1897, having witnessed railway development from the opening of the Liverpool & Manchester to the final 'Race to the North'.

Robert Riddles
1892-1983

Locomotive Engineer

Born	23 May 1892
Education	Premium apprenticeship at Crewe Works, under C. J. Bowen-Cooke and W. W. H. Warneford, 1909-14
Married	Irene (last name not listed in sources) during First World War (while serving in Royal Engineers)
Best-known works	Responsible for re-organisation of Crewe and Derby Works, 1925-30; as Principal Assistant to Stanier (qv), responsible for detailed design work on LMS 'Pacifics'; as Director of Transportation, Ministry of Supply, during Second World War, designed 'Austerity' 0-6-0ST ('J94'), 2-8-0 and 2-10-0; as CME of Railway Executive, responsible for BR 'Standard' designs
Honours	CBE, 1943 (for work at Ministry of Supply); Engineering Vice-President, LMS, 1946; 'Golden Key' to North British Hydepark Works
Died	18 June 1983
Buried	Private cremation after service at St Mark's Church, Swindon

Robert Arthur Riddles ('Robin' to his friends) has been described by his biographer Colonel H. C. B. Rogers as 'the last steam locomotive engineer' and 'the last man to wear the mantle of George Stephenson', in just the same way that his colleague and contemporary H. G. Ivatt has been described as 'the last CME'. Strictly speaking, I suppose these titles ought really to be accorded to someone in China, where steam locomotives have continued in use long after every other nation – but certainly the description is accurate for Riddles at any rate as far as the UK is concerned. He was responsible for the last British main-line steam locomotive classes, and his was the last flowering of the uniquely British apprenticeship-based, railway-company-oriented locomotive engineering tradition to which I referred in the Introduction to this book.

In some ways too (like Stroudley in the previous century) his career was that of the archetypal railway engineer. He began on the LNWR as a premium apprentice straight from school, with practical training by day and Mechanics Institute classes by night (unlike his LNER near-contemporary Thompson (qv) with his Cambridge degree and prior industrial experience elsewhere). He served as LMS Assistant Works Manager at both Derby and Crewe, and substantially redesigned the procedures for major locomotive overhauls at both places, introducing a conveyor belt system that cut the 'down time' for locomotive repairs by two-thirds. As Principal Assistant to the reigning CME (Stanier), he did much of the detailed design work on the LMS 'Pacifics' (for example, it was he, not Stanier, who fixed the 'Coronation' Class wheel diameter at 6ft 9in) and dealt quickly and efficiently with the blast-pipe problems on the initial 'Jubilees' and the fractured firebox stays on the initial 'Black Fives'. Finally, he became responsible for the design of a major series of locomotives – the 'Austerity' and BR Standard classes.

However – also like Stroudley! – there were ways in which Riddles's career was very untypical of the 'great tradition' of which he was the final example. One of these was due to the times through which he lived; his major career activities were punctuated, and influenced, by both World Wars in a way that was hardly true of any of the other designers in this book. Riddles never formally completed his full apprenticeship, for example; when war broke out in 1914 he was still in the erecting shop, and obtained special permission to join the Royal Engineers as a volunteer direct from there. This did no harm to his training, but it did leave him on return to civilian life with a commission, a fairly bad war wound, a wartime bride and no job to go to. Luckily, Bowen-Cooke gave him back his (fairly lowly) job as a fitter in the existing erecting shop, and H. P. M. Beames (Bowen-Cooke's successor) put him in charge of building a new one – the beginning of his career in works management.

The Second World War similarly affected his career in a drastic manner. When it broke out, Riddles had moved from being Stanier's Principal Assistant to being Mechanical & Electrical Engineer (Scotland), to make room for C. E. Fairburn, whom the Board favoured over him as Stanier's successor. He was just returning to Scotland after overseeing the American tour of the 'Coronation Scot' (see below) when he was 'poached' by the newly formed Ministry of Supply to become its Director of Transportation Equipment, a post he held till August 1943. Thus his first major foray into independent locomotive design was not for a railway company at all, but for the armed forces, where indeed it formed only part of his remit, which also included such things as cranes, Bailey bridges and the famous Mulberry pontoon harbours.

Riddles was asked by the War Office to provide freight locomotives for service both at home and abroad, as well as steam shunters of general 'Class 3' dimensions, and locomotives for the war effort in various colonial and Commonwealth territories. These last two requests were fairly easily answered: the 'colonial' requirements were met by Garratt orders from Beyer Peacock, and the request for a shunting tank design by adapting for mass-production under wartime conditions the really excellent Hunslet 'J94'-type standard 0-6-0ST, already widely used by industrial networks such as Stewarts & Lloyds steelworks at Corby. The freight engine needs were initially met by an order for 250 Stanier '8F' 2-8-0s, but the emerging requirements of wartime operation both at home and around the world meant that a locomotive even more basic, flexible and quick to build than the Stanier 'Consol' was needed. Riddles's response, worked out with the North British Loco Co at its Hydepark Works, was twofold – the 'Austerity' 2-8-0s and their successor for lighter tracks worldwide, the 1944 2-10-0s, both with parallel boilers and round-topped fireboxes to cut production costs, and flexible stays (which the uninitiated sometimes believed were broken!)

In January 1943 Riddles received the CBE for this work, and in June that year he returned to the LMS, first as Chief Stores Superintendent then, in 1946, as Engineering Vice-President, thus leapfrogging his colleague H. G. Ivatt, who had been appointed CME, apparently over his head, on Fairburn's death just a few weeks before. (In reality both appointments had been considered by the Board together: whether Ivatt's being announced first was political prudence or some lingering jealousy against Riddles's 'upstart' designing of locomotives without actually being a CME will probably never be known!) But in little more than a year, nationalisation meant that the LMS ceased to exist as a separate entity, and Riddles was urgently recalled from a 1947 farewell trip to America to find himself already a member of the five-man Railway Executive, with major responsibility for mechanical and electrical engineering (but, unlike a conventional CME, no single Chief Draughtsman).

Riddles's ideal objective for main-line haulage, based on both his upgrade experience of the LMS

Morecambe-Heysham line and his 1951 French experience of the Annecy SNCF trials, was electric power. However, the investment needed to make that practicable was some considerable time away. In the meantime, financial comparisons demonstrated that, at 1950 prices, steam power was still much more economical in terms of both £/lb TE and £/dbhp/hr (ie, both on starting and while running) than diesel-electric power (and very much more so than gas turbines). The result was the well-known series of Riddles BR Standard locomotive classes, formulated as the result of a report from a committee headed by E. S. Cox, and produced from 1951.

The characteristics of these locomotives are too well known to need more than a general comment here. They were all – except for the sole large Class 8 'Pacific' *Duke of Gloucester* – two-cylinder designs, with rocking grates, self-cleaning smokeboxes, self-emptying ashpans, and as many working parts as possible accessible for ease of maintenance. They were intended to incorporate the 'best practice' of all four previous companies (understandably, Swindon/Stanier/Ivatt practice tended to predominate), but design work was carefully shared out between various drawing offices so that, although all the types had a distinct 'family' resemblance to each other, none looked too specifically like the progeny of any one works. All were intended to work mixed traffic – freight and passenger alike.

Most of the designs were relatively trouble-free, thanks to the extensive preliminary research that went into their conception (again *Duke of Gloucester* is an exception to this rule). The best-known (and probably the best in practice) were the 'Britannia' Class 7 'Pacifics', which revolutionised train haulage in East Anglia in particular, and one late change to the scheme, the famous 'Class 9' 2-10-0s, which replaced a proposed 2-8-2 partly because Riddles had grown so personally attached to his Austerity 2-10-0 design. These were amazing engines, nominally freight locos but very free steaming and capable of speeds of over 90mph.

One of the most interesting characteristics of all the Riddles BR Standard engines, however, was the care taken with the design of the driver's cab, and this leads me back to the second way in which Riddles's career was untypical of the 'premium apprentice made good' tradition – he was much more of an actual engine-driver than almost any other locomotive superintendent or CME (apart, perhaps, from Joseph Locke, Matthew Kirtley and, of course, J. F. McIntosh (qqv)). However, Riddles, unlike McIntosh, never came up the full locoman's way – from cleaner through fireman to driver, progressing through the links. But – thanks partly to the labour troubles of the period – he did have much more footplate experience than is usual for someone on the design side; as a fitter at Rugby just back from the war, he took an engine out for the Holyhead mail during the 1919 strike (but did not actually drive it!), and he drove 'Prince of Wales' 4-6-0 *Edith Cavell* between Crewe and Manchester and Crewe and Carlisle on a variety of occasions during the General Strike of 1926.

His later work as Stanier's Principal Assistant further increased this experience. He was on the footplate (though not necessarily driving) for the high-speed Euston-Glasgow-Euston test run of *Princess Elizabeth* in 1936 and the famous record-breaking run of *Coronation* that so nearly demolished Crewe station's Platform 3. And finally, on the American tour of the 'Coronation Scot', which he was supposed to accompany in an executive capacity, Riddles in fact spent most of his time, as a result of the driver's illness, in turn driving and firing to the official fireman while he acted as driver (and, combined with fitting emergency repairs en route, got so dirty that in St Louis he was almost refused entry to his hotel). Indeed, his very last activity with British Rail was a footplate trip to Crewe on *Duke of Gloucester*.

All this meant that Riddles had a particularly acute sense of the importance of footplate and cab design both to staff comfort and to locomotive efficiency. He was known to say that more coal could be saved through good driving and firing of a simple, free-steaming design than by more complex attention to 'official' design for thermal efficiency. Thus his locomotives were robust and simple, free-steaming and easy to drive, and the cabs were so designed that the machine could be driven, if desired, entirely from a sitting position. Cab mock-ups, which working footplate crews were invited to examine, ensured maximum crew contribution to what must generally be seen as some of Britain's most successful steam designs.

The Transport Act of 1953 abolished the Railway Executive as a formal body, and Riddles took the opportunity to retire. He had, however, a considerable further career as a Director (and eventually Chairman) of Stothert & Pitt, crane manufacturers, with whom he had worked very closely while at the Ministry of Supply. He retired for the second and final time in 1967, aged 75, and died in 1983, aged 91.

John G. Robinson
1856-1943

Locomotive, Carriage and Wagon Engineer

Born	Elswick, Newcastle-upon-Tyne, 30 July 1856, son of Newcastle & Carlisle Railway engineer Matthew Robinson, who later that year moved to first Wolverhampton, then Chester when his friend George Armstrong became Divisional Locomotive Superintendent of GWR
Education	Chester Grammar School, possibly also privately, then apprenticed successively to Joseph Armstrong (George's brother) and William Dean at Swindon from 1872; later assistant to his father Matthew at Bristol
Married	Mary Anne Dalton, of Helston, Cornwall, Bedminster Parish Church, Bristol, 31 July 1884
Best-known works	As CME of Great Central Railway, 1900-22, carried out large-scale modernisation of locomotive stud; oversaw construction of Dukinfield Carriage & Wagon Works; developed superheating, including his own patent design with 24 or 28 elements against the Schmidt superheater's 18; designed fast 4-4-0s ('Director' Class), 4-4-2s and 4-6-0s for London Extension expresses, mixed traffic 4-6-0s for fast freight ('Fish' Classes), 0-8-0s and 2-8-0s for heavy freight work (the latter including wartime

	ROD standard 2-8-0s, later LNER Class 'O4'), and 4-6-2T design for London suburban trains (later LNER Class 'A5'); designed 'Barnum' centre-corridor excursion stock, restaurant, buffet and at-seat catered train sets for London and cross-country expresses, and modern suburban rakes
Honours	MIME, 1891; MICE, 1902; CBE, 1920
Died	'Koyama', Bournemouth, 7 December 1943
Buried	Bournemouth North Cemetery, alongside his wife (d 1938)

Born into a railway family that originated in the North East but subsequently moved to the Great Western, John George Robinson, like so many other famous British railwaymen, both served his apprenticeship at Swindon (under both Armstrong and Dean) and initially cut his teeth as a Locomotive Superintendent in Ireland. In 1884 (the same year as his marriage) he became Assistant Locomotive Superintendent on the Waterford, Limerick & Western Railway, becoming Locomotive Superintendent himself in 1888 on the death of his boss, remaining there till 1900. During his time he reorganised the WLWR's workshops and replaced most of the somewhat antiquated locomotives and rolling-stock.

In 1900, on Harry Pollitt's departure from the post, he returned to England to become Locomotive Superintendent of the Great Central Railway, becoming CME in 1902 when he also took over responsibility for carriage and wagon stock, a post that he then held until the Grouping of 1922-23. Initially Robinson continued the construction of Pollitt's final designs, but in late 1900 he obtained authority from the Board to begin a major upgrade and modernisation of the locomotive stock, concentrating initially on goods engines – the famous 'Pom Pom' 0-6-0s, followed in 1902 by the Class '8A' outside-cylindered 0-8-0 mineral engines, and the fast mixed traffic 'Fish' 4-6-0s of 1904.

It was clear that Robinson had grasped the point that the GCR's financial salvation had to lie in working up its freight business – a point re-echoed in his 1910 report to Fay (qv) that express passenger income was only 2s 2d per passenger mile, while express passenger costs were 3s 6d. Interestingly, however, this same report continued by sounding a warning against cutting off the express passenger business, essential to public relations and promoting business travel to gain freight orders:

> 'It would not be fair to take this figure as representative of what the company would save could the line be worked solely for goods ... but a rough estimate of what the passenger business costs.'

In other words, the passenger business should be kept, but was to be regarded as a 'loss leader', and locomotive building should be adjusted accordingly. (This report did lead to a temporary moratorium on new passenger loco construction, but only for one year.)

Passenger services, then, were certainly to be catered for, and indeed it is in many ways Robinson's express and suburban passenger designs that are the best remembered. For express work, a succession of fast 4-4-0s and 4-4-2s (often thought to be the most beautiful locos of early-20th-century Britain) were counterpointed by both two- and four-cylinder 6ft 9in and 5ft 7in 4-6-0s for heavier duties – fast heavy passenger and fish trains and heavy general merchandise respectively. These designs have two points of particular interest (apart from their shapeliness and – except for too small a grate and firebox on the four-cylinder 4-6-0s – their mechanical excellence, including superheaters to his own patent). The first is the extent to which they were mixed traffic designs, and the second the extent to which, although there were several smallish classes, many parts were standard, or near-standard, and interchangeable between them. (Both these points are likely to be traceable to his Swindon training.) Suburban traffic, for which he designed new, exceptionally comfortable but rather heavy five-car passenger rakes, was handled by the '9N' Class 4-6-2 tanks (later LNER Class 'A5'), possibly the most successful suburban passenger loco prior to Fowler's 2-6-4Ts for the LMS.

In addition to these suburban rakes, Robinson initiated other carriage-building programmes, including sets with catering vehicles, some designed for at-seat catering through the train, for both the London Extension and the cross-country services (some of these are further reviewed in my earlier book *Dining At Speed*). There was also something quite new, the roomy and tall 'Barnum' excursion sets, built to the absolute loading gauge maximum, with open-saloon centre-gangway coaches, tables at all seats, and some of the tables with folding flap edges for easier access. Many of his carriages had anti-telescoping buffers and fenders, a safety feature of his own invention. To provide for this massive additional build of carriages (and goods and fish wagons), Robinson developed a new Carriage & Wagon Works at Dukinfield.

But possibly his most famous locomotive of all was once again intended for freight work. This was the '8K' 2-8-0 design (later LNER Class 'O4'), developed from the earlier '8A' 0-8-0 mineral engines, superheated, making extensive use of standard parts, and itself developed in 1918 into the '8M', with a larger boiler and a Robinson instead of the original Schmidt superheater, which made it even more efficient. It was the '8K' design that was chosen by the Ministry of Munitions as the standard war heavy freight engine, and more than 500 additional locos were built to that design, some by the GCR itself and others by contractors (some were subsequently taken into stock by both the GWR and the LNWR).

In 1922 Robinson was 66, and the most senior CME of all the LNER's constituent companies. The LNER offered him the new expanded post, but he declined it on grounds of age, and recommended, in what must be one of the wisest and most selfless gestures in locomotive engineering history, that they appoint Nigel Gresley instead – with what results, we all know! In that year, too, his old boss Sir Sam Fay left to become Chairman of Beyer Peacock, and Robinson joined him there as a Director a year later. He lived for a further 20 years, dying in retirement at Bournemouth in December 1943.

Robert H. Selbie
1868-1930
Railway Manager

Born	Salford, 1868, son of Rev R. W. Selbie
Education	Manchester Grammar School and Owens College, Victoria University of Manchester, followed by clerical pupillage under Thorley (LYR General Manager)
Married	Florence Heyworth, Blackburn, date not given in sources
Best-known works	General Manager of Metropolitan Railway, 1908-30; introduced Pullman services on Aylesbury line trains; developed concept of 'Metroland' and Metropolitan Railway Country Estates Company
Honours	CBE, 1919
Died	Collapsed suddenly in St Paul's Cathedral, 17 May 1930, while attending confirmation service for his younger son
Buried	Cremated, Golders Green Cemetery

Robert Hope Selbie was to the Metropolitan Railway what Sam Fay (qv) was to the Great Central. Indeed, even their dates roughly coincided – Selbie took over as Metropolitan General Manager in 1908, and remained so till his death in 1930, while Fay became Great Central General Manager in 1902 and remained so till the 1923 Grouping. Both men, too, were highly ambitious for their respective lines, financially acute, and extremely publicity-oriented. Both had been recruited at a point where the lines concerned were in bad financial shape – the GCR from its London

Extension costs and the Met from the costs of electrification – and both were rivals for the outer-suburban commuter market beginning to develop on the two companies' Joint Lines. But though they were business rivals, there does not seem to have been any of the animosity between them that soured the relations between their predecessors William Pollitt and John Bell.

Sam Fay's fairly colourful career prior to coming to the Great Central has already been outlined. By contrast, Selbie's career before joining the Metropolitan was a good deal more conventional – no turning round of ramshackle bankrupt companies, just a steady efficient advance through the head office ranks of his home company, the Lancashire & Yorkshire, which he joined aged 15 in 1883, and for which he became Assistant Chief Traffic Manager in 1899.

So how did this apparently homespun Lancastrian come to be recruited to the Metropolitan Railway? The answer seems to lie with the legacy of former Chairman Sir Edward Watkin, himself a Manchester man. It seems that a custom had grown up in Metropolitan circles of looking to Manchester for its staff, just as it looked to the aptly named Metropolitan Amalgamated Company (later Metro-Cammell) of Birmingham, with whom it shared a Director, for its rolling-stock. In any case, Selbie was recruited as Secretary in 1903, and became General Manager in 1908.

In his new post, with a brief to reverse the company's current poor financial position that effectively gave him his head, Selbie's inherent strategic genius blossomed. Leaving aside its coal traffic to Neasden (which Selbie also actively fostered), the Metropolitan Railway's core business was carrying suburban commuters into, out of and through London; its main-line network stretched from Verney Junction beyond Aylesbury, Uxbridge, Hammersmith and South Kensington to Finsbury Park, Shoreditch and New Cross. The first two of these terminal points were rural and populated by relatively affluent potential customers; the rest were, as they still are, intensely urban and relatively proletarian in customer base. The answers to increasing turnover on such a customer base seem obvious to us now, though at the time it took a Selbie to see them: first, persuade more people to commute from the affluent areas of Uxbridge and the Chilterns (and if not enough lived there, persuade them to do so!); and second, persuade more people from the more urbanised areas to travel outwards on suitably advertised leisure excursions – into the Chilterns, or, for the less affluent, to closer places of pleasure such as Eastcote Park on the Uxbridge line.

Advertising and excursion fares took care of the second idea well enough. Putting the first into practice, however, was more complicated than it at first seemed. To begin with, there was the competition from the GCR, with its up buffet-car expresses making their last stop at Aylesbury often timed to poach 1st Class traffic from the Met's services, while especially after 1910 there were Robinson's fine new fast outer-suburban rakes, and the spanking new 'A5s' to haul them. Moreover, there was the question of how one catered for the wives and families of these affluent clients – what sort of London services were they likely to patronise?

Selbie's solution was initially sparked by the news in 1910 that Fay was considering a deal with the Pullman organisation (which in the end fell through); he went direct to the Pullman company and franchised them to run two Pullman cars (the famous *Mayflower* and *Galatea*) on selected trains from Aylesbury and Verney Junction right through to the City. I have described in detail in *Dining At Speed* how he rostered these Pullman cars to maximise their revenue-earning capacity. They catered not only for affluent business commuters to and from their City offices, but for their wives to go shopping in the West End – complete with their own tea rooms at Chiltern Court while waiting for the return Pullman – and their families to attend West End theatrical performances and enjoy supper on the way back. They were an immediate success, and only ceased operations at the outbreak of the Second World War.

Selbie's greatest stroke, however, was the creation of 'Metro-land'. Both the Metropolitan and the Great Central were actively pursuing additional customers for their suburban services by encouraging new building in their areas, and encouraging people to move out from London to 'the country', but the Met had one great advantage: it had found a way round the usual Parliamentary embargo on railways owning land for purposes other than actual railway operation. With the formation of the Metropolitan Surplus Lands Committee in 1885 it had been able to go into housing estate development business on its own account.

Selbie recognised as early as 1912 that the Surplus Lands operation could be sharpened up to produce considerable added value, both from the estates themselves and from the commuter traffic they generated. In 1919, accurately predicting the post-war boom in 'houses fit for heroes to live in', he formed the Metropolitan Railway Country Estates Company, nominally an entirely separate company from the Metropolitan but completely under its control, 'not merely to provide superior houses in the rural countryside ... but also to create new passenger traffic', with himself as one of the Directors. The already existing *Metroland* magazine – brilliantly re-titled by Selbie in 1915 from the prosaic *Guide to the Extension Line* – became the major publicity and marketing organ both for the new houses and for the excursion delights of the Chiltern countryside and small towns. It only remained for someone (probably Selbie himself) to coin the slogan 'Live in Metro-land' in opposition to the Great Central's much more ordinary 'Live in the Country', and the rest, as they say, is history.

The remainder of Selbie's career, which saw him from 1922 both General Manager of the Met and one of its Directors, was occupied by two things: capitalising on the successes of the ten years from 1910 to 1919 and asserting the independence and 'main line' status of the railway. He successfully avoided inclusion in the 1923 Grouping; the formation of London Transport in 1933, however, proved more difficult for the Metropolitan to avoid. Even so, he might perhaps have pulled it off had it not been for his sudden and untimely death in harness, just when he was negotiating with Herbert Morrison on the one hand and the Great Western (for a possible merger) on the other. Sadly, though, Selbie died on 17 May 1930, and the Met ceased to exist as a separate railway as from 1933. But his legacy both in 'Metroland' and in the promotion of leisure excursions to the Chilterns continued to survive long after him.

William Stanier
1876-1965

Locomotive Engineer

Born	Wellington Street, Swindon, 27 May 1876 (son of William Dean's chief clerk)
Education	Wycliffe College, Stonehouse, followed by apprenticeship at Swindon from 1892
Married	Ella Elizabeth Morse, Swindon, 4 July 1906
Best-known works	Continued LMS standardisation policy, restocking system with improved locomotive and carriage designs (locos incorporating best Swindon practice); major locomotive classes include 'Jubilee' and 'Black Five' 4-6-0s, '8F' 2-8-0s, 'Princess Royal' and 'Duchess' 4-6-2s
Honours	President, Inst of Locomotive Engineers, 1936; President, Assoc of Railway Locomotive Engineers and Inst of Locomotive Engineers (second term), both 1938-39; President, Inst of Mechanical Engineers, 1941; knighthood, January 1943; FRS, March 1944; President, Production Engineering Research Assoc, 1951; Gold Medal, Inst of Loco Engineers, April 1957; James Watt Medal, Inst of Mechanical Engineers, 1963
Died	Rickmansworth, 27 September 1965
Buried	Cremated, Golders Green Crematorium, London; memorial

service at St Margaret's,
Westminster

William Arthur Stanier was born into a railway family deeply steeped in the second ('Wolverhampton' as distinct from 'Brunel') Great Western railway tradition: his father had been specially brought from Wolverhampton Works by Armstrong, together with William Dean, to be Dean's 'confidential clerk' – a post that also involved such diverse activities as materials testing (which the elder Stanier initially did in his own home, for lack of facilities as Swindon Works!) and overseeing apprentice evening classes at the Mechanics Institute. The younger man was thus brought up from birth in a technically diverse railway atmosphere. Not surprisingly, he became what was later called a 'pre-apprentice', but in his day was termed an 'office-boy', at Swindon in January 1892, the earliest he could join the GWR, becoming an apprentice proper in May as soon as he reached 16.

Thus Stanier's early training took him right through the final years of the broad gauge and the massive efflorescence of locomotive and carriage design, under William Dean, that followed it. He actually worked as an apprentice on the 'convertible' 2-4-0/4-4-0 *Charles Saunders*, the first loco to have the Dean bogie, as well as many of the famous 'Dean singles'. Also, during his time in the drawing office, from 1897, he found himself involved with the introduction of the many Churchward innovations that began during Dean's later years, including domeless taper boilers and Belpaire fireboxes. This was followed from 1900 by extensive Running Department experience at both Paddington (under John Armstrong) and Swindon, the latter position including much experience of the new Churchward locomotives, with their characteristics of multi-cylinder layouts and superheating. In 1913, aged 30, he became Assistant Works Manager at Swindon, in

1920 Works Manager, and in 1922 Assistant to the CME (who by this time was C. B. Collett (qv)). In 1927 he accompanied Collett's finest new engine, *King George V*, to the B&O 'Festival of the Iron Horse' Centenary Exhibition in the USA.

Meanwhile, all was far from well on the LMS. The Midland legacy of rows between Deeley and Paget over divided authority that had continued between Fowler (qv) and Anderson, and the partisanship between Crewe and Derby, had been further exacerbated by a succession of short-reign CMEs – Hughes, 1923-24, Fowler, 1924-30, and Lemon, 1930-31. (The latter was really just a 'holding' operation, though he – or rather, his two principal assistants, Beames and Symes – did plan some interesting locomotives that were in the end never built, including a modernised 'Prince of Wales' 4-6-0 and freight 2-8-0 and 4-8-0 designs.) The LMS Chairman, Sir Josiah Stamp, accordingly resolved that a firm, completely 'outside' CME appointment was essential, and for a variety of reasons (including the fact that his chief, Collett, was only five years older than himself and the GWR management wanted him to 'go his full course'), Stanier of the GWR was the obvious candidate to approach. Accordingly, following some exploratory lunches at various London clubs in the best old-boy-network tradition, Stanier was invited to apply for the post.

Stanier was appointed CME of the LMS from 1 January 1932 with a mandate from Stamp to do two things. He was to provide sufficient locomotives for the system with the least possible number of standard classes, and he was to ensure that additional availability from each locomotive reduced the total number of locos needed across the system to as low a figure as possible. Interestingly, he was not charged by Stamp with introducing Swindon-style improvements as such (and, indeed, Crewe boiler construction practice turned out to be both as reliable as that at

Swindon and cheaper), but it seems unlikely that Stamp was unaware that his mandate to produce locos with maximum reliability and availability would inevitably lead someone with Stanier's background to do just that. Initially, of course, some of the 'transplanted' ideas caused problems – blast-pipe design on the early 'Jubilees' resulted at first in poor steaming, and low-temperature Swindon superheat was rapidly replaced by the more practical high-temperature version – but taper boilers, Belpaire fireboxes, long valve travel and a 28in cylinder stroke all proved themselves massively in the years that followed – not least during the unforeseen emergency of the Second World War.

The resulting tally of standard Stanier locomotives makes impressive reading, both in terms of efficiency and in terms of sheer numbers. In terms of efficiency, the overall number of locomotives in service was reduced from 9,032 when Stanier took over (itself a reduction under Fowler from the original 10,316 of 1923) to 8,138 in 1947. Some of this total includes further standardisation under Fairburn and H. G. Ivatt, but this itself was essentially a continuation of Stanier's policy, delayed by the circumstances of the war till after his retirement in 1944. In terms of numbers, the prize must of course go to the famous 'Black Five' mixed traffic 4-6-0s (842 built in all) and their '8F' 2-8-0 sisters, which just 'pipped them to the post' with a build of 852. The latter were identical in size to the LNWR build of Ramsbottom's famous 'DX' Class, the first ever mass-produced loco (though the extra 86 'DXs' built for outside users still puts them ahead even of Stanier's mass-production!). Even his 'bread-and-butter' 2-6-4Ts for suburban passenger services numbered 206 (343 if the three-cylinder variant is also included).

But pride of place must go to the 'Princess' and 'Duchess' 'Pacifics', including the famous streamlined series for the 1937 'Coronation Scot', with large superheaters, boilers and fireboxes to the very limits of the UK loading gauge, and the highest test horsepower of any British steam locomotive. Even this, though, did not exhaust Stanier's innovatory genius. The 'Princess' series included the only successful turbine-driven express locomotive in the British Isles (No 6202, later named *Princess Anne*), and in 1939 an even larger machine was proposed – a streamlined 4-6-4 with a mechanical stoker and 300psi boiler pressure, capable of taking a 500-ton train from Euston to Glasgow in 6 hours flat, to compete with air services. But alas, the war came along and stopped work on it.

Stanier's influence was also felt in areas other than steam locomotives. One of his first acts in 1932 was to rebuild an old Johnson 0-6-0T as an 0-6-0 diesel shunter, and this was followed in 1939 by a series of 0-6-0 diesel-electrics, of steadily increasing tractive effort, which had reached 40 examples by 1944 and formed the basis of the standard BR diesel shunter; there was also an experimental articulated three-car diesel set, forerunner of the BR DMUs, in 1938. He also had substantial influence on LMS carriage design, introducing flush-sided large-windowed stock with sliding ventilators to the upper part of the main window. His buffet-car designs, too, were even more innovative than Gresley's, with a true cafeteria-style 'tray track' and a separate queuing line for patrons awaiting service. However, this was a buffet too far – the punters preferred Gresley's more conservative approach, and the Stanier designs were subsequently converted.

By the time of his knighthood in 1943, Stanier's fame, both as an engineer and as a formidable team builder and manager able finally to reconcile the warring Crewe and Derby factions of the LMS, had already spread well beyond that company, and indeed even beyond Britain. He had served on two Committees of

Enquiry into Indian Railways in 1936 and again in 1938 (the first alongside Sir Ralph Wedgwood (qv)), and was to visit there again in 1944 as Chairman of the Machine Tool Mission. During the Second World War he chaired the Railway Executive Committee's Mechanical and Electrical Subcommittee (his '8F' 2-8-0s were one of the wartime standard locomotives) and was also Chairman of the government's Mechanical Engineering Advisory Committee and Scientific Advisor to the Ministry of Production, with a brief extending far beyond railways.

In 1944, aged 68, he retired as CME of the LMS, and was elected to a Fellowship of the Royal Society, only the third railway engineer to receive this honour (the other two were Robert Stephenson (qv) and Edward Bury). He also became Chairman of Power Jets Ltd, the government firm working on Frank Whittle's famous jet engine. He finally died, full of years and honours, including both the Loco Engineers' Gold Medal and the James Watt Medal of the Institution of Mechanical Engineers, in 1965.

George Stephenson
1781-1848

Early Railway Engineer

Born	Wylam, 9 June 1781
Education	No formal education; self-taught from age 18 (partly via local night classes in Walbottle, partly in process of educating his son Robert (qv)); attended Newcastle Literary & Philosophical Society with Robert
Married	(1) Frances ('Fanny') Henderson, Newburn Church, 28 November 1802 (d 1805); (2) Elizabeth Hindmarsh, also at Newburn Church, 1820 (d 1845); (3) Ellen Gregory (his housekeeper), Tapton, February 1848
Best-known works	Blucher, 1814; Stephenson safety lamp for mines, 1815 (long and erroneously ascribed to Sir Humphrey Davy); surveys and building of Stockton & Darlington line, 1821, and of Liverpool & Manchester, 1824; *Locomotion No 1*, 1825; *Rocket*, 1829 (with son Robert); founder (again with Robert) of the locomotive building firm that bears his son's name
Honours	Refused FRS, Fellowship of Institute of Civil Engineers, and (on several occasions) British knighthood, but accepted a Knighthood of the Order of Leopold from Belgium; first President of Inst of Mechanical Engineers, 1847

Died	Tapton House, near Chesterfield, Derbyshire, 12 August 1848
Buried	Holy Trinity Church, Chesterfield, beneath simple stone slab (current tablet in church bearing his name is a later addition)

Commonly (but inaccurately) described as 'the inventor of the steam locomotive' or, more accurately, as 'the father of the railway', George Stephenson's claims to fame lie primarily in two things – his capacity for bringing together the key concepts of locomotive steam power (individually invented by others) in a single design, and his tenacious vision (also originally conceived by others) of steam-powered public railways as a national or even international network. The son of a poorly paid fireman on the colliery steam pumping engines, he had no formal education whatever in childhood (with an income of only 12 shillings a week, the family was too poor), but from the age of 14 he rapidly learned a great deal of practical engineering as assistant fireman to his father, by the simple expedient of taking mine pumping machinery to pieces to repair it and putting it together again. After graduating to various positions (brakesman on a stationary winding engine, and repairman on a pumping engine at Killingworth), he became colliery enginewright in charge of all stationary engines at Killingworth, also overseeing other Grand Alliance pits in the area, in 1812.

George now turned his attention to other engineering matters, among them the miner's safety lamp that bears his name, and particularly – a natural extension, given his interest in stationary steam engines – to the development of steam engines that could run on rails and haul loads. This began with his *Blucher* at Killingworth (1814), and its sister locomotives *Wellington* and *My Lord* (a reference to

Lord Ravensworth, the Killingworth pit-owner's newly acquired title). As remarked above, Stephenson in no sense 'invented' the steam locomotive. If anyone could claim to have done that it was Richard Trevithick (qv), and William Hedley among others was already building locomotives at this time at Wylam. What he did do, however, was to bring together in one design a number of the key features that have characterised the steam locomotive ever since: the return-flue (later developed into the tubular) boiler, the blast-pipe, flanged wheels running on smooth rails, two cylinders, coupling rods, and (eventually, in *Rocket*) connecting rods driving the wheels direct from the cylinders. He also improved the design and construction of the iron rails on which these early locomotives ran, patenting a design manufactured under licence by Michael Longridge.

As the fame of Stephenson's locomotives spread, so did the demand for them. Between 1814 and 1821 he built 16 locomotives, for his own Killingworth colliery, for Hetton and for the Kilmarnock & Troon tramway. In June 1823, foreseeing continuing demand following the approval of the Stockton & Darlington Act the previous month, he founded, with his son Robert, the Darlington Quaker businessman Edward Pease (see below) and Longridge, the locomotive building firm of Robert Stephenson & Company, with works at Newcastle-upon-Tyne. Pease contributed the majority of the share capital (£1,600 of an initial total of £4,000), but George's son Robert was named managing partner despite being only 19. Opponents criticised the setting-up of the firm as an attempt to create a monopoly, but in fact it was more probably an attempt to put locomotive building on a proper professional footing, rather than something Stephenson did in between his other duties at Killingworth and increasingly elsewhere. The first two locomotives built by the new company (total order value £1,000) were for Pease's Stockton & Darlington Railway, including the famous *Locomotion No 1*.

Edward Pease was central to this phase of Stephenson's career. He not only backed the Newcastle locomotive works, but also (possibly at the railway promoter William James's instigation) appointed Stephenson first as surveyor, then as engineer to the Stockton & Darlington line; once again, Robert assisted his father in the survey. A clause in the new line's Act specifically empowered it to use locomotives to haul trains – which led Lord Shaftesbury to enquire what sort of animal a 'loco-motive' might be, and Stephenson to write annoyedly that 'Lord Shaftesbury must be an old fool. I always said he had been a spoilt child, but he is a great deal worse than I expected'. Even before the S&DR was opened the controversy and interest aroused by the new line led to Stephenson receiving enquiries and offers from other railway promoters, in particular the Liverpool & Manchester, to which also he became surveyor. He was dismissed from this post after wilting under a virulent cross-examination in parliament, leading to the L&MR Bill initially being defeated, but after the Act was passed, with John Rennie as surveyor, he was re-instated as engineer and, among other things, successfully carried the line across Chat Moss by 'floating' it on brushwood

The Stockton & Darlington Railway was the first public steam-worked line, but strictly speaking it was only a local line, even so. The Liverpool & Manchester, however, was a genuine main line, linking two major cities. It was thus crucial to the future acceptance of the steam locomotive as a means of transport that it should be the power unit of choice for that railway. However, an influential faction on the L&MR Board favoured stationary steam engines for haulage, claiming that the cost of goods per ton-mile would be twopence cheaper by this mode than by locomotive. To settle the matter, the Board in 1829 ordered a competition, the famous 'Rainhill Trials'. Five builders entered locomotives (one, *Cycloped*, worked by a horse and hence disqualified, may well have been intended as a joke). George and Robert Stephenson's entry, *Rocket*, won the trials, though on the line's opening day it was also involved in both the first fatal public railway accident and the highest speed attained to that time, 30mph (see the entry of Joseph Locke), both of which events one may perhaps also see as omens of the future).

From then on, the Stephenson 'team' – George, his sons Robert and James, and a variety of colleagues – became one of the two major forces in early Victorian railway engineering and promotion (the other, of course, being Isambard Kingdom Brunel (qv)). So much so that the 4ft 8½in 'standard gauge', derived from North Eastern colliery wagonways, to which many railways were built in the UK, Europe and America, became known initially as 'the Stephenson gauge'. George Stephenson himself became effectively a Victorian icon, a 'superstar' whose life exemplified the virtues of 'self help' preached by Samuel Smiles (who wrote his earliest biography), and the progenitor of the 'Railway King', George Hudson of York (qv), though his engineering, both civil and locomotive, became increasingly conservative following the Liverpool & Manchester, which many commentators regard as his peak of performance. He also became a very wealthy man, not only from his railway and locomotive engineering activity, but also from shareholdings and mine operations, especially the opening up of the Leicestershire coalfield, which was only discovered during cutting works by Robert Stephenson for the Leicester & Swannington line.

In these later years Stephenson also entered the world of the landed proprietors, with the purchase of two country houses, first Alton Grange in Leicestershire (near his coalfield), then Tapton House near Chesterfield (again near a coalfield, which he developed jointly with Hudson, at Clay Cross). It was from here that he 'saw off' two major challenges from Brunel – the so-called 'battle of the gauges' and the proposal to build an 'atmospheric railway' between Newcastle and Berwick. The latter was of particularly major importance, since had Brunel's scheme gone ahead it would effectively have blocked the subsequent creation of the East Coast Main Line to Scotland. When Stephenson's and Hudson's rival scheme for a standard gauge locomotive-worked line was accepted by parliament in 1845, 800 workers paraded through the streets with banners and music. His final railway-building project, also in 1845, was in Spain, for a railway from Madrid to the Bay of Biscay.

Robert Stephenson
1803-59

Early Railway Engineer

Born	Willington Quay, near Newcastle-upon-Tyne, 16 November 1803
Education	Long Benton village school to age 12, then Dr Bruce's Academy and the Literary & Philosophical Society, Newcastle, 1815-19; then apprenticed to Nicholas Wood, Killingworth Colliery (withdrawn in 1821 after only two years to assist his father on survey of Stockton & Darlington line); also attended Edinburgh University for six months, November 1822-April 1823
Married	Fanny Sanderson, Bishopsgate Parish Church, London, June 1829
Best-known works	Designed and built (some jointly with father George) *Locomotion No 1* (1825), *Lancashire Witch* (1828), *Rocket* (1829), *Invicta* (1830, for Canterbury & Whitstable Railway), *Northumbrian* (1830), *Planet* (1831) and *Atlas* (1833, the first locomotive to have steam brakes); managing partner of Robert Stephenson & Co, Newcastle locomotive builders, where above locos were built; originator of steam brake (but not of the valve gear that bears his name); constructed (some jointly with father) Liverpool & Manchester Railway (initial survey, with father George, 1821-22), Stockton &

	Darlington Railway (again with father, intermittently 1821-25), Leicester & Swannington Railway (1829), Canterbury & Whitstable Railway (1829-30), London & Birmingham Railway (1833-38), and Chester & Holyhead Railway (1845-50); built High Level Bridge, Newcastle (1849), Conway Bridge and Britannia Bridge, Menai Straits (1850), Royal Border Bridge, Berwick (1850), and Victoria Bridge, Montreal (1854)
Honours	FRS; President, Inst of Civil Engineers (1855) and (succeeding his father on the latter's death) Mechanical Engineers; MP for Whitby, 1847; offered knighthood, 1850, but refused (though accepted Belgian equivalent and French Légion D'Honneur); Order of St Olaf (Norway), 1853; honorary degree from Oxford, 1857
Died	Gloucester Square, London, 12 October 1859
Buried	Westminster Abbey, in Nave

As the summary above indicates, it is difficult to write of either of the Stephensons, father or son, without also writing of the other, at least during the first decades of their joint activity. In his early years, Robert Stephenson worked jointly with his father, and in many areas, from education to line survey, the older man seems to have regarded his brilliant son as an extension of his own powers and ambitions. Thus in several of their early joint locomotives, from *Locomotion* to *Rocket*, it is difficult to tell which Stephenson was actually responsible for such developments as multiplying the return flue into a 25-tube boiler, or repositioning the cylinders outside the boiler and at an angle to the vertical, to drive the wheels directly and more readily. Likewise, in their early joint surveys it is hard to tell which parts are the work of which.

The problem is similar with their joint locomotive building firm, Robert Stephenson & Co (for details of its setting up, see under George Stephenson), where advances in locomotive design often seem to be credited to the firm generally rather than to particular members of it. Thus, for instance, we know that the steam brake, first fitted on *Atlas* (built in 1833 for the Leicester & Swannington Railway) was actually designed by Robert, because he patented it, but the so-called Stephenson valve gear of ten years later, though invented at the Robert Stephenson works, was actually the product of two men called Williams and Howe (respectively at the time a 'gentleman-apprentice' and a patternmaker at the works) – interestingly, it was never patented.

Up until about 1824, then, and in some areas even beyond it, the two Stephensons, and indeed also their immediate entourage, seem to have functioned virtually as a joint entity – a sort of railway-making 'family' (in something approaching a Mafia-like sense of the word!). Two events, however, occurred between 1824 and 1838 to ensure and confirm Robert's personal and professional independence from his father. In 1824 he was offered, and accepted, a three-year contract to manage a group of Colombian silver mines on behalf of Thomas Richardson (another of the investors in the Newcastle locomotive building works) at a salary of £500 per annum. The venture proved beset with both technical and personnel problems, but undoubtedly it empowered Robert on his return in 1828 as his own man, in a way he almost certainly had not been before this overseas venture. (George took over his duties at the locomotive-building firm during his absence, and in fact does not seem to have been overly successful in building the business at that point.)

The second event that marked Robert Stephenson's emergence as a leading railway engineer in his own right was his appointment as Engineer of the London & Birmingham – the railway whose building is so graphically described in Dickens's *Dombey & Son*. If the Liverpool & Manchester was the world's first main line, then the London & Birmingham was the first main line of fully national importance, linking as it did the capital with England's second city – and eventually, via the Grand Junction (not engineered by Robert), with Carlisle and Scotland. It was also a line that involved overcoming some of the biggest civil engineering problems seen up to that time (Roade Cutting and Kilsby Tunnel, to name but two). Its successful completion in 1838 (albeit 100% over budget, with a total cost of £5.5 million) made Robert Stephenson the leading railway engineer (saving only Brunel) and locomotive builder of the time, with railway contracts from Norway to Belgium, and locomotive orders from Russia to Italy. Towards the end of his life, he was also regularly called in as a professional adjudicator in disputes over matters of railway engineering, and, as noted in the summary, was the first man to be President of both the Civil and the Mechanical Engineers.

Robert Stephenson also developed during his last 15 years an additional area of railway engineering expertise, in the building of box girder and tubular bridges. Three of his major railway engineering contracts – the Chester & Holyhead, the Newcastle & Berwick (originally surveyed by his father in 1836), and the Newcastle & Darlington – involved particularly difficult high-level river crossings, and in the case of the Chester & Holyhead also the crossing of the Menai Straits at a height sufficient to allow naval vessels underneath in full sail. Only one of his bridge solutions was conventional – the Royal Border Bridge at Berwick, with its 126-foot-high stone arches. Of the others, the High Level Bridge at Newcastle was a box girder construction with the railway on top and a road bridge below (still in use to this day, although an earlier box girder bridge across the Dee failed disastrously in 1847 when a train wheel broke and damaged the girders), while the Conway and Britannia Bridges (the latter so called from the Britannia rock on which one of the piers is anchored) were of welded tubular construction. Again international contracts followed for similar tubular bridges, two in Egypt and one in Montreal.

Robert Stephenson's last work was also on a bridge – repairing and strengthening the famous cast-iron bridge over the River Wear at Sunderland, the first but one iron bridge in the world (the first was of course Telford's, at Ironbridge), and the subject of the well-known transfer prints that identify the famous Sunderland lustre-ware pottery. His last overseas journey (officially a 'holiday and rest cure' for his failing health) was to Egypt. He died on returning from that journey in October 1859, just one month after Brunel, and was accorded what was virtually a state funeral, with a cortège passing through Hyde Park and burial in Westminster Abbey.

Patrick Stirling
1820-95

Locomotive Engineer

Born	Kilmarnock, Ayrshire, 29 June 1820, eldest son of Rev Robert Stirling, Church of Scotland minister and engineering inventor
Education	Apprenticed to James Stirling (his uncle) at Dundee Foundry, 1837-43, then 'improver' in Isle of Dogs, London, 1843-44; worked with Robert Napier & Co, Glasgow, 1844-46 (on marine engines); foreman at Neilson & Co's locomotive works, Glasgow, 1846-51; works manager at R. W. Hawthorn, Newcastle, 1851-53 (where he acquired his preference for domeless boilers)
Married	Wife's name recorded as Margaret in 1881 Census
Best-known works	Locomotive Superintendent, Glasgow & South Western Railway, 1853-66, and GNR, 1866, till just 11 days before his death in 1895; founded GSWR Kilmarnock Works; leading proponent of domeless boiler design (also used by his brother James and son Matthew on their locomotives); designed 8ft express 4-2-2s for GNR from 1870 onwards, among the fastest and most elegant express locomotives of their period
Honours	MIMechE, 1867; MICivE, 1878; Memorial Fountain at Doncaster, 1870; JP by 1881

Died	Highfield House, Doncaster, 11 November 1895
Buried	Doncaster, Thorne Road Anglican cemetery (St James's Church)

There is some evidence to suggest that mechanical engineering ability may have a tendency to run in families. One of the best examples of this is the Stirling family of Dunblane, Kilmarnock and eventually Doncaster, with Patrick Stirling playing the central role. His great-grandfather, Michael Stirling of Dunblane, developed one of the earliest threshing machines (1758); his father, the Rev Robert Stirling, developed a hot-air engine (1816) and helped in the development of the Siemens open-hearth furnace; and his uncle, James (with whom he trained), managed and eventually owned the famous East Foundry in Dundee – where Patrick's predecessor on the Great Northern Railway, Archibald Sturrock, also served his apprenticeship.

Looking forwards rather than backwards, three of Patrick's brothers (and three sons of a fourth) became railway engineers, mainly in South America except his brother James, who worked on the South Eastern Railway in England. Four of his own sons likewise entered railway engineering – Robert on the North Eastern Railway (Works Manager, Gateshead), Matthew as Locomotive Superintendent of the Hull & Barnsley Railway, Patrick junior on the Great Northern, like his father (Works Manager at Doncaster) and James on the Central London Railway. Finally, his grandson Harold (son of Patrick junior) was District Engineer for the South Indian Railway up till independence in 1948. Thus in 'our' Patrick Stirling we are dealing with not only an eminent locomotive designer but the central figure in a major locomotive engineering dynasty.

Although he had a varied career before joining the Great Northern – including the Locomotive Superintendent's post on the Glasgow & South Western

Railway, which also involved starting up the GSWR locomotive works at Kilmarnock, and where he perfected his domeless boiler and provided the first all-weather cab protection for engine crews – Patrick Stirling's real rise to fame took place during his long tenure of office as Locomotive Superintendent on the GNR, from 1866 till his death in 1895. He appears to have been personally head-hunted for the job by his predecessor, Archibald Sturrock, a fellow Scot who had, like him, trained under James Stirling at East Foundry, Dundee, and who in 1852-53 had ordered some famous and very speedy 2-2-2 'singles' for the GNR from Robert Hawthorn, with the building of which it seems likely that Stirling had been personally involved.

Stirling began his duties with an extensive tour of the various GNR outstations, which resulted in recommendations that to save costs heavy repairs should all be concentrated at Doncaster Works (still being extended when he took office), which should also be the centre for all new locomotive building. On the locomotive side, he identified an urgent need for more locomotives – the existing stock was heavily overstretched – as well as a need for standardisation. This latter was a common feature of railways in the mid- to late-19th century, but had been exacerbated on the GNR because that line's somewhat impecunious nature had resulted in Sturrock having to order engines in dribs and drabs, a few at a time. His initial recommendations were for 20 new 0-6-0s for coal haulage, and a further 20 2-4-0s for heavy express work. He also initiated the policy of 'cascading' displaced main-line engines to branch-line duties instead of building special new designs for each branch – again in the interests of both standardisation and economy.

These two initial batches of new engines were ordered from outside contractors, but once extensions to Doncaster Works were sufficiently advanced, in April 1867, Stirling sought Board permission to build new locomotives there as replacements for old engines as they became due for renewal, 'at about £400 less than [their] first cost', and to fund them out of the revenue account without requiring separate permission from the Board for each build. This mandate enabled him effectively to modernise and standardise obsolete stock at will for the next six years, until August 1873, providing – as well as further coal 0-6-0s, a standard boiler and a standard wheelbase design – the 0-4-2 'little Sharps', for mixed traffic and branch-line work, eventually numbering 45 in all. These performed very well (their other GNR nickname was 'little greyhounds'), but the 2-4-0s were less successful at speed, and this led Stirling to re-examine the case for single-driver locomotives on the fastest expresses, initially 2-2-2s, whose performance he carefully logged vis-à-vis his 2-4-0s on his journeys to and from King's Cross. As he himself said, 'the single engine had the best of it', and it appears that his mind was now made up to concentrate on 'Singles' for express work.

The result was, of course, the famous 'Stirling 8-footer' 4-2-2s, among the most famous express engines of the Victorian period. But the genesis of these magnificent machines was not quite as straightforward as may have sometimes been supposed. Stirling's initial preference, it will be recalled, was for a 2-2-2, not a 4-2-2, which with its front bogie and longer boiler is a larger engine altogether. Like many locomotive engineers of his generation, Stirling was by nature conservative over such matters as size, boiler pressure and wheel arrangement; furthermore, his conservatism extended similarly to carriage stock – he hated bogie carriages in particular for their excessive weight and size, though being a tall man himself he did at least insist on coaches that were not too low to stand upright inside. But like it or not, during the 1870s trains were getting steadily heavier, and the Great Northern, whose traffic was drawn principally from its outer ends (especially on the ECJS main line to Scotland) was in increasing danger of gaining an unenviable reputation for not keeping time.

It was this problem that the famous 'No 1' 4-2-2 was intended to solve, but although always beautiful and with an iconic number, she was not in fact a success as originally built. Stirling had made her bigger – 11,200lb TE at 120psi, or 13,065 if pressed up to 140psi, in the latter case not far off the tractive effort of the first Ivatt 'Atlantics' a generation later. However, he had not made her quite big enough where it mattered – her firebox was only 5ft 6in long with 93sq ft of heating, to power her long boiler and 18in by 28in horizontal outside cylinders. She seems to have tended to run short of steam, and there was no attempt to work her nearer to London than Peterborough. It looked as if Stirling might have to return to coupled express engines ('laddies rinnin' wi' their breeks doon' as he expressed it) after all, and his Chief Draughtsman, J. C. Park, actually prepared a design for an express 4-4-0 not long after No 1 was outshopped, retaining the front end of the 'Single', but with additional boiler tubes and a much larger (6ft 2in) firebox. (Its coupled wheels were to have been only 7ft in diameter, which would have brought the tractive effort up to 14,330lb.)

But Stirling decided to try one more trick. His second 8-foot 'Single', No 8, was built with the larger firebox and other modifications incorporated into the proposed 4-4-0 design. It was an immediate success, easily working to time over the gradients between Peterborough and London, and these modifications were incorporated into the rest of the class (36 engines in all), which thenceforth became the GNR's principal main-line express locos, though coupled passenger engines still continued to be built for certain duties, including nine 6ft 7in examples in 1881. The 'Singles' lasted long enough to receive two new leases of life – one from the adoption of cast steel wheels, which increased possible maxima from 75 to 86mph, and one from being fitted from 1885 with the Midland invention of steam sanding gear – the very same design that had made the late Johnson single-drivers (qv) possible. At the other end of the spectrum of power duties, Stirling also built throughout his long career a series of increasingly powerful 0-4-4Ts for London suburban traffic – and of course continued with the succession of goods and mineral 0-6-0s already mentioned above.

It has been suggested that Stirling, towards the end of his life, became increasingly conservative in his approach to locomotive design, and increasingly out of touch with the heavier traffic requirements that were emerging. There may well be some truth in this – he certainly had to be 'pushed' by Henry Oakley into sanctioning the construction of the new heavier bogie stock for the ECJS, and on his death in 1895 his successor Ivatt (qv) found himself with something of an underpowering crisis on his hands. But, to be fair, Stirling was designing locomotives for a specific set of main lines, of whose track limitations, especially as to safe axle weights, he was only too well aware. Had he campaigned for better track, and won, his engines might well have been bigger. But bearing in mind the cash-strapped nature of the GNR during most of his tenure – even the '8-footers' were mostly smuggled in as replacement locos – he probably wouldn't have won. And he may well have known it.

William Stroudley
1833-89

Locomotive Engineer

Born	Sandford, Oxon, 6 March 1833, son of a paper-mill machinist
Education	As a boy, sources describe Stroudley variously as 'self-taught' and 'educated at a Dame School'; initial technical training was in father's print shop; then apprenticed to Birmingham tubemaker and marine engineer John Inshaw, 1847-53, with a year (1848-49) seconded to the Vulcan Foundry, followed by various pupillages under Gooch at Swindon and S. W. Johnson and Charles Sacré at Peterborough, where he rose to be shed foreman
Married	(1) 1860, name and place not recorded in sources, but wife died some time after 1866; (2) 1877, Elise (or Eliza, as in 1881 Census) Brewer
Best-known works	Locomotive Superintendent of Highland Railway, 1865-70 and London, Brighton & South Coast Railway, 1870-89; introduced snowploughs on HR; completely rebuilt LBSCR's Brighton Works, and standardised to just five locomotive types, most famous being 'Terrier' 0-6-0Ts for suburban and branch work, and 'Gladstone' 0-4-2s for express haulage
Honours	Gold Medals in Paris 1878 Exhibition (for 'Terrier' design) and 1889

	Exhibition (for 'Gladstone' design); George Stephenson Medal, Inst of Mechanical Engineers, and Telford Premium, Inst of Civil Engineers (both 1884)
Died	Grand Hotel, St Lazare, Paris, 20 December 1889 (of pneumonia contracted while supervising tests of the 1889 prize-winning loco on PLM line)
Buried	Extramural Cemetery, Lewes Road, Brighton, Christmas Eve 1889, with major public funeral

William Stroudley can be seen as in many ways the archetypal mid-Victorian railway engineer. He was born of relatively humble parentage, just a little before the actual accession of Queen Victoria, and his initial training, at a definitely craftsman level (he has sometimes been called 'the craftsman of steam') was a good deal wider than simply locomotive engineering matters and eminently practical – he was shed foreman at Peterborough in the mid-1850s, for example. Both his Locomotive Superintendent posts were for railways that were permanently short of cash (a fairly common problem after the collapse of the 'railway mania') and on both he found himself faced with a rag-tag of expensive and semi-obsolete locomotives in urgent need of standardisation – features that could equally well be paralleled in the careers of Ramsbottom, Kirtley, Stirling and Dean (even Webb on the mighty LNWR had to deliver his services 'at minimum cost'). Again, like many of those just named, he is best remembered for a few key locomotive types – in his case the 'Terrier' 0-6-0Ts, with a competence out of all proportion to their diminutive size, and the spectacular and prize-winning 'Gladstone' 0-4-2 express engines in particular.

216

Stroudley was also in many ways an archetypal Victorian Locomotive Superintendent in his personal attitudes and staff relations. Like several of his contemporaries, he realised early on that the only way to achieve either standardisation or cost efficiency was for the railways to build their own locomotives at their own works, instead of ordering them from outside builders, and on the LBSCR he rebuilt Brighton Works extensively with that in mind. By temperament and early upbringing he was a stern disciplinarian – an aspect of his character probably fostered still further by studying, if only briefly, under Daniel Gooch – but he also had a paternalistic belief in earning his subordinates' respect, allocating every one of 'his' locomotives to its own crew, with their name and cumulative mileage inscribed in the cabs; and the latter were more than usually comfortable for the period (possibly a legacy of his Scottish experience – Patrick Stirling made somewhat similar provision).

Stroudley personalised each engine (except for the Class 'C' 0-6-0 goods locos) with its own name, often linking it to a station on the Brighton system. The engines were painted a splendidly deep gamboge, which he called 'Stroudley's improved engine green'. The fact that he was colour-blind may have had something to do with the misnomer (though the colour originated on the Highland, where the original engines were green). Nonetheless, the effect was both spectacular and motivating. Stroudley expected their proud crews to keep them in sparkling condition – and by and large they did. 'Surprise' visits to New Cross Shed (in fact, pretty well regularly after each of his weekly meetings with his Board) ensured that morale (and sparkle) was kept up to scratch.

In some ways, however, Stroudley was the very antithesis of the typical Victorian locomotive engineer. His concern for crew comfort in his cab designs has already been mentioned: this was not unique to him, as remarked, but it contrasts vividly with, for example, the bare spectacle sheets often provided by his near contemporary, Matthew Kirtley. More important, however, are some of the technical differences that set him aside from his contemporaries, even though he certainly believed with them in creating locomotives that were beautiful as well as useful.

To begin with, he had little or no truck with the then current express engine dictum that large driving wheels, on single-wheelers for example, were best powered by large cylinders fed by a relatively small boiler and firebox (a dictum that even tripped up the great Patrick Stirling (qv) on the first of his '8-footers'). Stroudley's 'singles', typified by No 151 *Grosvenor*, had big driving wheels and big cylinders – but also a generous boiler and a large firebox – as a result, they virtually never ran short of steam. Next, in a period that 'havered' greatly over train braking systems and, if anything, tended to prefer the steam brake, Stroudley stuck doggedly, after trials of both systems (again on *Grosvenor*) to the Westinghouse brake, persuading his Board in late 1877 to sanction the conversion of 50 locos and 500 carriages to the Westinghouse system. Furthermore, he disliked injectors (preferring feedwater heating), and despite the fact that almost everybody else seemed to be at least trying it experimentally, would have nothing to do with compounding.

Stroudley's biggest difference from his contemporaries, however, lay in his belief that front-coupled drivers were preferable to a front bogie. The received wisdom of the time was that leading bogies 'laid down the track' for the drivers that followed them. Stroudley by contrast believed passionately that 'large leading wheels ... [cause] less disturbance than small ones'. To demonstrate it, he built his 'D' Class 0-4-2Ts for fast suburban work, and when they proved highly successful, he rammed the point home with his prize-winning 'Gladstone' Class of 0-4-2 express tender engines of 1882 onwards. These engines were amazingly successful, despite their 6ft 6in leading coupled wheels, though we now know that this was primarily because of inspired springing arrangements on the drivers rather than Stroudley's maxim about large front wheels being correct – they had coil springs on the second (driving) axle but leaf springs, which are less flexible, on the leading coupled axle. Thus, although spectacular, the 'Gladstones' were something of a dead-end in design terms. And though at the end of his life Stroudley was considering a larger and longer 2-4-2 express engine (and companion 2-4-2T), when his successor R. J. Billinton wanted a larger express locomotive, he opted for the more usual wheel arrangement of 4-4-0.

It has been suggested that, had he lived longer, Stroudley's Board would have become somewhat disenchanted with him, largely because, though always economical, he was never quite as economical as they hoped he would be. But in the event, he died before any incipient disenchantment could surface. While attending trials of his 1889 Paris Exhibition prize-winning 'Gladstone' Class exhibit *Edward Blount* on the PLM line, he caught a chill that rapidly turned into pneumonia, and he died in Paris on 20 December 1889, aged 56. His body was shipped back to Brighton for a civic burial on Christmas Eve, with a half-mile funeral procession that included 74 marine officers and seamen, 1,600 men from Brighton Works marching four abreast, and, as author Tom Middlemass puts it, 'innumerable private carriages'. He was laid to rest in Brighton's oldest cemetery, the somewhat quaintly named Extramural Cemetery on Lewes Road.

Gilbert Szlumper
1884-1969
Railway Manager

Born	Kew, 18 April 1884, son of A. W. Szlumper, Chief Engineer of LSWR
Education	King's College School, Wimbledon; King's College London; engineering pupillage under Jacomb Hood in his father's department, 1902-05
Married	Jennie Margaret Sidber, Aldershot, 1913
Best-known works	Planning and initiation of major Southampton Docks extension; completion of Southern Railway electrification scheme
Honours	CBE, 1925; Territorial Army Officer, 1908, rising to Major-General, 1939; Lieutenant of City of London; Légion D'Honneur; Knight of St John; Commander, Order of Leopold
Died	18 Cranmer Court, London SW3, 19 July 1969
Buried	Not known

Although the first ten years of his railway career were in engineering, for almost a quarter of a century (1913-37) Gilbert Szlumper (the 'z' is silent) was Sir Herbert Walker's (qv) right-hand man, first on the LSWR and then the Southern. On both lines he served under him as Assistant General Manager, responsible for implementing many of his chief's major projects, including the major extensions to Southampton Docks and much of the large-scale Southern electrification. (Tasks of this size were something of a family speciality: his father had been in charge of the other great LSWR/SR project, the rebuilding and modernisation of Waterloo Station.) He has been described as 'tireless', 'a clear and forward thinker' and 'quietly efficient': certainly he seems to have had – in common with several of the great railwaymen of earlier times, Brunel for example – an almost infinite capacity for rising early and working continuously and extremely hard. Although a number of the accounts of the Southern between the two wars tend to down-play him in favour of his chief Sir Herbert Walker (whose salary, incidentally, was 2½ times greater), it seems unlikely that the more practical aspects of Walker's success would have been possible without him.

Szlumper took over from Walker as General Manager of the Southern in 1937, and appears to have intended to complete those areas of the massive electrification programme – namely the Kent Coast and the Bournemouth/Weymouth lines – that at that point remained steam-hauled. He also seems to have envisaged a future where the railway worked ever more closely with road transport, cutting out the need in particular for uneconomic, labour-intensive, frequent rural stations and goods depots. Unfortunately the coming of the Second World War put the first of those objectives on indefinite hold (it was later, of course, completed under British Railways auspices), while the same cause meant that the second, road/rail integrated services, barely had time to become more than a conceptual position.

Instead, Szlumper's military past caught up with him. He had been a Territorial officer since 1908, and had acted as Secretary to the Railway Executive Committee during the First World War. In 1939, now a Major-General (TA), the War Office requested his release on loan from the Southern to become Director-General of Transportation, a job that, among other things, involved overseeing the incredible logistic feat of supplying railway – especially Southern Railway –

support for the Dunkirk evacuation, averaging one Dunkirk train every 15 minutes across the evacuation period. In 1942 he formally retired from the Southern Railway to become Director-General of the Ministry of Supply (a key civil service post under the War Cabinet), and Sir Eustace Missenden replaced him as General Manager from then until Nationalisation. He died in London in 1969.

Edward Thompson
1881-1954

Locomotive Engineer

Born	Marlborough, 25 June 1881
Education	St David's School, Reigate; Marlborough School; Pembroke College, Cambridge (BA 1902)
Married	Edith Gwendolen Raven (daughter of NER CME Vincent Raven), 1913
Best-known works	Under Gresley, rebuilding ex-GER Holden 'B12' 4-6-0s and 'D16' 4-4-0s; post-Gresley, designed 'B1' ('Antelope') Class 4-6-0s, 'A2' Class 'Pacifics' (including rebuilds from Gresley 'P2' Class 2-8-2s), 'K1' 2-6-0s and 'L1' 2-6-4Ts, 'O1' 2-8-0s (nominally rebuilds of Robinson 'O4s') and 'B2' 4-6-0s (Gresley 'B17s' rebuilt with 'B1' boilers and cylinders)
Honours	Twice mentioned in despatches, First World War; OBE
Died	Brymbo, Wrexham, 15 July 1954
Buried	Not known

Edward Thompson was somewhat unusual for a British locomotive engineer. To begin with, he possessed a Cambridge degree, and second, he possessed wide experience outside the railway industry before being appointed as the Great Northern Railway's Carriage & Wagon Superintendent in 1912, exactly one year after Gresley took over as CME. At the formation of the LNER, he became Area Workshops Manager, moving during the 1930s to be Mechanical Engineer at Stratford, during which period he did the major work on the rebuilding (nominally by Gresley) of the Holden 'B12' 4-6-0s and 'D16' 4-4-0s, two pre-First World War classes that needed to be updated and retained for use on the lightly railed Great Eastern section until the arrival of Gresley's 'B17' 'Sandringham' Class in 1928-37. The 'B12/3' rebuilds, as they were known, though less attractive than the Holden Belpaire originals by virtue of their round-topped boilers, were particularly successful, and were subsequently used in a variety of other sections. Indeed, the sole surviving 'B12', currently the star of the North Norfolk Railway, is a Gresley/Thompson rebuild. Thompson later moved again, to be Mechanical Engineer Doncaster at the time of Gresley's death in 1941.

Gresley never had a nominated successor: the nearest person would have been Oliver Bulleid, but he had left to succeed Maunsell on the Southern in 1937. However, Thompson was the most senior of the various Divisional Mechanical Engineers, he had a proven track record at Stratford, he was already physically at Doncaster, and the middle of a war is no time to attempt to head-hunt top talent (unless you are the War Office). The LNER Board accordingly appointed him, despite the fact that he was already 60, and so could only expect to serve for five years (which indeed is precisely what he did).

Thompson took over at a time when the war demands on the railways were at their highest. The workshops were making everything from tank traps to aircraft components – everything, it sometimes seemed, except railway engines! Locomotive overhaul and repair, as well as new production, was cut as near the bone as could be managed (though clearly some repair as well as some production was still being undertaken). Working with depleted manpower, individual locomotives were being required to haul immensely heavy trains over air-raid-damaged track.

Accordingly, the simplest and most robust construction was essential, with maximum accessibility for quick repair and as long a life as possible between repairs. Two cylinders were infinitely preferable to three (except where power demanded three); conjugated valve gear, which was expensive and difficult to maintain, was to be eschewed; standard classes with interchangeable parts were a near essential, as distinct from Gresley's 'horses for courses' design policy; and Bulleid's beautiful aerofoil valances on the Gresley 'A4' 'streaks' were, if not actually anathema, something akin to the work of the Devil. War had shattered design continuity in more ways than one.

Thus, although much has been said about Thompson's anti-Gresley attitudes, and possible personal animosity between the two men, it was actually the imperatives of trying to run a railway in wartime (and during the post-war austerity that followed) that dictated Thompson's radical departures from Gresley's key practices. His accompanying dissolution of the Gresley design team and replacement by men of his own can likewise be rationally explained: if you are going to have to implement a radical change in design policy, it is better not to ask those emotionally associated with the old régime to carry it out. Nevertheless, there is no doubt that Thompson was personally opposed to certain aspects of Gresley's design practice – conjugated valve gear and 'horses for courses' small-class designs in particular – and would have been likely to 'ditch' these whether a war had existed or not. (It is of course always possible that some inkling of this had already reached the Board when they decided to appoint him. Given the wartime circumstances it would actually have made him an even more appropriate man for the job.)

Thompson's locomotive policy, then, was to initiate

a relatively small range of standard classes, of robust construction and easy accessibility, with as many standard interchangeable parts as possible, to include both rebuildings and new designs. In effect, he could be said to have been doing a Churchward (or a Stanier) on the LNER's locomotive stock. He estimated that around 1,000 new locomotives, together with rebuildings where relevant, would be needed to complete a post-war standard locomotive series. Although he retired before more than the initial stages had been completed, the final total of Thompson and Peppercorn locomotives (Peppercorn was his successor) reached 952, suggesting that his strategic vision was remarkably accurate – though, to be fair, this did also include 275 ex-WD locos of Riddles (qv) design.

The key locomotive design in Thompson's standardisation plan, and the one produced in most numbers, was the 'B1' or 'Antelope' Class mixed traffic 4-6-0. This had a boiler based on Gresley's 'B17' 'Sandringhams', but with higher pressure, 'K2' cylinders and 6ft 2in coupled wheels. From it was derived a new standard 'O1' Class 2-8-0, using the same boiler and cylinders, but the frames and wheel centres of the old Great Central 'O4s' – the highly successful standard freight locomotives of the First World War, many subsequently rebuilt by Gresley. The same front end (though with cut-away footplating) and cylinders, plus a smaller version of the boiler, when grafted on to the existing 'K4' 2-6-0 chassis and wheels, likewise produced Thompson's standard 'K1' 2-6-0 (which went on being built till 1950), and an all-new tank engine version, the 'L1' 2-6-4T, was designed for short-distance mixed traffic work (though the 'L1s' were not in fact particularly brilliant engines). Finally, a version of the Gresley 'V2', but with a front bogie, a redesigned boiler and cylinders with Walschaerts instead of conjugated valve gear, designated Class 'A2/1', formed the basis of the Thompson/Peppercorn 'A2' and 'A1' 'Pacific' classes – 6ft 2in and 6ft 8in 4-6-2 express engines respectively.

This brief description demonstrates, among other things, that Thompson was in fact less dismissive of the Gresley inheritance than has sometimes been supposed, in particular in his use of the 'B17' boiler and the rebuilt 'O4' and 'K4' chassis outlines. However, some of his other changes to Gresley's designs were a good deal less felicitous, and do smack somewhat of 'deGresleyfication' for its own sake. Particular examples of this are the conversion of the famous 'P2' Class passenger 2-8-2s into another batch of the prototype 'A2' 4-6-2s (with acute loss of the adhesion that was so essential on the routes for which they were originally designed), and the excessively expensive rebuilding of ten 'B17s' into an all but new two-cylinder 'B2' Class with entirely new cylinders and valve gear and a 'B1' boiler. It is on these two examples, in fact, that the belief of Thompson's personal opposition to all things Gresley – as we have seen, not quite so true as it might at first appear – is usually founded.

Thompson retired to Westgate-on-Sea, Kent, in June 1946, under the LNER's 'age 65' rule, and Peppercorn succeeded him for what was left of the LNER's independent life, as we have seen largely maintaining his predecessor's locomotive policies. Thompson died just over eight years later, in July 1954, in Wales.

Richard Trevithick
1771-1833

Early Steam Engineer

Born	Carn Brea, Camborne, Cornwall, 13 April 1771
Education	Initially at the local school at Camborne, then from slightly before age 15 (1786) in the Trevithick family's mining business (it would appear employed on a variety of tasks rather than as a formal apprentice)
Married	Jane Harvey, St Erth's Parish Church, 7 November 1797
Best-known works	Originated double-acting high-pressure steam engine; built earliest steam locomotives for both rail and road, including first loco (*Catch-me-who-can*) with direct drive from cylinders to wheels
Honours	No formal honours during his lifetime
Died	The Bull, Dartford, 22 April 1833
Buried	Dartford Church (in churchyard, at north end – grave now apparently lost)

The son of a Cornish mine manager and agent, Richard Trevithick participated from an early age in the tin-mining fraternity's efforts to improve the stationary mining engine (and incidentally evade Watt's patent monopoly) by harnessing high-pressure steam (at least in terms of the pressures then obtaining). In 1800 he built a double-acting high-pressure engine with crank, which became the basis for his world-famous 'Cornish engine', the standard early-19th-century stationary engine for mining, pumping or incline haulage.

Drawn to the possibilities of other uses for steam engines than stationary pumping or haulage, he next began experimenting with models for a self-propelled steam road carriage, and built three in 1801-03, running in Camborne, London and Coalbrookdale respectively. However, the poor condition of turn-of-the-19th-century roads meant that these applications were not practical. In 1804, for a wager, he built a steam railway locomotive with flywheel and 'trombone' slide drive (capable also of being disassembled and used for stationary work) for the Pen-y-Darren Tramroad in South Wales; the locomotive was successful in hauling a 10-ton load, though there were problems with cast-iron plate rails breaking beneath it. He built a second beam locomotive for Wylam Colliery, but the state of that line's wooden track made it impossible to use. Nevertheless, its presence there assisted William Hedley and Timothy Hackworth (qv) in their development of further steam locomotives, including some with features copied by George Stephenson (qv). Trevithick's third steam locomotive (1808, for public display near Euston) was *Catch-me-who-can*, the first loco to have direct drive from cylinders to wheels and hence the direct ancestor of all modern railway locos.

Beside the direct drive, Trevithick's other contributions to basic steam locomotive technology included the concept of adhesion of smooth wheels on smooth rails, the return-flue boiler, the blast-pipe, and coupled wheels. Other engineering activities (relatively unsuccessful) included a steam dredger for the Thames and a brick tunnel under that river, and work on a threshing engine, paddle steamers and a screw propeller – in essence, anything that could be operated by what he called 'strong (ie high-pressure) steam', eventually up to the then unprecedented figure of 150psi.

One of the reasons for Trevithick's relative lack of sustained business success (apart from in the field of the 'Cornish engine'), despite his well-recognised engineering brilliance, was his tendency to combine a talent for innovation, as evidenced by the range of designs and proposals just listed, with a restless desire to be on to the next innovative project – and a somewhat unruly temper (evident from his schooldays onwards). Politically a Liberal, towards the end of his life he became involved in a number of mining ventures in revolutionary South America, and eventually died back in England but penniless (though not strictly a pauper – his funeral expenses were borne by selling his gold watch). His son Francis, however, who had inherited his father's engineering genius without his predilection for constantly moving to new schemes, went on to become the first Locomotive Superintendent of the LNWR.

Henry Villard
1835-1900

Journalist, Financier and Railway Manager

Born	Heinrich Hilgard in Speyer, Bavaria, 1835
Education	Zweibrucken, Speyer and Pfalzburg gymnasia during 1840s (his father moved him from school to school to attempt to keep him clear of revolutionary political influences); emigrated to USA in 1853, aged 18, against his father's wishes, assuming his English name while on the boat
Married	Helen Frances ('Fanny') Garrison, daughter of anti-slavery crusader and newspaper publisher William Lloyd Garrison, Boston, 3 January 1866
Best-known works	Procured German bank and shareholder funding for various US railroads; as President of Northern Pacific (and majority shareholder) from 1881, completed transcontinental line, built feeder branches, restructured management, introduced emigrant sleepers and dining-cars
Honours	Personal friend of President Lincoln
Died	Thorwood Park, Dobbs Ferry, New York, 12 November 1900
Buried	Sleepy Hollow Cemetery, in family plot

O f all the 'famous railwaymen' featured in this book, the career of the German-American Henry Villard (born Heinrich Hilgard) in actual top railway management must be reckoned as one of the shortest – his Presidency of the Northern Pacific lasted slightly under three years. But during that time he not only completed what had been an ailing and almost bankrupt road, but established new and lasting management structures for transcontinental operation, carried through a 'comfort revolution' every bit as radical as that pioneered by James Allport (qv) in Britain, and established once and for all the dining-car as a major competitive marketing tool on long-haul US runs west of Chicago in the face of an 'anti-diner' cartel formed by all the other transcontinental providers.

Villard was the precocious and liberal son of a conservative German lawyer who emigrated to the USA at the age of 18 in the wake of the failure of the 1848 revolution, changing his name on the boat, possibly to escape connection with his family's conservative reputation. Arriving in the USA virtually penniless, he wrote articles for a German-language US newspaper and taught the language, while learning English sufficiently proficiently to read Law at Peoria College before becoming a political reporter, a war correspondent during the US Civil War, and a personal friend of Abraham Lincoln.

During recuperation from a bout of ill-health in Wiesbaden, back in Germany in 1871, Villard became interested in the US bonds and securities market (German bondholders had financed much of the early US railway boom). Subsequently, during the US financial crisis of 1873, bankers in Berlin, Frankfurt and Heidelberg persuaded him to join financial committees formed to protect German investment interests as a repayments negotiator. This led across the next eight years to his first becoming President of the Oregon & California RR, then, in 1881, of the O&C's major competitor along the Columbia River, the Northern Pacific.

When Villard took over the Northern Pacific, transcontinental construction had virtually halted, the company's contract with Pullman for passenger cars had been cancelled, and the company's finances were in shocking disarray. Villard injected $5 million of capital (with a further $5 million in reserve) to further transcontinental completion and a feeder branch-line network from a 'blind fund' specially established for the purpose, and established a scheme of management by function across the entire line (the other transcontinental roads managed each of their main sections separately). He also renegotiated contracts with Pullman to provide upgraded day- and sleeping-car comfort, and made specific provision for low-cost 'emigrant sleepers' able to offer affordable transport for immigrants from Europe to the farming states that the NP was designed to open up.

Finally, and perhaps most importantly, he pushed through, against some opposition from existing NP managers, a scheme for the purchase and operation of dining-cars on the NP's main transcontinental route right from the very start, beginning with the VIP trains to and from the 'last spike' ceremony of 22 August 1883. These cars were not intended as an additional profit stream in themselves: their purpose was to induce transcontinental passengers to leave the competing 'cartel railroads' (the Union Pacific, Burlington and Santa Fé), which had agreed to provide only refreshment halts west of Kansas City, and to transfer their allegiance to the NP instead.

The combined strategies, including the dining-car operations, were successful in this objective. By 1891 the Northern Pacific was carrying 45% of all westbound transcontinental passengers and almost 40% of all eastbound, passenger revenues had tripled, and all the competing 'cartel lines' were forced to run dining-cars of their own. The vindication had come too late for Villard's personal career, however, contractors' construction costs on the completion of the main transcontinental line had over-run by $14 million, well above Villard's personal reserve fund, and in the ensuing financial scandal he was forced to resign his Presidency on 4 January 1884 – a mere four months after the great opening ceremony. However, he subsequently managed to 'repair his fortunes' (*New York Times* obituary) back in Germany, and, after paying off outstanding debts in record time, returned to the Northern Pacific as Chairman of the re-formed Board of Directors from 1888 to 1898, though this time without Presidential executive power. He died in 1900, at his summer home in Dobbs Ferry, New York.

Herbert Walker
1868-1949

Railway Manager

Born	Paddington, 6 May1868, only child of Dr Stephen Walker MRCS
Education	North London Collegiate School and St Francis Xavier College, Bruges
Married	(1) Ethel Louisa Griffith, Llanwrst, 1895 (d 1909); (2) Lorina Elizabeth Shilds (née Webb), 1910
Best-known works	General Manager, LSWR, 1912-22, and Southern Railway, 1923-37; Director of SR from 1937; Chairman, Railway Executive Committee, during Second World War; responsible for rebuilding of Waterloo station, development of Southampton Port, third-rail electrification of suburban services, and Brighton/Portsmouth main lines; introduction of 'clock-face' timetabling; appointed (Sir) John Elliot as first railway PR officer; backed Dalziel's introduction of 'Golden Arrow' service and Pullman catering
Honours	Knighthood, 1915; Commander, Légion D'Honneur; Lieutenant of City of London; memorial plaque on Waterloo Station
Died	London, 29 September 1949
Buried	Cremated at Golders Green Crematorium, London

Herbert Walker joined the LNWR in 1885, aged 17, when a family financial crisis cut short his projected training for a career in medicine, rising eventually to be Outdoor Goods Manager, Southern Area, though the title did not actually do justice to the range of activities with which he was concerned, in particular his general reform of the North London Railway (1909). In 1911 he was head-hunted to become General Manager of the LSWR at the comparatively early age of 43. During the First World War he became Chairman of the Railway Executive Committee, for which he was knighted in 1915. On the formation of the Southern Railway in 1923, he first held joint General Managership with the GMs of the other two major constituents, but pressures from the LSWR's former Chairman, together with offers from the LMS to 'defect' to them, resulted in his becoming sole General Manager of the Southern in 1924. He remained in this post till 1937, when he retired, to be subsequently elected to the Board of Directors, a position in which he continued till his death in 1949.

Apart from the brief hiatus in 1923, Sir Herbert Walker was thus in charge of the LSWR and subsequently its larger progeny the Southern for a continuous quarter of a century, and in many ways his major activities carried on throughout that period with the main goals unchanged. Thus he began his term of office on the LSWR with the major rebuilding of the old (and chaotic) Waterloo Station. This had been under way since 1900 and was complete by 1921, but Walker's drive for modernity in station buildings continued throughout the 1920s and '30s, leading to a range of architecturally noteworthy 'art deco' stations including Wimbledon (1929), Surbiton (1935) and Malden Manor.

Other of Walker's major reforms likewise started with the LSWR and continued throughout his Southern days. The most far-reaching was the railway's massive third-rail electrification project, begun on the LSWR suburban lines, then extended at the Grouping to other suburban lines, and finally – for Sir Herbert's day – to the main lines to Brighton, Hastings, Eastbourne, Seaford and Portsmouth. The system used was the LSWR's third-rail system – not (or not merely) from personal pride on Walker's part, but because by 1923 it was already the largest Southern system, so it made economic sense for any others to change. Electrification brought cleaner trains (from 1933, cleaned by carriage-cleaning machines, saving substantial labour costs) and faster timings. It also brought a much more intensive service, with up to three electric services for every former steam service – essential where the London suburban market was concerned. Additionally, third-rail was much cheaper to install than an overhead system, and suburban EMU stock could readily be converted from existing steam carriages, likewise at low cost. Walker's plans were large, but his grip on financial control was tight.

Another major innovation – not actually original to Walker, but not used to anywhere near the extent before him – was fixed-interval or 'clock-face' train timetabling, where trains to a given destination depart regularly so many times an hour at certain minutes past each hour. This is so common a practice today that one forgets that on most railways, and even on the LSWR up until 1915, both suburban and long-distance services commonly ran at irregular intervals and timings, making consulting *Bradshaw* a task demanding the intellect of a Jeeves, if not an Einstein. Walker would have none of it – he wanted consistent intervals and times that one could remember. Thus a service of four trains an hour need not necessarily be exactly on the quarter-hour – it could be on the hour and 10, 30 and 40 minutes past, but not, say, 3, 14, 42 and 59 minutes past, and the chosen pattern would have to be repeated each hour throughout the main part of the day. Similarly, if West of England main-line services were going to leave on the hour, then they should do so every hour, or every other hour, depending on service frequency.

This innovation had two prime causes. It made for easier timetabling, and it was of course particularly suited to the increased frequency of the electric suburban services. It also made train times easier to remember, and a passenger who can easily remember a train time is all the more likely to decide to catch it. Keeping the railway in the public mind was also the object of a fourth of Walker's innovations, the hiring of John Elliot (later Sir John) from Fleet Street in 1925 to be the first UK railway public relations chief. A whole raft of measures followed under Elliot: a notable poster campaign, the introduction of the 'Atlantic Coast Express' and the naming of the 'King Arthurs', and a publication addressed to 'the man who lives in London', outlining how convenient Southern electrics made it to live in Surrey or Kent, and how easy it was to buy or build a house there.

Indeed, all these various innovations of Walker's can be seen to have had a similar objective – to improve services in such a way as to create additional custom. Walker was highly aware of the extent to which in the 1920s a combination of road transport competition and depression economics was eroding the railways' public transport near-monopoly, creating a need to attract custom and foster niche markets. Clean, modern, well-lit stations and clean, fast trains would attract that additional custom. Suburban electrification – together with appropriate PR activity – ensured that custom was increasingly middle-class rather than working-class commuters, tapping a market hitherto almost entirely restricted to Selbie's (qv) 'Metroland'. Such a market, even in the Depression years, would have more leisure and more disposable income than the old-fashioned closer-in working-class commuters, and electrification to Brighton and Hastings, again with suitable PR campaigns and discount day, weekend or monthly return fares, helped ensure that the Southern's other major niche market – holidaymakers – was likewise targeted, including travel by those same commuters in their spare time.

All this would without doubt qualify Sir Herbert Walker as one of the great railway managers of the 20th century, but the activity of his that will probably come first to mind where rail enthusiasts are concerned was his targeting of yet another niche market – the Pullman car user – jointly with Davison Dalziel (qv) and his successors. The already extant 'Southern Belle' was electrified as the 'Brighton Belle' in 1933 (and introduced a new concept – the luxury all-Pullman commuter train); the 'Golden Arrow', linking London and Paris, was introduced in 1929; the 'Bournemouth Belle' (which also served Southampton and, on weekdays, stations beyond Bournemouth to Weymouth) followed in 1931; and the 'Night Ferry', with its sleeping-cars on board, slipped back and forth across the Channel. Indeed, Sir Herbert was acutely aware of the Southern's unique position as an overseas gateway; he not only invested in cross-Channel services, but also in developing Southampton Docks as an ocean terminal, inveigling Cunard away from Liverpool. This gave even more scope for Pullman workings on the boat trains to serve the *Queen Mary* (from 1936 onwards), and of course even more revenue for the company.

Sir Herbert Walker retired as General Manager of the Southern in 1937, at the age of 69, but continued as a Director till his death in 1949, aged 81.

Edward Watkin
1819-1901

Entrepreneur and Railway Manager

Born	Salford, Manchester, 26 September 1819, son of Absalom Watkin, cotton merchant
Education	Details unknown (no records survive and even his own memoirs and speeches do not mention it), but he was working for his father by age 15
Married	(1) Mary Briggs Mellor, Oldham Parish Church, 3 September 1845 (d 1888); (2) Ann Ingram (née Little), widow of Herbert Ingram, founder of Illustrated London News, St George's Hanover Square, London, 6 April 1892
Best-known works	General Manager of MSLR, 1854-62, and Chairman, 1864-94; also Chairman of SER, 1866-94, and Metropolitan Railway, 1872-94; driving force behind MSLR (later Great Central) London Extension, intended with his Channel Tunnel project to create a main line from Manchester via London to Paris
Honours	Knighthood, 1868 (for work on Canadian Federation); baronetcy, 1880; Knight of Order of Redeemer, Greece, and of Order of Leopold, Belgium; MP for Great Yarmouth, 1857-58, Stockport, 1864-68, and Hythe, 1874-95; High Sheriff of Cheshire, 1874; Freeman of Hythe, 1886

Died	Rose Hill (family home built by his father but greatly extended by his first wife), Northenden, Cheshire, 13 April 1901
Buried	St Wilfrid's Church, Northenden (where there is also a memorial to him)

At the heart of any assessment of Edward Watkin there lies a mystery and a paradox. His career in railway management spanned half a century, yet he preferred to describe himself as 'a politician with railway interests'. At the height of his power, he was for more than 20 years (1872-94) probably the best-known railway management figure in Britain, rivalling George Hudson a generation earlier – yet he never controlled a first-rank line, and his companies paid only average dividends. In his dealings with other chairmen he was combative and bullying, yet among his own staff he inspired fierce loyalty. His plans for the Great Central's London Extension and onward via the Channel Tunnel to link Manchester with Paris were breathtaking in scope but economic nonsense: the route of the London Extension in particular served no new market whatsoever.

Politically he started life as a Manchester Radical and a supporter of the Operatives' Anti-Corn Law Association, yet he bought votes at the Great Yarmouth election, and his dealings with his own railway staff, though generally kindly, were paternalistic in the extreme (he refused to talk with trades union leaders, for example, if they were not members of his own staff). He was a voluminous correspondent, yet about some key areas of his life, such as his education, we know so little that it almost seems he was seeking to hide something. He was first knighted then ennobled by Queen Victoria for services to international politics, yet a number of his

241

contemporaries found him 'not quite a gentleman'. As we shall see, it is possibly this last statement that holds the key both to his career and to his 'workaholic', driven character.

Watkin seems from an early age to have felt himself an outsider. As noted above, we have no record of his education, but by the age of 15 he was working in his father Absalom Watkin's relatively modest cotton merchant's business. It appears that his father was throughout this period highly critical both of his mother for not maintaining a sufficiently 'middle class' household, and of Edward himself for paying attention to political affairs to the detriment of the business as he saw it – even though Absalom as a young man had done the very same thing. His mother in turn apparently was wont to accuse his father of extra-marital affairs – Hodgkins (see Bibliography) suggests that these accusations were unfair, but nevertheless the home and work atmosphere engendered by them would seem to have left Edward feeling both personally and socially insecure.

The final straw seems to have come when he sought in 1845 to marry Mary Mellor, the daughter of an Oldham manufacturer of considerable inherited wealth, and herself a woman of very substantial business acumen. By birth both his social and financial superior, to support her in the manner the young couple both desired he clearly needed a source of income considerably beyond what his by now more than a little uneasy role in the Watkin cotton business provided. He found it, it would seem, almost by accident, in railway rather than mercantile management, when a radical political colleague (possibly Edward Tootal) recommended him as an effective organiser to the Trent Valley Railway, which appointed him as Secretary.

The Trent Valley was only a tiny line, but it happened that the mighty LNWR was being formed at almost exactly that time, and the Trent Valley was among the minor lines gobbled up in the 1846 amalgamation that produced it. Mark Huish, the LNWR's first General Manager (and a past master of the slightly bullying, slightly devious diplomacy that was later to become Watkin's hallmark), took him under his wing, possibly again on Tootal's recommendation (Tootal was also a Director of LNWR). Watkin worked for the LNWR as Huish's assistant, specialising in detailed accounting and 'trouble-shooting', until 1854, when he was head-hunted by the MSLR, which was at the time over-capitalised and in a poor financial state, to take over as its General Manager and restore it to an even financial keel.

He remained the MSLR's General Manager until 1862, when he resigned in protest at actions taken in his absence in Canada when he was working as President of the Grand Trunk Railway, which he had also been invited to attempt to save from financial ruin. (He did indeed physically improve the Grand Trunk, and, as Queen Victoria recognised, contributed greatly thereby to the formation of the Dominion of Canada, but he himself described the attempt to reform its finances as 'futile' in a shareholders' report of 1868.) However, he returned to the MSLR in 1864 as Chairman, and followed this with chairmanships of the South Eastern (where his father-in-law was already a Director) in 1866 and the Metropolitan in 1872. In 1875 he became a Board member of the Channel Tunnel Company, though that project was eventually killed off by public opposition and military Francophobia (at one point a mob stormed his London house and broke the windows). He was also involved with the Athens & Piraeus Railway in Greece, and later (after his first wife's death) in India.

Watkin was invited to all three of his British chairmanships to restore ailing company finances, and in each case he did so, though always with average

243

rather than outstanding results. He remained Chairman of all three until his retirement in 1894 following a fairly severe stroke, which left him too debilitated to continue with such a workload. It is difficult to say precisely when his dreams of linking the MSLR directly with London and of forming a through route from Manchester to Paris took shape; Hodgkins dates the former to 1872, and the latter was presumably before the Channel Tunnel project in 1875.

The dream, however, certainly survived the demise of the Tunnel project, since under his direction the London Extension of the Great Central Railway (as the MSLR became) was laid out to continental loading gauge, and has been described as the most finely engineered line in Britain. The pity was that by the time the Bill authorising it was passed, all the genuinely remunerative routes between London and the North had been filled, and labour costs were rising, so that when it opened, five years after Watkin's retirement as Chairman (though he remained a Director till just before his death) and well over budget, it left the GCR with financial problems almost as great as those that Watkin had been imported to cure (and had cured) 45 years earlier. It would have made an ideal line for Eurostar – but economically it was redundant, and was closed as a through route in 1966.

Watkin may have envisaged a Continental through route, but he never amalgamated 'his' three companies to promote it; indeed, on the Metropolitan (in many ways the key link) he never even appointed common Directors with the other lines, apart from himself, so that after his departure rivalry between the Met and the GCR replaced co-operation. Once again, this seems characteristic of his driven, 'workaholic nature'. There is evidence in his life history of long-standing and frequent feelings of insecurity, even surfacing as a near nervous breakdown accompanied by panic attacks in 1851 – characteristically, he 'cured' himself by undertaking a fact-finding tour of US railroads – and actually leading to him being taken ill at a SER shareholders' meeting following overwork in the crucial year of 1868 already mentioned above. The one person he did seem to trust implicitly, despite his frequent absences from home, was his first wife Mary. He is said to have claimed that she 'entered into and grasped the complicated problems of [my] daily work', and certainly it was she who originated the idea of providing Provident Savings Banks for the workers in each of his three main companies, which was one of his main social advances.

Edward Watkin was also active in politics throughout his career. Despite the 'false start' in Great Yarmouth and some very odd behaviour at an early Stafford by-election, he was a major contributor to Liberal (later Liberal Unionist) affairs in Parliament, where he was a leading member of the 'Railway Interest' group of MPs in the fight against the imposition on railway land of the then punitive rating system. Following the crash of 1866, he became Chairman of the Select Committee that formulated the modern Limited Liability Company regulations, and he was one of 78 MPs who voted (in the end unsuccessfully) to extend the 1868 Reform Bill's suffrage to women. At the local level, Watkin was a leader in the campaign to promote public parks in Manchester, and to allow Manchester clerks a half-holiday on Saturdays.

Finally, to end this account with two more 'paradoxical' Watkinisms, he was also involved during his career with the New Hudson's Bay Company (which made him money) and a strange proposal to build a replica of the Eiffel Tower on the site of what is now Wembley Stadium (which didn't, and was abandoned when it reached a height of 155 feet). He attended the opening of his grand London Extension at Marylebone Station, aged 80, in a bath-chair, five years after his retirement. Two years later he was dead.

Francis Webb
1836-1906

Locomotive Engineer

Born	Tixall Rectory, Staffs, 21 May 1836, son of Rev William Webb
Education	At home till age 15, then apprenticed under Francis Trevithick at Crewe Works, LNWR
Married	Remained single, though some sources – eg Hamilton Ellis – have claimed he had an unsuccessful love affair with the daughter of LNWR Chairman Sir Richard Moon (qv)
Best-known works	Designed LNWR compound locomotives; developed cost-efficient techniques of locomotive construction and operation; pioneered use of steel in locomotive construction, radial axles, and use of telephones; proposed London-Glasgow electrification
Honours	Mayor of Crewe, 1886-87; Vice-President, Inst of Civil Engineers, 1904; JP for Cheshire
Died	Bournemouth, 4 June 1906
Buried	Wimborne Road Cemetery, Bournemouth, Grave E6 15N

After demonstrating remarkable engineering talent during his boyhood, Francis William Webb was apprenticed at Crewe under Francis Trevithick, the son of Richard Trevithick (qv) and Locomotive Superintendent of the newly formed LNWR. On completing his apprenticeship, he was retained at an increased salary, and two years later he became Chief

Draughtsman at Crewe under Trevithick's successor, Ramsbottom (qv). One of his many interests was in the manufacture and use of steel, and in 1866 he became manager of Bolton steelworks, moving back to manage Crewe steelworks in 1870, shortly before Ramsbottom's sudden resignation (over a salary dispute with Sir Richard Moon) led to Webb becoming Locomotive Superintendent in 1871.

Webb took over the locomotive (and carriage) design, construction and operation of what was at the time the largest joint stock company in the world, on which his predecessor had already begun a policy of construction standardisation and near mass-production, and at a time when public expectations of train comfort (and therefore train weight and speed) were about to increase dramatically. His remit from Moon was to provide 'the best possible equipment and services at minimum cost' (Simmons), and the fact that he went on to enjoy levels of salary far greater than that which had sparked Ramsbottom's departure indicates that the LNWR Board believed that he fulfilled that remit. Among his contributions to this policy (other than specific locomotive designs) were the increased use of steel for construction (of which more below); the development of radial-axle (and later bogie) compartment and saloon carriages with toilet facilities and offset vestibule connections (a design derived initially from Queen Victoria's pair of Royal Saloons constructed under his predecessor Ramsbottom in 1869), including the first paired kitchen-plus-dining-cars; and the introduction of the first British all-corridor through-vestibuled dining express (1893).

In the locomotive field Webb is chiefly famous (some would say notorious) for his compound locomotives, both double-single (2-2-2-0) and coupled, though they formed in fact a minority of his locomotive output by comparison with goods 0-6-0s such as the

'Cauliflowers' and 2-4-2 passenger and 0-6-2 'Coal Tanks' (and indeed some excellent simple 2-4-0 express engines). He has as a result often been portrayed as a dour, autocratic, stubborn, even stupid man, unable to admit that he was responsible for a series of bad designs and possessing such personal power that he could force them to be built. This canard, however, based on the dislike of certain elements in the technical press of the period of his particular compounding system, is far from the truth. Dour he was, and autocratic and stubborn he could certainly be, after the general fashion of high Victorian management (and any one fighting his corner against Sir Richard Moon needed both those qualities!) – but he was far from stupid, and although his personal power at Crewe was very great, like most locomotive superintendents of the time, his power to spend money without Board approval was strictly limited. The truth, as often, is rather different from the myth.

Webb's remit was to provide quality service 'at minimum cost'. Providing quality service meant catering for greatly increased train weights and speeds; minimum cost, however, meant avoiding as far as possible the associated increases in fuel costs that came with the larger engines required to do this job. One way to do this—already well attested in marine engineering – was by re-using each cylinder's-worth of steam to gain extra power – ie by compounding. Anatole Mallet had already experimented with compounds in France, and his 1879 paper to the Institution of Mechanical Engineers impressed Webb greatly. But to produce the high-pressure steam, a compounding system required a large firebox, which in turn led to the driving axles of Webb's initial 'double-singles' needing to be 10 feet apart in order to clear that firebox. Webb's studies in steel meant that he was aware that with the technology available at that point (1882) connecting rods longer than 9 feet were liable to be structurally unsafe as a result of uneven tyre wear on the wheels they joined; hence the decision to go for the 'double-single' layout, despite problems of wheel synchronisation. Fifteen years later, when advances in steel technology meant that longer connecting rods could be forged, Webb duly changed to coupled compounds.

The 'Webb compounds', as a group, were not the best of performers – but they were not as bad as is sometimes portrayed, and they certainly did achieve their primary purpose of cutting the LNWR's coal and water bills. At their worst, they were sluggish and heavy on maintenance costs, but at their best, they could run well – *Adriatic*, already five years old at the time, averaged 64mph from London to Crewe in the 'Race to the North' of 1895, and two years earlier *Greater Britain* had run for six consecutive days between Euston and Carlisle at an average speed of 47.7mph overall. And, to be fair, far from relying totally on the compounds, Webb did also continue to build his 2-4-0 simple expansion 'Precedent' Class (nominally as rebuilds of Ramsbottom's 'Newtons', but actually new engines) from 1887 to 1894.

Webb's concern with technical innovation continued throughout his working life. In 1882 he built the first dynamometer car to be used on a British railway other than the Great Western. In 1890 he patented the electric train staff, and in 1897 the electric signalling frame, and in his very last year as Locomotive Superintendent at Crewe he adopted steel-framed tenders as standard in place of the older wooden-framed ones, and modified the valve gear on his final set of compound 4-4-0s (the 'Benbows') to enable the high-pressure valves to be notched up independently while low-pressure was in full gear – a modification that H. F. Livesey claimed 'was a very successful alteration'. He also became in his later years a protagonist of the railway's use of the telephone, and –

himself an early motorist – advocated as early as 1896 the electrification of the London-Glasgow West Coast route across a 15-year period, to permit speeds of 100mph in competition with what he saw even then as the coming threat from road transport.

Webb retired from the LNWR in 1903 at the age of 67, Hamilton Ellis claims in a fit of pique caused by the announcement of George Whale as his eventual successor while he was still in office, but more probably because he knew he was already incurably ill. He died in Bournemouth in 1906, leaving large sums to charitable and civic concerns in his long-time home town of Crewe.

Ralph Wedgwood
1874-1956

Railway Manager

Born	Barlaston, Staffs, 2 March 1874 (great-grandson of potter Josiah Wedgwood)
Education	Clifton School, then 1st Class Honours Moral Sciences degree from Trinity College, Cambridge, followed by traffic apprenticeship with NER
Married	Iris Veronica Pawson, Farnley, Leeds, 1906
Best-known works	Chief General Manager, LNER, 1923-39; instituted decentralised area management, 'continuous improvement' strategy, buffet-car services, Pullman and streamlined luxury trains
Honours	CMG, 1917; CB, 1918; knighthood, 1924; baronetcy, 1942; Officer of Légion D'Honneur; Order of the Crown (Belgium)
Died	Leith Hill, Dorking, 5 September 1956
Buried	Barlaston Cemetery

Arguably along with Sir Herbert Walker one of the greatest British railway managers of the 20th century, Ralph Wedgwood joined the North Eastern Railway in 1896 as its first-ever 'traffic apprentice', armed with (of all things!) a Classics degree from Cambridge. His innate ability as a manager was reflected in a meteoric rise: Company Secretary by 1905, Chief Goods Manager by 1911, Deputy General

Manager (following First World War service as Director of Ports) in 1922, and General Manager in 1923, the year of the Grouping when the NER became part of the LNER. His obvious ability and relative youth (nearly 20 years younger than his rivals in the other constituent companies) made him the clear choice for Chief General Manager of the enlarged but financially precarious concern.

Wedgwood's management style had four great strengths: delegation, strategic planning, 'continuous improvement' (apart from Pullman (qv) he may well have been the first to use that now-fashionable term), and an ability to forge close personal relationships with his key team players – in particular William Whitelaw as Chairman and Sir Nigel Gresley as CME. Because it served areas especially prone to the effects of the Depression, the LNER was always even more strapped for cash than the other 'Big Four' companies. It was also always vulnerable to competition from improving road transport, and eventually, on its longer routes, from air transport, where the more up-market services were concerned. Wedgwood delegated considerable autonomy for everyday management to the various regional Divisions, and this largely avoided the rivalries and jealousies that so devastated the early days of the LMS. More important still, it left him and his top team free to concentrate on genuine strategic policy. His famous strategic watchword, 'continuous improvement coupled with continuous economy', encapsulated this policy, and addressed simultaneously both the key threats to the new organisation.

The effects of this management stance can be seen in a whole range of different innovations and developments. On the economy front, Wedgwood's inspection teams (the so-called 'razor gangs') probed the costs and benefits of every aspect of the line's services, whether it was a matter of rationalising depots, persuading over-manned staff to take early retirement (in the days before full pension schemes), or cutting back train services to specific days of operation to save coal on uneconomic runs. But equally, under Wedgwood top management didn't ask the rank and file to do things it wouldn't do itself. When railwaymen's wages were cut (as they were on all the companies several times during the Depression), the Board cut its salaries and fees by exactly the same percentage. And if the numbers of workers was reduced by a somewhat enhanced natural wastage, so too was the number of Directors. The policy survived Wedgwood's departure: even at Nationalisation, the final compensation payments to Directors were abrogated in order to offer the shareholders a slightly better final dividend.

Wedgwood's policies were far from being solely about economy, however. Like Walker (qv) on the Southern, he constantly strove to improve services in order to attract, grow and retain custom. The LNER did not have the dense suburban base of the Southern (apart from the ex-Great Eastern 'Jazz' services), but it did link London with a major (if recession-bedevilled) industrial heartland and a well-loved sea-coast popular with 'Wakes Week' tourists from that same heartland, and it had the long, level East Coast Main Line to Scotland. These factors gave Wedgwood, ably aided and abetted by Gresley in particular, the opportunity to develop three distinct approaches to growing the inter-war passenger market: the buffet-car tourist excursion trains, the East Coast Pullmans, and finally the record-breaking streamlined expresses of the 1930s.

The buffet-car trains – apart from the unsuccessful experiment on the old Great Central, the first of their kind in Britain – in fact owed their genesis fairly directly to Wedgwood's Cambridge origins. In the early 1930s he learned that the King's Cross-Cambridge services were being badly eroded by competition from the recently upgraded A1 road. Gresley wanted to offer a service of steam railmotors, as he was already doing on the line to Hunstanton, but Sir Ralph had a firmer grasp of what the inhabitants of his alma mater wanted, and seems to have pretty well twisted Gresley's arm to put on fast, frequent, light buffet-car services instead. He was correct: despite Gresley's initial misgivings, the undergraduates flocked to the 'beer trains' (as they nicknamed them) in droves. The weekend excursionists loved them too, and Gresley went on to build more and more buffet-cars, first for Wakes Week 'tourist excursion' stock, then to provide enhanced services on major secondary lines, such as Newcastle-Carlisle, which did not warrant a dining-car. Meanwhile, traffic on the Cambridge route thoroughly recovered.

The East Coast Pullman trains – in conjunction with Davison Dalziel (qv) – catered for the opposite end of the market. Here the problem Wedgwood needed to address was how to locate and grow the most economically remunerative market for the existing Pullman cars that the LNER had inherited from the Great Eastern. New money wasn't involved – the existing contract still had years to run – but Wedgwood and Dalziel both needed to ensure that the services operated made the maximum profit for the LNER and the Pullman Company, at a time again of increasing financial constraint because of the Depression. What was needed was a route (or routes) that combined civic pride and snob appeal with the maximum likelihood of attracting such well-heeled business clientele as still remained. Harrogate furnished the first element (subsequently extended to Edinburgh), and, after a brief unsuccessful experiment of running to Sheffield, a combination of Leeds (extended via Edinburgh to Glasgow) and an increased provision of 3rd Class Pullmans provided the second. The

'Harrogate Pullman', later the 'Queen of Scots', and her Yorkshire sisters were born. At the same time, Wedgwood upgraded the facilities and improved the timing of various leading non-Pullman expresses – most particularly the 'Flying Scotsman'.

But the tour de force for Wedgwood's 'continuous improvement' policy came from 1935 onwards with the world-beating streamlined trains 'Silver Jubilee' (1935) and 'Coronation' (1937). The initial impetus for these services seems to have been a fact-finding visit that Wedgwood and Gresley paid to Germany to sample the Hitler régime's new diesel express, the 'Fliegende Hamburger'. Neither man liked it, though they were impressed by its speed; Wedgwood is said to have commented that an 'A3' 'Pacific' hauling ordinary stock between London and Newcastle could do as well – Gresley had a go with No 2750 *Papyrus*, and Wedgwood again proved to be right. It took a mere six months and three weeks for the streamlined, steam-hauled result to enter service, burning North East coal (an important patriotic publicity coup) and bringing Newcastle within a day-return distance of London. The train was an immediate success: it loaded to 86% and stimulated a 12% rise in Newcastle-London passenger traffic overall. Wedgwood recommended two further high-speed streamliners, the 'Coronation' (London-Edinburgh) and the 'West Riding Limited' (London-Leeds); these too were successful, though the timings of the 'Coronation' were not well thought out in loading terms, and a fourth less-high-speed streamliner, the 'East Anglian', was eventually added (London-Norwich).

The publicity value of these high-speed streamlined services was central to Wedgwood's drive for 'continuous improvement', which he once defined as increasing, year on year, the number of services operated at an average of 60mph or over. But in terms of route utilisation and safety planning, operating trains at maxima regularly in excess of 90mph led the

NER (and to a lesser extent the LMS with its Coronation Scot' service) into uncharted waters. Drivers were unused to the speeds (and in some cases downright frightened by them); braking requirements meant that additional signalling block sections had to be left empty ahead of the speeding streamliners; and a fair number of the LNER's distant signals on the high-speed routes had to be repositioned further from their corresponding home signals in order to be seen in time. To be fair, Wedgwood himself did take action, in the two years between the introduction of the 'Silver Jubilee' and the 'Coronation', to order that at least some of these problems be put right, but one cannot help feeling that even his strategic mind had failed to realise quite what a new operating world he was moving his company into.

Wedgwood also served on several key Government Committees, including the Weir Committee on main-line electrification, the Indian Railways Standard Enquiry Committee (1936) and the 'Square Deal' campaign over freight traffic rates. He retired from the LNER in 1939 (and had an 'A4' 'Pacific' named after him), but continued as Chairman of the wartime Railway Executive Committee till 1941. He died in 1956.

Appendix

Engineering Apprenticeship 'Families'

It is a commonly known fact that – whether by genetic predisposition, cultural transmission, or a mixture of both – railway engineering talent, like music, often runs in families: the Drummond, Stirling and Billinton families are particularly good examples. What is perhaps a little less well known, though, is that the nature of engineering apprenticeships, especially in the earlier part of the railway age, similarly means that a sort of 'family likeness' runs through designs created by engineers that have trained under masters at particular works, whether they are connected by actual genetic families or not. Thus, for instance, we may reasonably talk about the Crewe, Horwich, Derby or Swindon design 'families'. Furthermore, these 'families' of design training are themselves related.

This Appendix attempts to set out, in the form of a series of 'family trees', how the design training of the main railway engineers covered in this book is related. I have given each 'family' a name (usually that of the Works where it originated). The name(s) of the initial engineer(s) whose influence set the 'family likeness' in motion is/are given in **bold type**. Their subsequent pupils (or pupils' pupils) covered in this book are then listed in ordinary type. Names of engineers who form an important link in this 'family tree', but are not among the 50 covered in this book, are given in *italics*. Vertical lines indicate pupillage or influence by succession (eg Johnson as successor to Kirtley, McIntosh as successor to Dugald Drummond) – horizontal lines indicate friends or colleagues.

I start, of course, with the oldest 'design family' of the lot – that of the early North East enginewrights.

THE 'GEORDIE' FAMILY

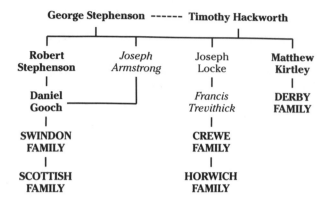

THE SWINDON FAMILY

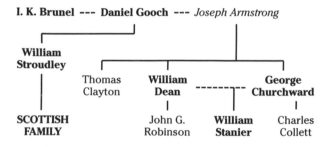

THE CREWE FAMILY

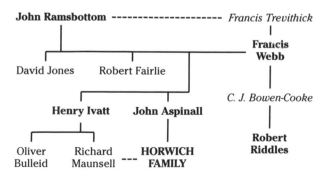

THE DERBY FAMILY

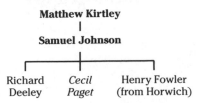

Matthew Kirtley
|
Samuel Johnson

Richard
Deeley
    Cecil
Paget
    Henry Fowler
(from Horwich)

THE HORWICH FAMILY

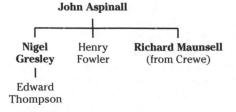

John Aspinall

Nigel
Gresley
|
Edward
Thompson
    Henry
Fowler
    Richard Maunsell
(from Crewe)

THE SCOTTISH FAMILY

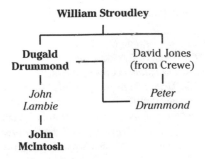

William Stroudley

Dugald
Drummond
|
John
Lambie
|
John
McIntosh
    David Jones
(from Crewe)
|
Peter
Drummond

Bibliography

ᴧn, Ian *abc British Locomotives 1944* (London, Ian Allan Publishing, 1944; new ed Hersham, 1992, rep 2001)

ᴧtkins, P 'Richard Mountford Deeley, Author and Polymath' (*Midland Record*, 20 (New Series), 2004, pp11-12)

Bagwell, P. and Lyth, P. *Transport in Britain* (London, Hambledon & London, 2002)

Bailey, B. *George Hudson: The Rise and Fall of the Railway King* (Stroud, Sutton Publishing, 1995)

Barnes, R. *Locomotives That Never Were* (London, Jane's, 1985)

Beddoes, K., Wheeler, C. and Wheeler, S. *Metro-Cammell 150 Years of Craftsmanship* (Cheltenham, Runpast Publishing, 1999)

Behrend, G. *Pullman in Europe* (London, Ian Allan, 1962)

Body, G. *Great Railway Battles* (Wadenhoe, Silver Link Publishing Ltd, 1994)

Booker, F. *The Great Western Railway, A New History* (Newton Abbot, David & Charles, 1977)

Brooks, Rev Dr E. C. *Sir Samuel Morton Peto, Bt, 1809-1889: Victorian Entrepreneur of East Anglia* (Bury St Edmunds, Bury Clerical Society, 1996)

Brooks, P. R. *Where Railways Were Born* (Wylam, Wylam PC, 1975, rev 1979)

Brown, F. A. S *From Stirling to Gresley* (Oxford, Oxford Publishing Company, 1974)

Great Northern Locomotive Engineers (London, George Allen & Unwin, 1966)

Nigel Gresley, Locomotive Engineer (London, Ian Allan Ltd, 1961)

Bryan, T. *All In A Day's Work* (Hersham, Ian Allan Publishing, 2004)

Bulleid, H. A. V. *The Aspinall Era* (London, Ian Allan Ltd, 1967)

Bulleid of the Southern (London, Ian Allan Ltd, 1977)

Master Builders of Steam (London, Ian Allan Ltd, 1963)

Burton, A. *The Orient Express* (London, Amber Books Ltd (David & Charles), 2001)

Richard Trevithick, Giant of Steam (London, Aurum, 2000)

Casserley, H. C. and Johnson, S. W. *Locomotives at the Grouping – London, Midland & Scottish Railway* (London, Ian Allan, 1966)

Chacksfield, J. E. *Richard Maunsell – An Engineering Biography* (Usk, The Oakwood Press, 1998)
C. B. Collett – A Competent Successor (Usk, The Oakwood Press, 2002)

Commault, R. *Georges Nagelmackers* (Paris, Éditions de la Capitelle, 1972)

Cornwell, H. J. C. *William Stroudley, Craftsman of Steam* (Newton Abbot, David & Charles, 1968)
Forty Years of Caledonian Locomotives (Newton Abbot, David & Charles, 1974)

Cox, E. S. *Locomotive Panorama* (London, Ian Allan, 1965)

Davies, H. *George Stephenson* (London, Weidenfeld & Nicholson, 1975)

Day Lewis, S. *Bulleid – Last Giant of Steam* (London, George Allen & Unwin, 1964)

Deeley, R. M. *A Genealogical History of Montfort-sur-Risle and Deeley of Halesowen* (London, Charles Griffin & Co, 1941)

Dow, G. *Great Central* (3 vols) (London, Locomotive Publishing Company, Vol 1 1959, Vol 2 1962; Ian Allan Publishing, Vol 3 1965)

Edwards, D. and Pigram, R. *The Golden Years of the Metropolitan Railway* (London, Baton Transport, 1985)

Edmondson, John B. 'To Whom Are We Indebted for the Railway Ticket System?', (*English Mechanic & World of Science*, 697, 2 Aug 1878, p525)

Farr, M. *Thomas Edmondson, Transport Ticket Pioneer* (Weston-super-Mare, Avon-AngliA Publications, 1982, rev ed 1987)
Thomas Edmondson and his Tickets (Andover, published by the author, 1991)

Fletcher, M. and Taylor, J. (eds) *Railways, The Pioneer Years* (London, Studio Editions, 1990)

Fryer, C. *British Pullman Trains* (Great Addington, Silver Link Publishing Ltd, 1992)

Green, O. and London's Transport Museum *Metroland for 1924* (British Empire Exhibition Issue, new ed with extended introduction, London, Southbank Publishing, 2004)

Hamilton Ellis, C. *Four Main Lines* (London, George Allen & Unwin, 1950)
Some Classic Locomotive Types (London, George Allen & Unwin, 1949)
The Midland Railway (London, George Allen & Unwin, 1955)

Twenty Locomotive Men (London, Ian Allan Ltd, 1958)

'Famous Locomotive Engineers I: William Stroudley' (*The Locomotive*, 15 May 1937, pp149-152)

'Famous Locomotive Engineers II: David Jones' (*The Locomotive*, 14 August 1937, pp253-256)

Harris, M. *British Main Line Services in the Age of Steam* (Sparkford, Oxford Publishing Company, 1996)

Hills, R. L. and Patrick, D. *Beyer, Peacock: Locomotive Builders to the World* (Glossop, Transport Publishing Company, 1982)

Hodgkins, D. 'Writing the Biography of Edward Watkin' (York, Inst of Railway Studies Lecture, May 1999)

The Second Railway King (Whitchurch, Merton Priory Press Ltd, 2002)

Holcroft, H. *An Outline of Great Western Locomotive Practice, 1837-1947* (London, Locomotive Publishing Co Ltd, 1957)

Hughes, G. *LNER* (London, Guild Publishing, 1986)

Klapper, C. F. *Sir Herbert Walker's Southern Railway* (London, Ian Allan Ltd, 1973)

Jackson, D. *J. G. Robinson: A Lifetime's Work* (Headington, Oxford, The Oakwood Press, 1996)

Jenkinson, D. and Essery, Bob *Midland Carriages* (Shepperton, Oxford Publishing Company, 1984)

LMS Standard Coaching Stock (3 vols) (Shepperton, Oxford Publishing Company, 1994-2000)

Johnson, P. *An Illustrated History of the Welsh Highland Railway* (Sparkford, Oxford Publishing Company, 2002)

Livesey, H. F. F. *The Locomotives of the LNWR* (London, The Railway Publishing Co Ltd, 1948)

McKenzie, William A. *Dining Car Line to the Pacific* (St Paul, Minnesota Historical Society Press, 1990)

MacLeod, A. B. *The McIntosh Locomotives of the Caledonian Railway* (Staines, Ian Allan, 1944)

Marshall, J. *A Biographical Dictionary of Railway Engineers* (Newton Abbot, David & Charles, 1978)

Middlemass, T. *Encyclopaedia of Narrow Gauge Railways of Britain & Ireland* (London, Guild Publishing, 1991)

Stroudley and his Terriers (Easingwold, Pendragon Partnership, 1995)

The 'Scottish' 4-4-0 (Penryn, Pendragon Books (Atlantic Transport Publishers) 1994)

Milligan, E. H. *Quakers and Railways* (London, Sessions Book Trust, 1992)

Morel, J. *Pullman* (Newton Abbot, David & Charles, 1983)

Mullay, A. J. *Streamlined Steam* (Newton Abbot, David & Charles, 1994)

Nock, O. S. *British Locomotives of the 20th Century* (2 vols) (London, Guild Publishing 1984)

The Locomotives of Sir Nigel Gresley (2nd ed) (Sparkford, Patrick Stephens, 1991)

The Railway Engineers (London, Batsford, 1955)

Sir William Stanier, an Engineering Biography (Shepperton, Ian Allan Ltd, 1964)

The Caledonian Dunalastairs (Newton Abbot, David & Charles, 1968)

Peacock, A. J. *George Hudson, 1800-1871, The Railway King* (2 vols) (York, Viking Press, 1988/89)

Peacock, A. J. and Joy, D. *George Hudson of York* (Clapham, Lancs, Dalesman, 1971)

Platt, A. *The Life and Times of Daniel Gooch* (Gloucester, Alan Sutton Publishing, 1987)

Pratt, G. J. *Midland Railway Memories* (Derby, Harpur & Sons, 1924)

Radford, J. B. *Derby Works and Midland Locomotives* (London, Ian Allan Ltd, 1971)

A Century of Progress: Centenary Brochure of the Derby Carriage & Wagon Works (Derby, 1973)

'Railway Ancestors' (*Family History Society* Issue 27, Summer 2002, Vol 7, No 3; Great Central Railway Issue)

Ransom, P. J. G *Narrow Gauge Steam* (Sparkford, Oxford Publishing Company, 1996)

Reed, M. C. *The London & North Western Railway* (Penryn, Atlantic Transport Publishers, 1996)

Robotham, R. *The Great Central Railway's London Extension* (Shepperton, Ian Allan Publishing, 1999)

Rogers, Col H. C. B. *The Last Steam Locomotive Engineer: R. A. Riddles CBE* (London, George Allen & Unwin Ltd, 1970)

G. J. Churchward, A Locomotive Biography (London, George Allen & Unwin Ltd, 1975)

Ross, D. *The Willing Servant: A History of the Steam Locomotive* (Stroud, Tempus, 2004)

St John Thomas, D. *GWR Locomotives – Names, Numbers, Types & Classes* (Newton Abbot, David & Charles, 1971, rep of GWR books of 1911, 1928, 1938 and 1946)

St John Thomas, D. and Whitehouse, P. *SR 150: A Century and a Half of the Southern Railway* (Newton Abbot, David & Charles, 1988)

Simmons, J. and Biddle, G. (eds) *The Oxford Companion to British Railway History* (Oxford, OUP, 1997)

Smith, D. J. *Robert Stephenson* (Princes Risborough, Shire, 1973)

Smith, M. *Steam on the Underground* (Shepperton, Ian Allan Publishing, 1994)

Stretton, C. E. *The History of the Midland Railway* (London, Methuen & Co, 1901)

Tyldesley, J. 'Who Lived There?' (*BackTrack*, November 2000, p637)

van Riemsdijk, J. T. *Compound Locomotives* (Penryn, Atlantic Transport Publishers/Pendragon Books, 1994)

Vaughan, A. *Isambard Kingdom Brunel, Engineering Knight-Errant* (London, John Murray, 1991)

Weaver, R. 'Francis William Webb – A Reappraisal' (*Railway World*, Sep/Oct 1986, pp538-543, 606-611)

Webster, N. W. *Joseph Locke, Railway Revolutionary* (London, George Allen & Unwin, 1970)

Whitehouse, P. and St John Thomas, D. *The Great Western Railway* (Newton Abbot, David & Charles, 1985, rep 2002)
The Great Days of the Southern Railway (London, BCA, by arrangement with David St John Thomas, 1992)
LMS 150 (Newton Abbot, David & Charles, 1987, new ed 2002)
LNER 150 (Newton Abbot, David & Charles, 1989, rep 2002)

Whitehouse, P. B. and Snell, J. B. *Narrow Gauge Railways of the British Isles* (London, Book Club Associates, 1986)

Williams, R. *The Midland Railway: A New History* (Newton Abbot, David & Charles, 1988)

Wilson, R. B. (ed) *Sir Daniel Gooch, Memoirs & Diary* (Newton Abbot, David & Charles. 1972)

Wragg, D. *The Southern Railway Handbook, 1923-1947* (Stroud, Sutton Publishing, 2003)

Young, R. *Timothy Hackworth and the Locomotive* (Shildon, Stockton & Darlington Jubilee Committee, 1923, rep 1975)

The Railway Magazine: Issues for Dec 1900, April 1902, Oct 1908, June and Sept 1912

The Times: sundry issues from 1885 to 1983

Website http://www.steamindex.com: various citations